Enemies of the State

ENEMIES
of the
STATE

Gary Murray

S I M O N & S C H U S T E R

LONDON·SYDNEY·NEW YORK·TOKYO·SINGAPORE·TORONTO

First published in Great Britain by
Simon & Schuster Ltd in 1993
A Paramount Communications Company

Copyright © Gary Murray, 1993

Introduction Copyright © Tam Dalyell, 1993

Simon & Schuster Ltd
West Garden Place
Kendal Street
London W2 2AQ

Simon & Schuster of Australia Pty Ltd
Sydney

A CIP catalogue record for this book is
available from the British Library
ISBN 0–671–71194–6

Typeset in Melior 11/14 by Florencetype Ltd, Kewstoke, Avon
Printed and bound in Great Britain by
Butler & Tanner Ltd, Frome

Contents

Dedication

This book is dedicated to the late Hilda Murrell, an elderly anti-nuclear campaigner, who was abducted and murdered on the 21st March 1984. May her spirit rest in peace.

Author's Note

My reasons for writing this book are twofold. First, I want to highlight the fact that for over thirty years private investigators in Great Britain have been allowed to operate without any form of legislation to control their activities. This state of affairs has led to a gradual expansion of private espionage, with unregulated 'civilian' spies working for British and foreign Intelligence services. Security-conscious professionals like myself find this completely contrary to public or defence interests and it is our earnest wish that some kind of legislation will be introduced to control the private detective industry.

Second, I believe that a number of illegal acts, including violence and murder, have been committed by agents of British Intelligence – in some cases with the connivance of members of Her Majesty's Government. One particularly important case is that of Hilda Murrell, who was murdered on the 21st March 1984. This and other cases are cited in this book.

I hope my efforts have not been in vain and that someone somewhere will take some action, ideally by way of a public inquiry into the allegations contained in *Enemies of the State*.

The following glossary is to help readers to understand the general duties of the agencies referred to:

MI5:

A unit of the Security and Intelligence Services, its *official* role is to combat espionage, subversion and terrorist activities within the United Kingdom and British overseas territories. Regrettably this has not always been the case: much of their work has been directed to targets that have merely been declared subversive by the government of the day. Until very recently, MI5 was never officially acknowledged as even existing. MI5 agents do not have powers of arrest – yet.

MI6:

Another unit within the Security and Intelligence apparatus, hidden within the administration of the Foreign and Commonwealth Office. MI6 agents operate mainly overseas and are responsible for providing intelligence on any kind of perceived *external* threat to the realm. Like MI5, until recently MI6 did not officially exist. The agents of this unit do not have powers of arrest – yet.

SAS (Special Air Service):

A regiment within the British Army, the SAS can be deployed in any overseas fighting or 'domestic' combat against a foreign enemy or intelligence-gathering role. They are experts at surveillance and covert operations.

SB (Special Branch):

The arm of British police forces set up initially to counter the activities of the Irish Republican brotherhood. Until 1958, SB was controlled exclusively by the Metropolitan Police, but now all provincial police forces have such units, whose officers hold normal constabulary powers of arrest. Special Branch liaises with the Security and Intelligence Services and, like MI5, directs some of its energy to political and domestic targets.

GCHQ (Government Communications Headquarters):

The tasks of this organisation are signals intelligence and communications security. All information collected by GCHQ is done by electronic eavesdropping and while its official role is to monitor military and diplomatic signals of foreign nations, it is not unusual for GCHQ to harvest information from domestic and international communication lines on behalf of other intelligence or law enforcement departments. There is regular liaison with MI5, MI6 and Special Branch.

Operational Controller/Handler:

A staff Intelligence Officer working for the Security and Intelligence Services or Special Branch who runs a freelance agent on a person-to-person basis. Depending on the relationship and nature of the work being carried out by the agent, it is not unusual for the Handler to threaten, bribe, or even blackmail their sources. Trickery and coaxing are all part of the Handler's methods of operation.

On the 27th December 1992 a *Sunday Express* headline heralded the setting-up of Britain's first 'Security Police' force. Writer William Massey revealed that MI5 was demanding new powers of arrest for its operatives. One Security and Intelligence Officer said: 'Powers of arrest would be appropriate in matters of Official Secrets and Prevention of Terrorism Acts.'

Whilst the granting of such authority to MI5 agents will be operationally convenient, in that the use of police will no longer be required, there is a sinister element in this proposed legislation. The thought of secret agents having the power to arrest anyone they consider is a threat to the state is just too horrific for words. In effect, it means that the faceless men and women representing Whitehall would be able to gag and prosecute any British citizen.

All I can say to that prospect is, God help the outspoken anti-nuclear protesters, environmental groups, writers, and others probing into the murky activities of Government and the Security Services. It would appear that Big Brother is here to stay.

Foreword

A depressing feature of our times is the emergence of the 'so what?' factor. Shame-making events can be accurately chronicled; can go unchallenged; and can be conveniently forgotten. Grasshopper-like, public interest alights on the next sensation. Politicians are probably more to blame than any other group; like a flight of starlings, we flock from one perch to another, on the heels of a headline readily provided for us by instant TV.

Yet, if *Enemies of the State* were to be met by the all-too common 'so what?' response, it would be deeply discreditable to the British State. Because Gary Murray penetrates sensitive areas at the very heart of governance, as Enoch Powell used that word, of that State.

So what? So a heck of a lot.

For starters, the whole sordid and brutal murder of the Shrewsbury rose-grower Hilda Murrell must be re-opened. As elsewhere in *Enemies of the State*, Mr Murray's energy and professionalism have produced completely new material, hitherto unknown to those of us versed in the events surrounding that grim Friday 24 March 1984, when the body was found in the Hunkington copse. In particular, the truly astonishing and remarkable affidavit reproduced on pages 199–203 demands a detailed response from the highest authorities in the land. Whatever else, it cannot just be left to accumulate dust in some pigeonhole. Grave, grave allegations against the behaviour of the State are implied.

Not only would it be a stain on British honour to do nothing, it would be a dereliction of duty not to make every effort to create the conditions where it is less likely that such gross events will ever take place again in our country. There is one glimmer of hope that this is not quite an indulgence in wishful thinking. Hilda Murrell's murder is one of those rare episodes that will not go away and is somehow lodged in the collective British psyche. Nearly a decade has passed, and still I get several letters a month on the subject. And, at least among the middle-aged and more senior members of the Shropshire community, concern is unabated after all this time. Gary Murray adds a new dimension to the mystery and fuels the need for a new enquiry.

Enemies of the State also fuels the need for something else: a serious attempt to regulate and control the activities of free-lance detectives, and the nature of the work and tasks which the State – that is, you, the tax payer – asks them to perform. I have read and reviewed a number of excellent books by both journalists and academics focusing on this area of activity. But Gary Murray's contribution is altogether different. He is not an academic. He is not a commentator. He is an insider. He is a candid gamekeeper who, in my experience of him, both knows and is activated by the difference between right and wrong. He is constructive and not destructive, patriotic about the values that it is truly worth being patriotic about.

On a personal note, I am thankful that Gary Murray explodes the notion that Hilda Murrell might have been murdered on account of her critical views of the Sizewell reactor project. I regarded the culpability of the nuclear industry as a quite preposterous suggestion. As the Chairman of the Atomic Energy Authority put it to me, it is not the business of the Central Electricity Generating Board or the Atomic Energy Authority to contract for the murder of septuagenarian rose-growers!

Gary Murray's chapter on the Security Services should be required reading for any decision-maker involved in the current debate on the future role of MI5 and MI6. Before powerful Ministers tread too far along the road to conferring on the Security Services responsibility for terrorism, hitherto in the domain of the police, they should reflect on what Gary Murray felicitously terms 'less than legal'. Any anti-terrorist organisation should be made to justify itself in an open court of law, and to my mind Gary Murray's riveting first-hand account of life at the operative's sharp end makes the police–court relationship, which perhaps we take for granted in Britain, well-nigh impossible. Would MI5 with police responsibilities be prepared to allow its personnel to appear in a witness box? And, what kind of figure would be cut before a British jury by an organisation which, according to Gary Murray, has resorted on occasion to assassination as an instrument of policy?

Perhaps an endless series of revelations have combined to anaesthetise the British public against shocked outrage. But, again, as in the case of Hilda Murrell, Gary Murray's quite new material cannot just be left in limbo by any self-respecting Parliament in the throes of an argument about the control of the Security Service – and control of subversive cliques within the Service, who have become a law to themselves, as Harold Wilson graphically pinpointed as far back as his anguished evidence to the Royal Commission on the Press in 1977. Nowhere have I read such an instructive account of the crucial handler-agent relationship as that given first-hand by Gary Murray. Imagine the feelings of Paul Henderson of Matrix Churchill when he felt abandoned by his recent friends in MI6 as soon as he got into hot water with the Customs and spent the night in the clink.

As a Member of Parliament with thirty years' and more seniority in the House of Commons, I am determined to bring Gary Murray's chapter on the Security Services to the attention of Lord Justice Scott, and to the attention – for answers – of the Defence Secretary, the Trade Secretary, the Home Secretary, the Foreign Secretary, the Lord Chancellor and, above all, the head of the Security Services, the responsible Minister, the Prime Minister.

Tam Dalyell MP

Acknowledgements

A lot of people have contributed to this book, far more than I originally envisaged. Of the numerous members of the private detective and security industry many must remain unmentioned, for the simple reason that their lives could be at risk. In any case, these witnesses could well become vital to an official investigation into serious criminal offences. To these necessarily unidentified contributors I tender my sincere thanks.

A similar situation exists with serving members (and former members) of the Security Services and Special Branch who, inhibited by the Official Secrets Act, were unable to go 'on the record' in any great detail with regard to their work. However, after seeking legal advice, it was possible to engage in sensible, restricted discussion with these sources, who considered it legitimate to assist on unclassified matters. I must stress that at no time did these contributors discuss anything of a classified nature. My thanks to them all.

A very special thank-you must go to former Military Intelligence Officer (MIO) Captain Fred Holroyd, author of *War without Honour*, who despite his own personal problems and circumstances since resigning his commission has never failed to offer expert advice and friendly assistance to the numerous writers and television producers who have knocked on his door.

The cloak and dagger world of espionage is permanently awash with contradictions and false trails, many of which have been set up by evil individuals seeking to distort the truth. Fortunately, the media employ a number of very competent journalists who are in effect capable 'spies' in their own right, admittedly confined to journalism. Nevertheless these writers, researchers, broadcasters, and TV producers regularly engage in delicate covert operations without any form of protection, moving in areas very alien to those of their normal expertise. As media undercover agents they have achieved tremendous success, and I am proud to have worked with many of them, some of whom have provided invaluable assistance during the writing of this book. They are:

Duncan Campbell, Chairman of the Board for *New Statesman and Society* magazine, probably the most well known investigative journalist in Britain. I am most grateful for opportunities to work with him at irregular intervals between 1979 and the present time.

Many thanks to Mark Hollingsworth of Granada's 'World in Action' for his assistance and advice during a period when it was necessary to track down and interview important witnesses. A special thank-you to Clare Powell, also of 'World in Action,' whose skills as a researcher have been invaluable in sections of this book. Her friendship and advice are also greatly appreciated.

It is impossible to catalogue in detail the particular roles played by other media contacts. Suffice it to acknowledge here their valued assistance in one form or another:

Jack Saltman – Thames Television
Nick Davies – formerly of the *Observer*
Ian Trueman and Graham Jones – *Daily Star*
Andrew Fox – Central Television
Paul Foot
Gerry Gable – *Searchlight* magazine
Brian Barr – BBC
James Cutler – Yorkshire Television

Sebastian Cody – Open Media
Vanessa Chapman – London Weekend Television

It goes without saying that I am also grateful to the many witnesses who have come forward to speak out concerning the death of Hilda Murrell.

First and foremost I would like to thank Catriona Guthrie (Trina), who not only put herself at risk by infiltrating areas closed to me but also gave valuable advice in the construction of Hilda Murrell's background activities and personality. My thanks to the many other witnesses mentioned in the relevant chapters.

I am particularly grateful to Commander (retired) Rob Green, former Naval Intelligence Officer and Hilda Murrell's nephew, for his continuing availability and time during our numerous discussions regarding Hilda's murder. His continuing silence over the Falklands and the sinking of the *Belgrano* is to be respected and admired.

Without the co-operation of ECOROPA, whose directors Fern Morgan-Grenville and Edward Goldsmith opened their files to me, it would not have been possible to clarify important aspects of Miss Murrell's work. My thanks to all concerned, also to Gerard Morgan-Grenville, and Peter Bunyard of the *Ecologist* magazine.

No writer can succeed without a support team. In my case I am fortunate in having my wife Ursula, who is an expert word processor operator and whose unsurpassed skills have proved invaluable throughout the writing of this book. Ably assisted by my daughter, Alison, and son, Ben, between us we have been able to prepare the manuscript for publication.

An important part of an investigative writer's work is locating and interviewing witnesses, who in some cases refuse to talk! I am fortunate in having met a number of very co-operative people, some of whom are described in the chapters relating to 'Other Victims' and 'The Libyan Connection'. I would like to thank all who agreed to go on the record, particularly Hassan Assali who, despite being incarcerated in one of

ACKNOWLEDGEMENTS

Her Majesty's prisons, was able to arrange for me to examine valuable evidence relating to his work and conviction.

Last, but certainly not least, I would like to thank my literary agent, David O'Leary, my editor, Nick Austin and Nick Webb of Simon & Schuster for making this book possible.

Preface

Private detectives, security consultants, and other individuals and companies trading under various euphemistically obscure business titles are currently part of an extensive civilian espionage network covering the British Isles. Many of these spies are engaged in unorthodox, and at times highly illegal, covert intelligence operations on behalf of the Security Services (MI5) and foreign governments. Others have, as will be seen in this book, managed to obtain access to confidential information from classified official sources. This data has in turn been passed on to unauthorised persons for massive commercial gain. In a lot of cases the official 'contacts' inside the government department from where the information was stolen have escaped punishment.

It is important to understand that not all spies are engaged in unlawful acts. To appreciate what I mean, readers should examine the *Collins English Dictionary* definition of the word spy: 'One who watches and reports secretly.' This description can apply to many people engaged in the gathering of information. For example, writers, journalists, television researchers and even marketing consultants occasionally watch and report secretly. But this does not necessarily mean that they are spies engaged in nefarious deeds. The same can be said for operatives within the intelligence services and other official agencies, who somehow manage to go about their watching and secret reporting without breaking the law.

As far as my own work as a spy was concerned, I would like to think that I was one of the 'good guys', as they say. Having said that, I am surprised that I was able to operate within the law, given all the circumstances surrounding my official work.

These circumstances, plus the total lack of regulation over the private detective and security industry, resulted in many occasions where I was tempted to use tactics frequently adopted by more unscrupulous members of the profession.

However, this was not the case and now that this book has been published, I hope that commonsense will prevail and that some kind of legislation will be enacted to control Britain's private spies – and that a public hearing will be commissioned to look into the murder of Hilda Murrell.

Introduction

Investigating the activities of individuals and organisations is not as easy or as straightforward as one would believe. Even highly experienced detectives and intelligence agents must never forget that local conditions and numerous other variables regularly affect undercover operations. One oversight or omission can lead to compromise – or something even worse. My own experience of such a situation occurred on a cold rainy night in January 1982 when I set out on surveillance of a group of anti-nuclear protesters suspected of planning a raid on a top secret Ministry of Defence base in Berkshire.

Frustrated and distracted by problems I was experiencing over my freelance work with MI5, I neglected to carry out my usual pre-surveillance reconnaissance and status checks of the objective. The result, in aviation terms, could be described as a 'near miss'.

Having received a vague, unimpressive briefing from an intoxicated client, I travelled to Hackney in East London where, just after midnight, I hastily parked my car in what I (wrongly) assumed would be the most suitable place to keep watch on the small terraced house suspected of being used by protesters.

The narrow, dimly lit residential street did not lend itself to a static surveillance of this kind, and it did not take me very

1

long to realise that I had been negligent on a number of counts, including my choice of position. My brief was to note the registration numbers of vehicles visiting the 'target' address where, according to my client, a London cell of anti-nuclear protesters intended to meet.

Having settled down in the back seat of my car, I went unenthusiastically about the business of setting up my tape recording equipment, only to discover that the batteries were flat. To add to my frustration, bordering by now on utter misery, heavy rain was causing condensation which greatly inhibited visibility, and as vehicles began to arrive all I could do was scribble into a notebook what little I could observe.

By 2 am my kaleidoscopic state of mind began playing tricks on me, so much so that it became impossible for me to remain in my car any longer. If only I had carried out my usual pre-surveillance checks, the difficulties of the assignment could have been anticipated. Also, if I had used a proper covert vehicle rather than an ordinary saloon car, a trouble-free operation would more than likely have resulted.

Mumbling obscenities to myself and wondering what the hell I was doing outside an address in Hackney at two o'clock in the morning in pouring rain, I stumbled out of my car and floundered towards Mare Street in search of an all-night coffee house and, I hoped, a toilet. Despite the annoyance of having my spectacles steam up, it was refreshing to feel the rain pounding against my face. By the time I had reached the main thoroughfare I was feeling less sorry for myself and quite alert – certainly alert enough to discover I was being followed.

Cruising slowly down Mare Street, behind me, was a dark Ford saloon car. In addition to the driver, I could see one front seat passenger who appeared to be holding something to his mouth. Another larger-looking male was slouched in the rear. I continued walking and increased my pace to cross the main road into Lamb Lane. I remember muttering to myself: 'What the bloody hell?'

Initially, I toyed with the idea that maybe these people were muggers, or even protesters bent on revenge. But this idea did not ring true: although capable of breaches of security and even other criminal offences, anti-nuclear protesters did not have a reputation for being violent.

I rapidly formulated the opinion that this was a 'job' car, and that perhaps the occupants were either police officers or from some other law enforcement agency on routine night patrol. Suddenly, the car accelerated and screeched to a stop alongside of me. The driver and the back seat passenger left their vehicle at speed and, in what was obviously a well rehearsed drill, grabbed me, applied an incapacitating lock to my right arm, and slammed me over the bonnet of their car. Not a word was spoken, and for some inexplicable reason I shouted: 'You've done this kind of thing before, then?' Swiftly, they searched and 'frisked' me, presumably to check for weapons.

The larger of the men dropped a plastic identity card on the bonnet, under my nose. Forcing my head down to look at it, he whispered in my ear: 'OK, Gary Murray of Euro-Tec Private Investigators, what's your game?' Staring at the ID card, I realised that it was my own. I was now firmly convinced that these unfriendlies were police officers and, remembering that I was in Hackney, a patch that was policed by the Met, a Force which did not enjoy a reputation for good conduct, I decided to adopt a polite, cool attitude to the situation. Apologising profusely, I replied: 'I'm dreadfully sorry, officer, there must be some mistake. I work for a firm of private investigators and I'm on a divorce case, it's rather confidential and I'm not able to discuss it'.

My identity and occupation were, of course, correct, but the divorce line was one of the many cover stories I adopted when working for Government clients. At this stage in the proceedings I felt confident I would be released.

No such luck. My head was lifted and then slammed violently down onto the bonnet of the Ford. This was followed by a vicious punch to the lumbar region, which caused partial disablement. My mind conjured up past experience of training

3

in Resistance to Interrogation. Somehow, I had to exaggerate my condition, in the hope they would lay off the violence and release me. At 45 years of age, although I was in reasonable condition, I had little or no chance of dealing physically with these characters.

A different voice rasped sarcastically: 'So, you're a private eye. Who is your client, and what are you doing watching nuclear protesters if you're on a divorce case?' Before I could respond, another fist pounded into my kidneys, followed by a slap around the ear. Gasping with pain, I started to speak: 'Look, officer . . .' But before I could continue Mr Backseat sneered: 'Officer? Who says we're police?' An ominous silence descended, broken only by the patter of rain on the bonnet and roof of the car.

Suddenly, there was the familiar sound of an Ultra High Frequency (UHF) radio transmission from inside their vehicle. It was now apparent that the front seat passenger was in fact the radio operator of this group, and that the remaining two thugs were a driver plus observer. It was difficult to work out who was in charge. In any event, this analysis did not really alleviate my worries: if anything I felt worse.

Desperately seeking to ease the pain in my right arm, I managed to wriggle into a position where I was able to look down at the ground under my pinioned limb. What I saw made me even more confused and alarmed. I could see the feet of one of my captors. He was wearing desert boots, the hallmark of the Special Air Service. Unexpectedly, the radio operator called out, presumably through either the open window or door of their car: 'He's ex-RAF SIB, operates his own agency called Euro-Tec, he's on the alpha list.'

At this point I was released, which was just as well as I was about to vomit all over the bonnet of the car. To this day I don't know if they were worried about my health, their paintwork, or the fact I was on some mysterious list. Suddenly it was over. Without any explanation, they returned to their car, the only comment coming from the driver as he got behind the wheel:

'You should have stayed in the SIB, old son', he said.

Within seconds they had vanished like spectres into the night. The whole incident had taken less than 10 minutes. For me, it seemed much longer. After gathering up the contents of my wallet, notebook, identity card and keys, which were scattered on the pavement, slowly and with great difficulty I returned to my Volvo.

The activities of the occupants in the terraced house were no longer of any interest to me. My primary concern now was my physical state, which was not good. As I drove home, my secondary thoughts were taken up with recent unpleasant events involving thugs wearing SAS desert boots. How did they have access by UHF radio to information confirming my occupation and the fact I had served with the Air Force Special Investigation Branch (SIB)? And just what was the alpha list?

CHAPTER 1

The Beginning

The Royal Air Force Police are responsible for criminal investigations, counter-intelligence and general police matters concerning the Royal Air Force. They are established at RAF Stations in the United Kingdom and abroad. Investigations are the responsibility of Headquarters Provost and Security Services (UK) which functionally controls a number of subordinate Units.

The overall controlling authority for the RAF Police is the Ministry of Defence (Air) Directorate-General of Security (RAF) based in Northumberland Avenue, London, and the Commanding Officer (CO) normally holds the rank of Air Commodore. At the time of writing, the CO is Air Commodore A C P Seymour, whose full title is Director of Security and Provost Marshal (Royal Air Force).

The SIB (Special Investigation Branch), as it was originally named, comprises two élite departments within the RAF Police, their respective tasks being criminal investigations and counter-intelligence duties.

There is also a highly efficient and respected police dog branch whose canine detectives enjoy a worldwide reputation for their specialist skills.

All RAF police, including Special Investigators, are graduates of a central training establishment based at RAF Newton, near Nottingham, where the quality of basic and advanced training is such that Air Force Investigators are held in high regard throughout the world. RAF 'spooks' have played an integral part in numerous undercover operations, and have contributed to the detection and apprehension of a number of foreign agents, both in the United Kingdom and abroad.

I was fortunate enough to serve in the RAF police as a junior non-commissioned officer (NCO), first as a station policeman-dog handler, graduating to the complete No: 44 Special Security briefing course, followed by No: 10 Investigators course which I successfully concluded on the 28th March 1962 at the then Training School at Debden, Cambridge. I gained operational experience on criminal and counter intelligence units at No: 4 RAF Police District, Innsworth, as it was then known.

My overall service was reasonably uneventful, with a General Service Medal for active service in the Far East and, apart from the occasional reprimand for insubordination or fighting in out-of-bounds areas, I managed to conclude my service with my conduct being assessed as 'Very Good'. Ability as a tradesman was reported on my Certificate of Service as being 'Good'.

At the conclusion of my service in the Sixties, I set out to win fame and fortune as a musician-entertainer. However, this was not to be and eventually, in 1968, I joined forces with David Sandry, a former Army SIB Investigator, and together we formed Euro-Tec (Private Investigators), offering a world-wide 'secret service' to businessmen and private clients. This was my first step into the secretive world of private intelligence operations. Had I realised then that in years to come I would be beaten, shot at, manipulated by the Security Services, divorced, and attempts made on my life, it is highly likely that I would have stayed in show business.

The development of the private detective industry must surely be one of the most extraordinary social phenomena of the twentieth century. It is difficult to comprehend how a profession, once dominated by sleazy little men in raincoats, has been transformed into an ubiquitous multi-million-pound-a-year private intelligence industry.

Contrary to popular belief, modern private detectives are nothing like their television versions. The media and the public's wishful thinking have created the image of down-at-heel trenchcoated individuals engaged in various acts of anti-social skulduggery. Nothing could be further from the truth. The 'traditional' gumshoe, now in reality consigned to history, has been replaced by an entirely new breed of high-tech private investigator.

Completely free from any form of statutory regulation or control, these investigators skilfully act as private intelligence agents for the business community as well as for government departments – including the security services of Great Britain and the USA. The intelligence services of the erstwhile Soviet Union were also known to utilise the expertise of western private investigators. The GRU as well as the KGB found established detective agencies an excellent method of expanding Soviet covert operations. Past Soviet intelligence operations contracted out to British detective and security agencies penetrated the very heart of the British Defence Ministry and other official departments.

Types of assignments undertaken by private detectives vary, according to the individual's background and capability. Some agencies survive very well on 'bread-and-butter' work passed to them by solicitors and finance houses. The more qualified and adventurous operators revel in a greater variety of work, including spying for the British and foreign security services already mentioned.

Many British and American private investigators have varied qualifications acquired from service with a number of different specialist government organisations. These include the Police, the Customs and Immigration Service, the Special Branch, Military Intelligence and the Special Air Service (SAS). In the United States, former members of the CIA and the Federal Bureau of Investigation (FBI) have formed private detective agencies that have become household names.

Ideally suited to clandestine investigations, these highly experienced men and women earn millions of pounds and dollars a year satisfying information-hungry clients, and it is not uncommon for these agents to risk their lives, as well as their liberty, in order to conclude a mission successfully.

In addition to these high-quality members of the business, because of the lack of official regulation the industry is forced to accept a number of unqualified types who have no formal training or 'trade' qualifications.

Despite this lack, some of these 'amateurs' have managed to build up successful businesses and now boast images of respectability and professionalism. The truth is, some of these individuals are criminals, very skilled in the art of extorting or conning vast amounts of money from their clients.

The clandestine gathering of confidential information has been a key activity of government for hundreds of years. The samurai warriors of old Japan excelled in the covert acquisition of information, for example. It was not until the year 1817, however, that private investigation materialised as an organised profession, when Frenchman François Eugene Vidocq opened a detective agency in Paris, France. He later went on to achieve notoriety by publishing his memoirs, which became in effect the first-ever detective stories.

Shortly after the creation of this Paris agency, Glaswegian Alan Pinkerton emigrated to America where, in 1830, he established the first American detective agency. This firm, specialising in criminal investigation, was known as The Pinkerton Detective Agency and was responsible for the tracking-down of some of the most dangerous outlaws of the day.

Pinkerton's agency liaised and worked with official law enforcement departments, including, in the twentieth century, the FBI. Despite operating initially at a time of extensive police corruption, Pinkerton's managed to retain an image of total professionalism and integrity. However, public respect waned for a while after Pinkerton began to involve his firm in political and strike-breaking undercover investigations which resulted in a number of deaths of industrial workers.

The Pinkerton Detective Agency has since returned to its former glory and is now one of the largest, most prestigious investigation and security organisations with branches throughout the world, including Britain.

Private detective agencies in Britain began to spring up around the middle of the nineteenth century. However, compared to the work of their American counterparts that of the British 'enquiry agents' was vastly different. It appears that the profession of enquiry agent was an off-shoot of the security industry, which at that time was responsible for supplying men to guard factories and other premises.

The introduction of the Matrimonial Causes Act of 1857 paved the way for the British enquiry agent to undertake divorce investigations. This kind of work was eventually to become a lucrative source of business for Britain's private eyes.

These early detectives expanded their operations to include supplying prostitutes, mistress-minding, pimping, and even fixing divorces. Without realising it, these pioneers had created an image that was to stay with the profession for over 50 years.

One notorious Victorian detective, Harry Benson, discovered an excellent method of encouraging his clients to part with vast amounts of money. He excelled in uncovering scandals involving members of the aristocracy – and he would then blackmail his victims, whose families were only too anxious to pay for his silence.

By 1901, agencies had expanded their operations to include various other types of assignments. The first multi-purpose detective agency in London was created by a man called Garner, who was directly responsible for setting the pattern for the twentieth century private eye.

Meanwhile, in America the Pinkerton Detective Agency had

extended its services to include security duties. Other agencies were also formed around this time, and many famous American names came into being, among them Wells Fargo.

Since these very early days, British investigators and security firms have been allowed to trade without any form of official regulation, and this has resulted in the gradual development of a private intelligence network covering the whole of the United Kingdom. From about 1960 onwards spying appears to have become an increasingly important part of the profession's operations. Newspapers began reporting on the activities of certain individuals who were undertaking industrial espionage assignments.

In 1967, Sir Richard Powell, Director General of the Institute of Directors, London, voiced his concern: 'There are certain organisations that have been sent to steal industrial secrets to sell to a large organisation in Switzerland. To my certain knowledge there is another that exists in Tokyo, and they are prepared to suborn anyone in order to get this information, which is worth many thousands of pounds. Ten years ago you never heard of industrial espionage in this country, but now it is clear that it is something which has to be dealt with. It is a nuisance which we've got to try to get rid of.'

The growing Japanese and American influence on business intelligence was a major factor in detectives becoming involved in espionage assignments, so much so that the Younger Report referred to a private eye who said that he had handled about 50 cases involving industrial espionage between the years 1969–70. Vincent Carratu, a respectable commercial investigator, described his case load: 'At this particular moment I have four cases that involve espionage. I reckon to get 40 or 50 cases a year to investigate.'

Over twenty years have elapsed since the widespread introduction of espionage-allied assignments, and the continued absence of official regulations has resulted in an uncontrolled growth of these activities, with operatives willing to steal secret information, tap telephones, burgle, and even carry out acts of assassination on behalf of their clients.

Government agencies – MI5, MI6, and Special Branch – have used the services of the private sector on confidential assignments for more than twenty years. In the United States, where it is not unusual for official departments to set up their own civilian firms, the CIA and FBI also employ civilian undercover agents.

My first experience of a secret *ex officio* mission occurred when, along with my colleague David Sandry, I accepted what *appeared* to be a simple matrimonial case. This, it transpired, was not what it seemed, and I unwittingly became a victim of a disguised intelligence operation centred on Berlin, that Mecca for clandestine agents. Of course, now that the Wall has been removed and the Cold War ended, there must surely be a lot of unemployed spies lounging around the bars of Berlin. Things were different 22 years ago.

In February 1970, Mainline Investigations and my own firm, Euro-Tec (Private Investigators), undertook jointly to work together for an American millionaire who told a convincing story of a delinquent missing wife. The client, Charles Schneider, reported that his wife, Christa, had vanished and that he was anxious to get her back.

I spent several hours discussing the best way to trace Christa Schneider with David Sandry. Our respective experiences with the Army Special Branch and the Royal Air Force Security Services ultimately played an invaluable part in what turned out to be a bizarre investigation.

The personal background of the subject of enquiry was very interesting. It transpired that she was a German national, most of whose family and friends lived in various areas of Germany, including Berlin. Despite this, the client failed to suggest that enquiries might well have to be carried out in these areas. On the contrary, he gave us the impression that his wife would be somewhere in England, and that the task of tracing her would be reasonably straightforward.

Sandry and I rapidly eliminated the sources of possible

clues in the UK, and our enquiries eventually reached a stage where it was obvious the investigation would have to be extended to relatives and friends in Germany. However, the client appeared reluctant to authorise such investigations, and we found ourselves having to persuade him that, if success was to be achieved, it was vital to dispatch one of us to Düsseldorf, where Christa's parents lived. Finally Mr Schneider agreed, and I was elected to handle the German end of the assignment on the 11th May 1970.

Research in and around the area where the parents lived quickly revealed that Christa was resident and working in East Germany. Unable to make personal contact with the client, I took the initiative and, after leaving a message with Sandry in the UK, departed for Berlin.

On arrival at Tempelhof Airport I was greeted unexpectedly by a well-spoken Englishman identifying himself as David Cartwright, a friend of the client. There was no way of checking with Schneider, and in any event Cartwright's knowledge of the case was impressive enough to convince me that there was nothing to worry about.

A small but comfortable room had been arranged for me at the Plaza Hotel on Kurfürstendamm Ecke Knesebeckstrasse, in the Western Sector, and by 4pm I had set up my headquarters in room 221. Left to my own devices, I set about hiring a vehicle (suitable for surveillance) and visited the 'target' address to carry out the usual pre-surveillance 'recce'. All went according to plan, and at dawn the next day I was secreted in the rear of the Volkswagen hire car, keeping watch on number 6 Sachsicher Strasse, which was immediately opposite the Hotel Eden.

The first day's surveillance was unproductive. Even personal 'pretext' visits to the address failed to confirm that Christa was associated with any of the flats in the building. By now I was experiencing a feeling of mild concern. At 9pm I terminated surveillance and returned to the hotel, to be met by David Cartwright who suggested a late night snack.

13

At first, the meeting seemed like a straightforward social occasion, until I found myself faced with an unexpected proposition. Cartwright explained: 'Certain good friends of mine need – urgently – a service they reckon you can provide'. He then produced a photograph, obviously taken in England (Sloane Square, in fact) and described what was required: 'Your observation point is located very close to the Hotel Eden. My friends would like to confirm the movements of the man in this photograph. They would be particularly grateful for details of any address he visits tomorrow after he leaves the hotel at about 9am. If you could follow him into the Eastern Sector, my friends would be eternally grateful.'

I was astounded, and immediately realised that perhaps the assignment on behalf of Schneider was bogus. Or maybe a covert intelligence agency was taking advantage of my 'tourist' status in Berlin. My many queries were answered with explanations like: 'This is nothing more than a delicate industrial matter that my friends are confident you can handle.'

After a lengthy discussion, it was finally agreed that I would extend my surveillance to the Hotel Eden and that in the event the subject of the new investigation entered the Eastern Sector, I would follow and rendezvous with an East German operative who would take over the 'tailing'.

Cartwright also explained to me that, before returning to the West, it would be necessary for me to wait at a particular café, where the East German operative would return with details of any address visited by the 'target'.

After a restless night, I prepared myself for what I anticipated would be a lengthy surveillance. Because of the operational risks involved in such work, many private security agents and investigators refuse such duties. However, if the truth be known, my enthusiasm for the uncertainty and thrill of one-man surveillance was the main reason for accepting this assignment.

In the main, surveillance agents function in small groups

when tailing their targets. Contact with each other is maintained via hand-held personal VHF radios so that the risk of being observed, or losing the target, is reduced to a minimum. In the trade, one-man operations are avoided whenever possible.

Despite the notorious difficulty of solo tailing, certain investigators and security men have emerged as experts in such duties. I was among them and had, over a number of years, developed my own unique system of one-man tracking. My reputation was so well-known in the industry that other detective agencies and security firms would regularly sub-contract such assignments to me. On one occasion in 1969, having accepted a mission to follow a suspect from Twickenham, ostensibly to where they worked in nearby Hounslow, I found myself at Gatwick Airport boarding a flight to Spain! Fortunately, being an ever-ready type of detective, I had my passport with me and was able to acquire a place on the same flight as the target. Ten days later I returned to England with a comprehensive report for the client.

The morning of the Berlin surveillance was cold and dull, so I started by devouring a hearty breakfast. I then prepared a shoulder bag which contained a camera, planning to photograph the subject of investigation if possible, not for the mysterious Mr Cartwright but for my own benefit. My curiosity was well and truly aroused.

Armed with a street map of the Western Sector, plus my 35mm camera and the ability to speak only Linguaphone German, I positioned myself at a small coffee bar from where I could observe the Hotel Eden. The photograph supplied by Cartwright was useful for identification purposes, and I was confident that the quarry would easily be spotted leaving the building. According to the information, time of departure would be between 8.30 and 9am. At 8.50am the subject walked out of the hotel and stood on the pavement. He paused, looking up and down the street as though checking for anything unusual. My immediate reaction was to curse silently: 'Shit, he's expecting a tail', I said to myself.

Things were not improved when suddenly the target turned and walked towards the café where I was sitting at an outside table. However, as an experienced hunter I was adept at following a target not only from behind but also in front, so as he walked towards the café I left the observation point quickly and took to the street where, by discreet use of shop windows, I was able to monitor and anticipate his direction. The fact that he was wearing a very conspicuous overcoat in a large square design was a great help, I remember nicknaming him Mr Check Overcoat.

For 30 minutes we walked the streets of West Berlin on what was obviously a counter-surveillance exercise. There was a ten-minute stop at a small café opposite a garage on Pariser Strasse, and then the journey continued to the Europa Centre, close to the Zoologischer Garten. During this time I found myself exercising every skill in a desperate effort to stalk my quarry around the Centre.

Suddenly, he appeared to relax and on leaving the Europa Centre he turned east and walked for a further 20 minutes. By this stage I had switched my surveillance mode from front to rear. I unexpectedly lost sight of the subject, and in a panic ran into Friedrichstrasse to be confronted with what I remember as an awesome sight. There, approximately 100 metres away, was the Allied Checkpoint into the Eastern Sector – 'Checkpoint Charlie' itself.

The sight of Checkpoint Charlie induced maximum trepidation and I thought seriously about aborting the mission. Although I had agreed to extend the surveillance into the East, I had secretly hoped that I wouldn't actually have to. But after a few moments of inner panic and disorientation I gathered my wits and continued on.

Ahead was the stark, grim outline of East Germany peeping over the Berlin Wall. The conspicuous Communist observation towers manned by armed troops advertised quite clearly the penalty for any breach of security. I mused over the delight my (soon-to-be-ex-) wife would experience if anything happened to me.

The first task was to re-spot my prey, and to ensure that we did not end up face to face whilst going through the checkpoint. Approaching the Allied section of Checkpoint Charlie, I suddenly noticed away to the right a viewing platform used by members of the public for looking over the Wall and there, staring into the East almost as though he was searching for someone on the other side, was Mr Check Overcoat. After a few moments, he hunched over what appeared to be a notebook in which he was writing something.

It was at this stage that I decided to attempt a photograph. This was done by entering a small museum immediately behind the viewing rostrum where, by poking the camera through the West-East viewing window, I was able to capture a photograph of the target as he hunched over his notebook. The time was 12 noon, and I was becoming aware that there was a growing possibility of being caught in the Eastern Sector during the hours of darkness. This was something I was very keen to avoid.

After 20 minutes or so of looking into the East, my quarry left the rostrum and approached the checkpoint. From the museum window, I watched him enter the guardhouse controlled by the Eastern authorities. Within five minutes he left, and walked down Friedrichstrasse into East Berlin. Taking a deep breath, I followed reluctantly.

I entered the guardhouse nervously and handed over my passport to a female East German border guard who held it out of sight underneath a security counter, presumably checking my details against the list of suspect Western Intelligence agents. The passport described me as a 'business consultant': this discrepancy was to play on my mind throughout the stay in the Eastern Sector. Eventually, having changed Western currency for the appropriate East German money, and after describing myself as nothing more than a tourist, I was issued with a short-term permit. A few moments later I crossed the area known as 'no man's land' and finally walked into East Germany.

I remember the weather was very cold when I cleared the checkpoint. I could see the troops in the observation towers looking at me through their binoculars, and this made me very nervous. As I walked through no man's land, I was aware of the minefields and the automatic machine guns positioned along the Eastern side of the Wall. The trauma of going through the Berlin Wall seriously inhibited my operational effectiveness for the whole of my stay on the other side.

I walked quite slowly along the southern side of Friedrich-strasse, frantically looking for Mr Check Overcoat. For several minutes I could not see him at all. After walking about half a mile, the street became quite busy and isolating individuals for identification was extremely difficult. Suddenly, approximately 20 yards ahead on the opposite side of the street, I saw my target bobbing along in the crowd.

By now I was becoming very apprehensive. My instructions were to hand over the surveillance to someone else – but I had no way of identifying my contact. As I approached a built-up area near a railway station, I decided to decrease the distance between myself and Mr Check Overcoat. I was in the process of closing with him when suddenly a man in a black leather raincoat bumped into me and whispered: 'Guten Tag, Herr Murray, alles ist in Ordnung, bis bald'. I understood this to mean: 'Good day, Mr Murray, everything is in order, see you later'. I remember experiencing an overwhelming feeling of relief.

A few moments later I was alone on the streets of the most sinister city in Europe. Messrs Check Overcoat and Black Leather vanished into the crowd, leaving me to continue with the next stage of the assignment: to locate the café and wait. It took me less than ten minutes to establish myself in the small café/bar situated very close to the railway bridge on Friedrich-strasse.

After an hour and a half (at 3.30pm) I was becoming aware

that dusk was approaching rapidly, and that the checkpoint would soon be closed for the night. By 5pm I was seriously contemplating a change of location when in walked Mr Black Leather. He approached the bar, ordered a beer and sat at the table next to me.

At 5.15pm he left his seat and walked to the exit. As he passed me, he dropped a small piece of rolled-up paper discreetly into my lap. A few moments later, in the café toilet, I unfolded the paper and was mightily relieved to see an address written on it. I memorised the information and then flushed the paper down the toilet.

I walked back to the checkpoint allowing enough time to comply with the entry-exit regulations. However, my return to the West was not without incident. I was taken to a small cubicle, where I was strip searched and questioned for one hour about my afternoon visit to the other side. After sticking religiously to my 'tourist' cover story, I was eventually allowed to return to the Western sector. I subsequently learned that the stop, search and question process was a routine course of action adopted from time to time by the border authorities. On my return, I fully expected Cartwright to be waiting for me. However, he was nowhere to be seen. No message, nothing.

At midnight, Cartwright telephoned and apologised profusely for his absence. He then requested details of the address. Reluctantly, I gave them over the telephone and during the course of the conversation Cartwright indicated there would be an envelope left at the hotel – 'in which will be a token of our appreciation', he said.

The following morning, as Cartwright had promised, an envelope was indeed left at the hotel, addressed simply to 'G Murray'. Inside was £200 sterling – not bad for a day's work in 1970.

Later that day I reactivated the original surveillance on 6 Sachsicher Strasse where, much to my surprise, I observed the elusive Christa Schneider coming and going. I was able to monitor her activities and obtain photographs without undue difficulty. In fact, her general conduct was such that I soon believed that she was aware of the surveillance.

Over a period of three days I gradually constructed a dossier on the activities of Mrs Schneider: photographing and following her to various locations in the Western Sector was easy. Eventually I confirmed with my colleague David Sandry that the assignment had been concluded, after which I arranged a flight back to London through a local travel agent.

I returned to my hotel room at 3pm to discover my personal belongings had been ransacked. Reports and operational notebooks, even my camera bag, had been searched. Fortunately, the several films used through the week were intact, along with the assignment notes.

My flight was not until 8am the following day and I decided that it would be unwise to remain in the hotel any longer. Within 15 minutes I had settled my bill and was speeding to Tempelhof Airport in a large Mercedes taxi. After a very uncomfortable sleepless night at the airport I eventually boarded the 8am flight for London, arriving at the home of the client at noon.

My first question to Mr Schneider was: 'How long have you known this man Cartwright?' Looking straight into my eyes, he said 'Cartwright? What are you talking about? I don't know anyone of that name!'

Having completed the Berlin assignment, I set out to track down the mysterious Mr Cartwright. I spoke with contacts in various branches of the armed forces, Special Branch, Army Intelligence, and even the Foreign Office: no one had any knowledge of such a person operating in Berlin. The mystery deepened when, while I was trying to solve the riddle of this assignment, my close friend and colleague of long standing, David Sandry, abruptly announced his resignation from the business. Within days of this announcement he vanished, and has not been seen or heard of for over 22 years.

If it were not for the fact that Sandry had primary control of the Schneider/Berlin case, I might have thought that perhaps he had decided just to vanish into obscurity. However, his knowledge and operational responsibilities concerning the case were such that I now believe there was much more to the project than just tracing a missing wife. There were also his links with Army Special Branch and the British Secret Intelligence Service (SIS).

Despite intensive searching, no trace of David George Sandry has been found to date in England, Australia, New Zealand, Gibraltar, Germany, Singapore or other areas of the Far East. Even extensive enquiries in the United States and Canada have failed to uncover any clues. I believe the only conclusion one can reach about this puzzle is that Sandry is no longer alive. I find it hard to believe that a friend and colleague would just vanish without explanation – no telephone call, letter, not even a Christmas card. It is very strange that shortly after these bizarre incidents, the man in charge of a major investigation should vanish so completely.

As far as the Cartwright saga was concerned, obviously some kind of covert Intelligence assignment was 'laundered', either through my detective agency in London or, because of my presence in Berlin, a British or American unit decided to activate a disguised covert operation.

Because of my personal operational circumstances, I could not spend too much time searching for either Cartwright or Sandry. It was obvious that I had been duped by a cloak and dagger unit into providing a service – admittedly one for which they had paid. I therefore decided to abort my search for the truth, and concentrate on a very different type of work. Although what some new clients wanted was potentially chancy, my firm, Euro-Tec, agreed to infiltrate British trade unions.

CHAPTER 2

Infiltration of Trade Unions

On the 11th May 1970 at 9.30pm, ensconced in my office on the top floor of my modest semi in Sunbury-on-Thames, I was just about to close up shop for the night when the telephone reserved for business calls emitted its familiar ringing sound. Impatiently, I snatched the handset off its cradle, answering with an abrupt 'Hello, Euro-Tec, can I help you?'

'Gary, it's Dennis, can we meet in half an hour?' a well-spoken voice asked.

Dennis was a serving Special Branch officer, introduced to me by Army SIB friends working in Old Scotland Yard. A social relationship had developed, and occasionally I would pass snippets of information to him. I guess he considered me a useful contact.

We rendezvoused at our usual spot, a small Heathrow pub close to the Police Station at London Airport. What he had to discuss was interesting. 'I've put your firm up for a job investigating trade unions. Are you interested?' he said.

'You bet. Who will I be dealing with?' I asked.

At this point Dennis avoided going into details, and simply informed me that I would be contacted the following day. As we parted he shook my hand and said: 'There's just one small proviso about the job: there might be something in it for us so don't be surprised if you see me around from time to time. I might even ask you occasionally to expand on some aspects of your reports'.

I shrugged. 'That won't be a problem', I replied.

While trade unions obviously protect the working rights of their members, there have been numerous occasions when union activity has greatly affected not only the business operations of specific organisations but also the lives of individual British citizens. There was also the strong possibility that some unions were being infiltrated by Eastern Bloc agencies keen to destabilise the British political scene. Perhaps this was why some British industrialists decided to establish a union monitoring service, staffed by undercover private detectives based in London. Which is where my firm, Euro-Tec, came in. We agreed to form an undercover squad of industrial intelligence agents whose brief was the long-term infiltration of specifically named unions.

Between June 1970 and July 1972, this top secret operation resulted in a steady flow of data concerning the activities of a number of British trade unions. Shop stewards were monitored, as were numerous union officials, along with their families and friends. Talk about Reds under the bed!

Confidential reports were regularly supplied via solicitors to a committee of industrialists who insisted that their only reason for these extraordinary espionage measures was to monitor the activities of individuals whose conduct was considered prejudicial to the interests of management – and the State. The arrangement with my Special Branch friend continued throughout this period.

This undercover operation, codenamed 'Big Red', involved 11 private detectives who successfully infiltrated trade unions by obtaining manual or white collar jobs in various UK firms. Once in place, they cultivated and recruited 110 informants over a period of two years. A good example of these union intelligence operations is provided by the 1972 National Dock Strike.

In June 1972, along with a number of fellow undercover detectives, I was called to the offices of Messrs Bircham & Co., St Vedast

House, 150 Cheapside, London EC2, a firm of solicitors who outlined a serious union problem involving a London cold storage depot and dock workers. After an initial briefing, we were dispatched to the headquarters of The Midland Cold Storage Depot, 35 Waterden Road, London E5. Incidentally, I should point out that the firm Bircham & Co. were not involved in any way in the undercover operation 'Big Red' as mentioned above.

On arrival at the Cold Storage Depot, we noticed that the entrance was blocked by a number of pickets waving signs displaying a variety of messages including 'This is dock work, keep out', or 'This Depot is BLACKED, keep out.' After some difficulty we managed to get into the Depot, where I talked with the management and their solicitors. The problem was that dock workers were picketing a number of similar depots in the London area on the grounds that the use of cold storage staff to load and unload containers meant considerable loss of work for the members of the relevant unions.

The request was simple: 'We want you to identify the union ringleaders of the pickets and to collect evidence that can be presented to the National Industrial Relations Court.'

This particular undercover assignment was unusual in that the presence of secret agents had been requested in a court of law, for the purpose of giving evidence. Whilst we had no objection to this, I immediately realised that the undercover intelligence squad, Big Red, which we had successfully operated for two years, would have to be abandoned once the identities of the Euro-Tec operatives became public knowledge. There was no indication at the time that we were about to become involved in a sequence of events that would culminate in a national dock strike, with hundreds of protesters marching through the streets of London.

Initial research revealed that three unions appeared to be involved in the proceeding: the TGWU, USDAW and the National Amalgamated Stevedores and Dockers, their joint representation being in the form of the Shop Stewards Committee of the Port of London who, according to the

General Manager of Midland Cold Storage, had virtually taken over from the official unions in the London Docks. Manager and Director Robin Bray said: 'The Committee has taken upon itself the job of protecting London dock workers' jobs, and the Committee is trying to expand the dockers' sphere of work, basically by the use of violence or threats.'

The method of operation adopted by Euro-Tec agents was to position a large derelict van a few yards from the main entrance to the Midland Cold Storage. This vehicle was convincingly disguised to give the impression that it had been abandoned. The truth was that hidden inside were surveillance men armed with hand-held VHF radio telephones, in touch with colleagues positioned nearby who were close enough to be immediately available in the event of trouble. The vehicle was adapted in such a manner that photographs could be taken of the pickets and car registration numbers of the apparent ringleaders noted and passed to nearby mobile surveillance operatives, who would then follow these organisers to their home addresses.

The derelict van remained in place for weeks, successfully transmitting vital information that enabled Euro-Tec detectives to follow the main organisers of the picketing to their homes and to secret strategy meetings held in various public houses in and around London. By posing as sympathisers and locals, we were able to tape record all of these meetings.

The most difficult aspect of this investigation was the daily installation of the static surveillance agents. The only method we could use was for the observers to enter the vehicle every morning at 5am and to leave at 11pm. The toilet arrangements necessitated by this lengthy daily confinement are best left to the reader's imagination. There were many occasions when the workers, some of them extremely violent, actually congregated around the van to discuss their strategy. This lucky break made it possible to eavesdrop and tape record conversations. However, a number of tense situations developed when drunken dockers attempted, fortunately unsuccessfully, to get into the van. On one

25

occasion there was even talk of setting fire to our listening post.

The investigation and surveillance was an overwhelming success: we were able to report in detail on the daily plans and intentions of the picketing dockers. Obvious ringleaders were identified and tailed to their homes, and dozens of confidential meetings were infiltrated, not only those of the pickets but also those of top-level union officials. Even their wives were approached and 'chatted up' about the activities of their husbands.

Operatives were wired for sound, enabling them to tape record virtually every remark. They concentrated particularly intently on the advance plans of the strikers and pickets. One agent, disguised as a tramp, actually managed to get himself 'adopted' by the pickets on duty at the Midland Cold Storage Depot, where he bravely tape recorded hours of conversations. Even when caught in a pub toilet installing a fresh tape in his recorder, he convinced his challenger that he had stolen it from an electrical shop. The result of that confrontation was that one drunken docker offered our 'tramp' £20 for the recorder. To maintain credibility, he was forced to accept . . .

The investigation progressed throughout June 1972, until the evidence collected was sufficient to support an application by the Midland Cold Storage Company to the National Industrial Relations Court for an injunction prohibiting the picketing of the Midland Cold Storage Depot.

The Union defendants finally identified and named in the court action were Victor Turner, Bernard Steer, Derek Watkins, Anthony Merrick, Cornelius Clancy, Ronald Hedges and Edward Hedges. In addition to these individuals, various trade unions were also named: the Joint Shop Stewards Committee of the Workers of the Port of London; the Union of Shop Distributive and Allied Workers; the National Amalgamated Stevedores and Dockers; the Transport and General Workers Union.

As is normal with any court case of this nature, to ensure the attendance of the defendants at the trial official summonses were issued, naming the seven individuals.

Solicitors acting for the plaintiffs then had the task of ensuring that the court documents were served upon the defendants. They chose to use my firm, Euro-Tec. This was unusual in that infiltrators and collectors of evidence are not normally used in the serving of legal documents issued for a case in which they are also covertly employed.

Nevertheless, we decided that, with our intimate knowledge of the defendants, we were ideally suited for this task, which turned out to be a complicated operation successfully executed over a period of two days. The defendants were most displeased and took extreme measures to avoid the summonses.

A potentially dangerous situation developed on Saturday 8th July 1972 when I set out personally to serve summonses on the defendants. Realising full well that I could be identified as one of the undercover agents who had been mixing with and spying on the strikers, I came face to face with the first defendant, Edward Hedges, at 15 minutes past midnight. Service was completed as quickly as possible, leaving him no opportunity to identify me. I was aware, however, that he would immediately telephone his co-defendants. This made us even more apprehensive about delivering the remainder of the documents.

At 11.45am on the same day, I successfully intercepted Ronald Hedges and served the papers on him. From there I journeyed to the home of Tony Merrick, who immediately recognised me and challenged me as to my true identity. At first he refused to accept service of the court documents: fortunately I was able to talk my way out of the situation, leaving the summons with him.

By now, it was obvious that the defendants were aware of the papers to be served on them – and of the fact that one of the actual undercover detectives was performing this duty. Therefore, when I reached the Kent home of Derek Watkins, at 1.20pm, it was no surprise that he became aggressive and immediately identified me. I was able to serve the court documents on him, but he refused to allow me to leave the premises and a rather unpleasant argument developed, with Watkins accusing me of being a Special Branch Fascist spy who was responsible for all manner of hardships experienced by the dockers. Watkins even produced a newspaper displaying a photograph of myself accompanied by fellow detective Ian Laslett.

As usual in circumstances like these I stuck to my cover story which was simple and, on this occasion, true: I was a court process server authorised to deliver the summons and I was not obliged to give my name and/or address. Watkins was furious, so much so that I fully expected a one-to-one physical confrontation with him. However, I felt sure that I would be able to deal with him before he injured me. Fortunately, this was not necessary. I was able to persuade him to escort me to the local police station where he could make a complaint against me. I knew that once we were inside police premises I would be safe.

Sure enough, within minutes of Watkins 'delivering' me to his local station I managed to persuade the Constable on desk duty to separate us and, after a couple of minutes with an Inspector, I was ushered out of the station and allowed to go about my business of serving summonses on the remaining defendants.

At 4pm I arrived at the home of Bernie Steer, one of the principal agitators in the strike, and observed his blue Mini Estate, XYM 614G, parked outside. He was served without any undue difficulty.

The only other defendant to cause difficulty was Cornelius Clancy, who refused to answer his door despite visits at various times of the day and night. Eventually, I decided to tackle him actually on the picket line, on Monday 10th July 1972 at 7.40am. By this time we had managed to infiltrate the dockers' ranks with new undercover agents, so I was not unduly concerned at my own identity being confirmed. As I approached Clancy, he vanished into a circle of burly dockers. My colleagues, located nearby in covert and overt vehicles, had strict instructions to 'pile in' if I was attacked.

As I approached the protective circle around Clancy, I was told by one docker 'Try and get him and you're a dead man'.

This was now a personal issue with these men, and I must confess it was also a tremendous personal issue as far as *I* was concerned. Clancy was the last defendant I had to serve a summons on, and I was determined to get him.

I stared at the ring of dockers and could just about see Clancy's head bobbing around in the middle. I spoke, firmly but politely, to the ringleader. 'Don't be stupid, you know as well as I do if you start anything now your case is finished.' The dockers mumbled to each other and anxiously looked at the television camera crews who were watching. I shouted over their heads at Clancy: 'You know what this is, Clancy, don't you?' 'Of course I bloody do, and you can piss off', he replied.

The rules concerning service of court documents are simple: the defendant must be aware of what the papers are and they must be left with him. Touching him with them is accepted as 'good service'. My job, therefore, was half complete. All I had to do was to ensure he received the documents. My method was classically simple: I rolled the summons up into a baton-like shape and threw it over the heads of the dockers, not really expecting to achieve personal service.

However, I was elated to see the documents bounce off his shoulder and had great pleasure in shouting at Clancy 'That's legal service, you're served'.

I fully expected an outbreak of violence at this, as, no doubt, did the television and radio crews who were hovering like piranha fish waiting for their breakfast. But apart from a few obscene remarks, the dockers simply huddled together with the defendant to examine the documents.

With the service of summonses on the defendants completed, it was naturally assumed they would attend the trial held in the National Industrial Relations Court. Not so. The defendants formally declared that they did not recognise the court, they refused to attend and the application by the Midland Cold Storage Company for an injunction restraining the seven named dockers and the unions from picketing developed into an ugly affair.

On the opening day of the trial, a surprise witness complained that the plaintiffs had commissioned private detectives to spy on the dockers. This revelation was immediately followed by Counsel for the Midland Cold Storage Company asking the court to hear evidence 'in camera' (closed court) because certain witnesses feared their businesses would be ruined if they were identified.

The trial gradually developed into a controversial public issue, involving the rights of union members to picket. Two of the seven named defendants, Bernie Steer and Vic Turner, who had also been involved in the picketing of another cold storage depot, were committed to prison for failing to obey court orders. However, they were saved from 'martyrdom' by the intervention of the Official Solicitor. When eventually interviewed by the press actually on the picket line, they said 'We will not appear voluntarily before the court. They know where to find us, let them come.'

Throughout the trial the Judge heard allegations of violence, and requests for evidence to be heard in a closed court. In referring to the application for the court to sit in camera, Mr Alan Campbell, QC for the plaintiffs, said: 'Certain evidence is only available on the basis that it is given in confidence. It has been difficult to get anyone to come forward, because of intimidation and blacking activities.'

The expression 'blacking' referred to a system of blacklisting visiting drivers by placing their names and lorry registration numbers on what was commonly known as 'The Cherry Blossom List'. Getting on this list was very damaging for drivers, whose duties involved visiting the docks to unload their employers' goods. It meant the goods would not be unloaded and this could, in some cases, cause smaller transport firms to go out of business.

During the trial, Euro-Tec undercover agents – some of whom had actually infiltrated the picket lines, posing as dockers and taping incriminating conversations – provided a regular stream of valuable data on the activities of dockers. In an attempt to collect evidence of actual intimidation, one agent, Christopher

Burch, drove a van through the picket line and attempted to gain access to the cold storage depot. Carrying a concealed tape recorder, he engaged the dockers in conversation. On returning to operational headquarters for a debriefing, he was horrified to find that he had forgotten to switch on the recorder. The verbal report he gave was so valuable that I insisted he made a return visit. Burch agreed reluctantly, and fortunately returned eventually with the necessary evidence. He was a capable and brave undercover agent who took grave risks to complete his mission. The last I heard he was working as an airline pilot.

As an undercover operation, the investigation of the dockers and infiltration of the various unions was 'state of the art.' There had been very little time to conceive and execute a foolproof plan and almost all operational decisions, because of the unusual circumstances surrounding the project, had to be spontaneous. So it was inevitable that the identities of the detectives involved would become known to many dock workers who had taken part in the picketing and subsequent marches held in London.

The day of reckoning for us arrived when it was formally announced that Counsel for the plaintiffs would be calling private detectives to give evidence. The presence of undercover agents reporting on their covert methods of collecting evidence created an uproar among the hundreds of dockers now involved, or interested, in the outcome of this controversial case. The streets surrounding the then National Industrial Relations Court in Chancery Lane became crowded with marching, banner-waving protesters, incensed at the duplicitous methods used to collect evidence for the plaintiffs.

Left-wing elements of the media branded my colleagues and me as fascist spies working for Special Branch. And one very tenacious Communist reporter actually managed to acquire copies of confidential surveillance reports, which were eventually published in their entirety. At this point we became very concerned for our safety, so much so that we refused all interviews with the Press and arranged to enter and leave the court via a side entrance. This did very little to protect us.

As with most applications for injunctions where defendants refuse to attend court, it was eventually ordered that the seven named dockers be committed to prison for their contempt. So they were arrested and escorted to prison, thereby gaining the type of publicity normally reserved for genuine martyrs. Thousands of marchers took to the London streets, and the national dock strike that resulted from this case caused industrial chaos throughout the country. At the same time, trade unions which had been infiltrated by Euro-Tec took every opportunity to exaggerate the true circumstances of this use of private detectives.

I personally was branded as the ringleader of the whole operation, and found myself the victim of false newspaper reports accusing me of tapping telephones. Fortunately, after seeking legal advice, I was able to obtain written apologies from the newspapers responsible. However, the allegations suggesting that I was acting for Special Branch as a sideline to the main project caused considerable embarrassment. The fact that I had been seen in the company of a Special Branch officer at a London hotel during the dock case tended to add fuel to the speculation about official involvement.

From the moment the identity of Euro-Tec detectives was announced formally in court, we received a continuous stream of abusive telephone calls, uttering threats of death and other forms of violence. On a number of occasions our cars were followed at high speed by a group of men who attempted to force us off the road. Attempts were even made to immobilise vehicles at times we were expected to attend court to give evidence. The culprits were never identified, and all I know for certain is that the people responsible were not the seven defendants named in the court proceedings – they, of course, were in custody at the time.

Such experiences are common in the private investigation industry, especially for those agents engaged in tricky operations that can develop into violent confrontations. Under such circumstances it is up to the individual to take suitable precautions to ensure his or her own safety.

For me personally, this was the end of union infiltration. A number of unions, however, are still under investigation and as far as I am aware Special Branch and MI5 liaise with dozens of undercover investigators working as 'moles' on behalf of security firms linked to government agencies. Since 1972, technical methods of collating intelligence data have improved, and today electronic eavesdropping (bugging and telephone tapping) plays an integral part in undercover work. More of this later.

My career changed direction somewhat after the national dock strike when I unexpectedly joined a Special Air Service unit based at Chelsea Barracks, London.

The 21st SAS is a reserve unit utilising the expertise of civilian volunteers who are supervised and trained by career instructors from 22 SAS. My brief, unimpressive flirtation with this élite outfit enabled me to undergo specialist training, including courses at the Army Intelligence Centre in Kent. My duties with the Operations Intelligence cadre of 21 SAS brought me up to date with certain aspects of covert intelligence work. On a personal front, I'm not ashamed to admit that what was required of SAS men was far beyond my capabilities.

I also met and cultivated contacts in the Secret Intelligence Services – MI5 and MI6 – many of whom diverted potential clients to my detective agency. My expertise as a private pilot also proved very useful in this work.

This newly developed business lifestyle also meant that I was able to employ, quite unofficially, on a freelance basis, serving members of official units, on assignments compatible with their professional skills. This was an invaluable facility for a civilian detective agency, so much so that during the mid-1970s my firm, Euro-Tec, regularly employed operatives from MI6, Army SIB, the Immigration Investigation Branch, the Royal Military Police, the Special Air Service and the Parachute Regiment.

There was never any question of impropriety or abuse of my connections with these officers: all signed contracts of employment and even had their photographs taken for Euro-Tec identity cards, and at no time did I ever have access to official information protected under the Official Secrets Act. As far as I was aware, all had the permission of their Commanding Officers.

On reflection, I now realise that this was a period of metamorphosis, in that I was becoming gradually more involved in assignments of a clandestine nature.

My regular contact and my gradually developing personal relationship with government friends resulted in an influx of new clients who would telephone my office and say 'Your name has been given to me by so-and-so in Security. Can we meet?'

A good example of how informal and 'cosy' these unique official-unofficial relationships eventually became can be seen in a letter, dated 3rd June 1983, from an Army Special Branch officer to myself:

> 13 Detachment, 76 Section
> Special Investigation Branch
> Royal Military Police
> British Army of the Rhine
> British Forces Post Office 41
> Detmold Mil 238
> 3 Jun 83

'Mr Gary Murray M.I.P.I.

'Dear Gary,

   I have been a member of the I.P.I. since Feb. 81 (Ml52) and I am writing to you in response to your article "Recruiting" which appeared in the Newsletter published in February 1983.

   'I would like to recommend one of my investigators for membership to the Institute, Sgt. R.E. Meacham of the above unit, who initiated the enquiry on learning I was a member.

   'To be considered for SIB, individuals are required to pass examinations on British Criminal Law, Evidence and Procedures, and legislation appertaining to offences against the person, property and the public. A detailed knowledge of the Judges' Rules is essential and they too are tested by examination. Sgt. Meacham has passed all the required examinations and has proved himself to be a very competent and professional investigator, being able to work unsupervised during many serious and complex enquiries.

'I have no hesitation in recommending Sgt. Meacham for membership to the Institute and would further recommend that he be exempt from taking the entrance examination, as I consider his academic and investigational capabilities are above the minimum required for acceptance to I.P.I.

Yours Aye
(signed)

This letter clearly shows that, along with colleagues in the Institute of Professional Investigators (IPI), I was enjoying close links with Military Special Branch officers. Had I been inclined (for any reason) to get hold of any kind of secret information, it would have been possible to cultivate any one of these contacts to my advantage.

As it was, as a private pilot flying a civilian helicopter, I was allowed to use the Army Special Branch Training School cricket pitch to visit their base on an occasion I attended a weekend training seminar, where private investigators received lectures from SIB instructors in VIP protection. We also used military shooting facilities provided by our hosts.

Army Special Branch is not the only official unit to provide instructors to the private sector. The Royal Air Force Special Investigation and Counter Intelligence departments also provided training for private detectives, including myself, in surveillance and interrogation.

In 1977, when my expertise was in demand abroad, it became evident that other detectives were creating reputations for themselves as espionage agents. Their activities were more flamboyant and, while they obviously rendered a useful service to their clients, they were, at times, so unorthodox in the way they went about their business that it was not uncommon for some of them to end up in court, mavericks who had broken the law.

CHAPTER 3

Maverick Spies

It is not unusual for members of specialist professions to share a strong esprit de corps. But in any such fraternity, especially one where its members pursue an adventurous trade, it is inevitable that some operators will become more prominent than their colleagues. This usually leads to frequent and, at times, controversial publicity, with the creation of images peculiar to specific individuals. The private detective industry certainly has its share of such personalities who over the years have developed their own 'unconventional' reputations. Without any doubt, Britain's earliest 'maverick investigator' was Barry Quartermain.

For over a decade, Quartermain traded as one of Britain's most successful 'gumshoes of fortune' – until his exciting and controversial career came to an abrupt end in the criminal court when he received a three-year prison sentence.

At the time of Quartermain's arrest and conviction a number of government officials, including police officers, voiced a certain amount of sympathy for him. One senior officer, who has recently passed away, had this to say about Quartermain's conviction: 'Official regulation of the private detective industry has been totally ignored by Government. If this state of affairs is allowed to continue, and as long as clients have a requirement to employ these detectives for the purpose of tapping telephones and bugging premises, then I can see no curtailment of these spying activities in the foreseeable future.

'In my opinion, clients are as guilty as the perpetrators of these offences. There is also the question of government departments ignoring the problems associated with the activities of certain private detectives. Anyone who is in a position to control the illegal offences of another, and who ignores his legal and moral responsibility to legislate over such criminals, is as guilty as the accused.'

This particular informant was very forthcoming, and described in candid detail numerous cases where the authorities had refused to prosecute a number of private spies for serious offences. He concluded by saying: 'In some cases the perpetrators have been liaising with government agencies, passing on very useful data. This is one reason that, on occasions, criminal acts are ignored.

'I worked on a number of cases involving private investigators and I got to know Barry Quartermain quite well. In my personal opinion, he was a capable operative who exuded total loyalty to his clients. He was a victim of a legal situation that encouraged him to act in an irresponsible manner, which led to his imprisonment. He was, in effect, a victim of Government lethargy and lack of interest. If the law had been constructed to regulate the detective industry there would have been at least some form of deterrent, and this could well have resulted in Quartermain, and others, acting in a more responsible manner.'

This informant's expert testimony aptly illuminates the state of the profession, and just how British private detectives were getting out of control. But what about Barry Quartermain, and how did he find himself incarcerated at Her Majesty's pleasure?

The first public report on the activities of this former member of the Royal Air Force appears to have been in 1962, when the *Daily Express* reported details of a court case involving his agency:

40-year-old Mrs Mary Fredaline of Clarendon Road, Notting Hill, London, appeared at Marylebone Magistrates' Court, where she accused Quartermain of assaulting her. Mrs Fredaline alleged that he broke into the bedroom of her flat at 2.30am by forcing open the door. According to Mrs Fredaline, Quartermain was accompanied by two women, plus an Alsatian dog. At the time, she was in bed with a Mr Cole from Byfleet, when suddenly the door burst open and there stood Quartermain, a female assistant (23-year-old Pat Smith), and Mrs Cole, the wife of Mrs Fredaline's bed partner.

According to the complainant, Quartermain, armed with a flash camera, said: 'I am a CID officer from Kingston police, and I am here to get divorce evidence.' A struggle then followed, during which Mrs Fredaline was dragged, naked, from her bed and photographed three times by Quartermain. Eventually, she was knocked unconscious.

At the time of this incident Barry Quartermain was a relative newcomer to the detective industry, but had already built up a list of regular clients, including solicitors and finance companies as well as a number of official public service departments.

By 1966, he was described in the press as 'running Britain's largest detective agency'. He was then trading from Kingston-upon-Thames, Surrey, and had established a reputation as an expert in electronic surveillance. This expertise with bugging equipment led to the downfall of a number of wayward marital partners who had cheated on their spouses.

After providing evidence in one of his 'electronic' divorce assignments in 1966, a divorce Judge described Mr Quartermain's skill at bugging as 'a distasteful invasion of privacy.' Quartermain's reaction to the Judge's remark was 'I did nothing illegal, I used a tape recorder which anyone can buy.'

In fact, Quartermain was only speaking the truth. His actions were not illegal, and the result of this particular case was that his evidence was accepted and a divorce decree granted to his client. For his services, he received a fee of five hundred pounds.

In 1966, to tape record conversations secretly required a

certain amount of skill and knowledge of electronics. In those days equipment was still rather unsophisticated and bulky, which meant that the 'spook' had to conceal the machinery concerned very skilfully to achieve success.

Quartermain's method proved very successful and involved the use of an automatic sound-activated tape recorder, measuring approximately 18 inches by 18 inches. This machine, with self-charging batteries, was capable of unattended automatic operation for days at a time. On one occasion he planted the recorder near a swimming pool, 100 yards from the main house. He then extended yards and yards of wire, hiding it in flower beds. On the transmission end of the lead was a small microphone which he installed behind the bedhead. The whole installation was skilfully engineered, resulting in the collection of a lot of evidence that was useful to his client. When asked to comment on his electronic skills, Quartermain said 'The whole lot was invisible, I would defy anyone to find it.'

The late 1960s was a very lucrative period for the Quartermain empire. His business expanded and he radiated affluence. However, 1968 saw the beginning of a decline in the fortunes of the man described in national newspapers of June that year as 'the private eye with a pickaxe approach.'

Quartermain got this reputation as a result of some new and controversial work undertaken by his detective agency. The lucrative contracts passed to private eyes by local Councils, and other clients who required their own private 'effective' bailiff force was, and still is, a financially rewarding business. In Quartermain's case, he was recruited by a client to evict squatters from premises in Ilford.

Accompanied by twelve colleagues, all wearing fibreglass protective helmets, he set about his squatter eviction mission in such a manner that a pitched battle broke out on the streets of Ilford at 5am. Only police intervention stopped the public highway becoming a virtual battleground. On arrival, the police were greeted by the sight of screaming women running around in their night clothes and sinister helmeted private detectives armed with pickaxe handles and throwing bricks through the windows of the houses occupied by the squatters.

This incident ignited an intensive investigation by police into the activities of the Quartermain Detective Agency which, by 1969, was described by a number of national newspapers as 'the most powerful organisation in the country'. When questioned about this new kind of violent and unusual 'detective' work, Quartermain said 'Evicting these people is quite outside my personal life. These squatters don't bother me, they don't live with me, and when I go home to bed I certainly don't have them on my mind.'

Shortly after the Ilford street battle, questions were asked in the House of Commons about the activities of private detectives and their methods of operation. The MP for Hampstead at that time, Ben Whitaker, put a question before the House demanding an investigation into the activities of Quartermain and other private detectives, and asking in particular what legislation could be introduced to regulate their activities. Meanwhile, back at the headquarters of Quartermain's investigation group in Surrey the star of the show was enjoying a number of press interviews, and describing details of his business activities to the various journalists now interested in his international organisation.

The private eye in the public eye described how he entered the detective industry after leaving the RAF. It all appeared to start while he was serving in the Air Force. He had submitted a feature article to a Fleet Street newspaper who were so impressed with his effort they passed a number of projects to him on a freelance basis.

Eventually, Quartermain left the Air Force and set up a news agency in Kingston-upon-Thames, Surrey, from where he actually worked as a journalist. In 1955, he eventually formed the Kingston Detective Agency and by 1969 he claimed to control 13 such firms, all involved in detective or related operations.

When asked to comment on his success with electronic surveillance equipment, he said 'We were the first detective agency in this country to harness the use of electronic devices for the purposes of executing our work.'

In 1969, the Quartermain Investigation Group brochure lavishly described the services on offer. It displayed photographs of a fleet of radio-controlled cars, including a Rolls Royce. His motto at that time was: 'Knowledge, plus experience, equals successful knowhow.'

After fifteen years of private practice, Barry Quartermain appeared to have reached the pinnacle of his success. He enjoyed a luxury home with all the trappings, and was very fortunate to have numerous prestigious clients, including legal firms and banks, as well as industrial and commercial organisations who regularly used his clandestine services. When asked about the mention of industrial espionage in his company brochure, he denied undertaking such work and claimed that reference to such activity in his brochure was a misprint. Following the Ilford squatters incident, the Metropolitan Police mounted an official investigation into his activities.

The inquiry, which lasted for nearly two years, was spurred on by reports in the *Guardian* suggesting that a number of Britain's private spies were engaged in the illegal buying and selling of official secrets. It was alleged that this secret data had been obtained from various government departments, including the Inland Revenue and the police Criminal Records Office as well as various Whitehall departments. Immediately after this extensive examination of the industry, the Government announced certain safeguards to deny sensitive information to unauthorised individuals.

The investigation was led by Detective Chief Superintendent John Hensley who stated that he wanted to interview Barry Quartermain, proprietor of what was by now Britain's largest detective agency. At this time Quartermain was trying to avoid prosecution for drink-driving offences, and appeared to have taken evasive measures to avoid arrest.

Eventually, on the 16th April 1973, after he had failed to attend the Inner London Crown Court to answer the motoring charges, a warrant was issued for his arrest. And in a message to 100 countries who were members of Interpol, Scotland Yard announced that they wished to question the elusive gumshoe in connection with enquiries they were making into allegations of blackmail and conspiracy to pervert the course of justice.

By September the same year, Quartermain was still at large. In the interim a 2,500-page dossier on his activities had been handed to the Director of Public Prosecutions. This extensive report had been compiled by a special Scotland Yard 'Leaks Squad', set up following disclosures by the *Guardian* that government information was being systematically obtained for commercial use by private investigators.

The investigation culminated in a raid on the offices of Southern Commercial Investigations in Surbiton, Surrey, the headquarters of the Quartermain operation. Shortly after being interviewed, Quartermain vanished out of the country with his secretary who, it transpired, was also his girlfriend. Thirty detectives were involved in the two-year investigation which, apart from the Great Train Robbery, was one of the largest ever mounted by Scotland Yard around that period.

Quartermain remained at large until 1974 when he was arrested in Durban, South Africa. He was discovered by the authorities working as a private detective again, along with his attractive blonde secretary, Marilyn Harrison. Although there was no extradition treaty between the UK and South Africa, the offences for which Quartermain and Harrison were arrested involved passport and immigration breaches so it was decided to deport both of them back to England where, on the 17th January 1974, Quartermain was arrested at Heathrow Airport.

Finally, Quartermain appeared at the Central Criminal Court where the judge and jury heard the Crown Prosecutor describe how the defendants had adopted a 'Day of the Jackal' system to obtain passports in the names of dead people. Despite a tenacious defence, he received a three-year sentence for various offences.

Described in court as The Saint and Callan rolled into one (although his television appearances other than on news reports had been restricted to one appearance on David Frost's programme), Quartermain left behind a wife and four children when he went to prison Divorce proceedings quickly followed and court injunctions were issued, freezing all of his cash and assets. His conviction and imprisonment was said to be 'the end of the largest private espionage empire in England.' The court was told that his agency and network of spies had a veritable Watergate-type armoury of advanced bugging and telephone tapping equipment, used to collect data for their clients. It was also revealed in court that Quartermain and his colleagues acquired official information from government records.

When asked about the case and legislation, a serving senior civil servant had this to say on the 1st January 1989: 'If we could turn the clock back to 1974 when Quartermain was convicted, the correct course of action for the Government at that time should have been to activate an official method of regulating private detectives. For over twenty years these people have had a free hand, and now look at what we are faced with. We are a country where one senior police officer can spy on another via the use of detectives skilled in bugging.'

I assume that this informant is referring to author Michael Prince and his book *God's Cop*, in which he describes the use of London private eyes to bug the home of the Chief Constable of Manchester, James Anderton.

Little is known of the current activities of Barry Quartermain, except that he is no longer working as a private investigator. Rumours circulating within the business suggest he was last heard of running a hotel somewhere on the South Coast.

One would have thought that the publicity generated by the

activities of the Quartermain group of companies would have led to some kind of Government legislation to control Britain's private detectives. This was not the case: the appropriate departments totally ignored the situation, despite cries from Members of Parliament and the media. It was not surprising, therefore, that other budding gumshoes decided to involve themselves in espionage-type assignments. In fact, throughout the period of extensive Scotland Yard investigation into the Quartermain affair many other firms were also gathering official information.

Despite further arrests and convictions, the private spy business boomed, with many gumshoes undertaking some very bizarre and unorthodox assignments. Despite their questionable methods, one could not help but admire the operational success they achieved. They infiltrated organisations, bugged top secret meetings and generally accomplished the kind of goals normally associated with their official counterparts in Special Branch or MI5. Within the trade they created reputations, albeit notorious ones, that in some cases still exist today.

Operatives of this type include Ian and Stuart Withers who for twenty years have provided an impressive world-wide intelligence service to hundreds of clients. Their successful continuing presence in the industry today indicates that there is a continuing demand for such expertise.

In 1968, the Withers brothers found themselves the victims of adverse publicity when the *Sunday Times* reported that the then Home Secretary, James Callaghan, had been asked to carry out an inquiry into the activities of their Surrey-based detective agency, Christopher Roberts & Company. The hysteria that gripped Parliament and Fleet Street at the time was the result of unsubstantiated, hysterical allegations accusing the brothers of spying for the South African Government. However, there was no evidence to suggest that any member of the Christopher Roberts agency had committed any criminal offence. Ian and Stuart Withers strongly denied infiltrating the anti-apartheid movement or bugging a meeting of the United

Nations Special Committee on apartheid. Similar denials were also issued in respect of an alleged undercover investigation into John Lawrence, author of *Seeds of Disaster*, a controversial exposé of the South African Government's propaganda techniques.

The *Sunday Times* of the 19th November 1968 alleged that an undercover agent employed by the Christopher Roberts agency had investigated the activities of Lawrence, a former South African citizen living in London. According to the report, the agent, a Mr Sunderland, had been seen keeping watch on Lawrence's house and was subsequently traced, via his car registration number, to the offices of the detective agency. (Even today there are a number of South African exiles living in London who go in fear of their lives.)

A former Special Branch officer, with extensive experience of the South African Intelligence set-up in the United Kingdom, said 'I remember this incident involving private detectives and the South African Government. No criminal offences were ever committed, and as far as we were concerned work carried out for any overseas government was none of our business, unless of course there was a crime or breach of British security.'

The excitement over the South African business eventually subsided. However, in 1970 it was reported again in *The Times* that a private investigator had disclosed he was the mastermind behind the infiltration of the Anti-Apartheid Movement, and that a covert operative had posed as a voluntary worker in order to penetrate the organisation. The detective named was Ian Withers of the Christopher Roberts Agency.

This revelation came about as a result of Withers being approached by a Member of Parliament with a request to investigate circumstances surrounding the mysterious circulation of a letter on House of Commons notepaper announcing the tenth anniversary of the Sharpeville massacre.

This revived the 1968 hysteria over private spying operations for the South African Government, this time with accompanying cries demanding a full enquiry into the use of Commons notepaper and exactly what role undercover agents had played on behalf of the South African Bureau of State Security (BOSS).

The Christopher Roberts agency finally admitted working for the South African Government, but insisted that their work was non-political. No official action was taken by the authorities, and once again there was no suggestion of any criminal offence being committed by any member of the Christopher Roberts agency.

In 1971, radio amateur William Borland, a civil servant of Bromley, Kent, and a licensed radio ham operating under call sign G3EFS, started receiving mysterious transmissions from a man talking to a dog called Bess during the course of a routine radio session. These conversations fascinated Mr Borland so much that he decided to use his radio direction-finding equipment to trace the source. He eventually tracked down the signals to a hotel in Westmorland Road, Bromley, where the manager, a Mr Edwards, was known to have a Dalmatian dog named . . . Bess.

Mr Borland told the *Daily Telegraph* 'When I told him what I had been receiving, he was amazed. We searched the hotel, and found a bugging device in the bedroom.' A police investigation was mounted, and eventually a number of private detectives appeared in the dock, charged with conspiracy to contravene the Wireless Telegraphy Act by installing and using unlicensed radio transmitters. The accused included Ian and Stuart Withers, along with other members of the Christopher Roberts agency, who pleaded guilty. They received a nine-month prison sentence, suspended for three years, and heavy fines. On leaving court to be interviewed for television, Ian Withers said 'I think the sentences were extremely fair in all the circumstances.'

'TWO JAILED FOR SECRETS SNOOP' – this screaming 1973 *Daily Express* headline introduced readers to a lengthy report on an extensive Scotland Yard investigation culminating in an Old Bailey trial. The defendants were once again Ian and Stuart Withers, on this occasion trading under the name The London Bureau of Investigation.

According to the report, the events leading up to the trial began in 1971, immediately after the conviction of the Withers brothers for bugging the Bromley hotel bedroom, when a newspaper editor became interested in their boasts that they could find out anything. The editor decided to mount his own investigation into their activities. It turned out that, for a fee of £125, the brothers would cheerfully probe his tax affairs, along with the private lives of his editorial staff.

Immediately following this newspaper exercise, Detective Chief Superintendent John Hensley, with colleague Detective Inspector Bernard Davis, seized from the agency all files and records dating back for three years. The investigation that followed uncovered a whole new world of freelance espionage and illegal acquisition of secret information.

Eventually, Ian and Stuart were charged with a string of offences, including the theft of nine National Insurance cards and conspiring to contravene the Firearms Act by possessing a gas gun. The main charges involved conspiring, on divers occasions between 1968 and 1971, with persons unknown to effect a public mischief by obtaining Government information as well as confidential information from banks and building societies.

The final outcome of this case was to become the most controversial legal decision involving private investigators so far given in the United Kingdom.

Throughout the lengthy trial, the jury heard how the defendants, over a number of years, skilfully penetrated the files and records of banks, building societies, Government departments and even Scotland Yard. Their methods were so successful that opposition leader Harold Wilson and Liberal leader Jeremy Thorpe even called for a ban on the passing of information by telephone.

The system was simple, involving posing as government officials while making a telephone call to others. If the data required was held by a bank or similar institution, then the perpetrators would simply pose as officers from another branch. This enabled them to collect virtually any type of confidential information: bank balances, criminal records, ex-directory telephone numbers, traffic offences and driving licence data, as well as car registration details. The Inland Revenue was also penetrated with relative ease.

At the end of the trial, Mr Justice Caulfield said 'This form of prying could be extremely dangerous, and has very great potential for evil.' There were also strong protests from the National Council for Civil Liberties. Even the then Prime Minister, Edward Heath, set up a top level probe to be conducted by Scotland Yard.

Stuart and his brother Ian (a former policeman) both received prison sentences on conviction of intent to effect a public mischief by unlawfully obtaining private and confidential information. Their wives were also given suspended sentences. However, the case did not end with the Crown conviction. Immediately after the trial, an appeal was lodged and in 1974 the two private detectives, plus their wives, won their appeal in the House of Lords against the public mischief offences. Five law lords ruled that there was no offence in law of 'conspiracy to effect a public mischief.' Viscount Dilhorne said: 'If this left a gap in the law, it was up to Parliament to fill it.'

Prior to the House of Lords decision, the Appeal Court had altered the original sentences by imposing a reduction and suspension, accompanied by fines. Refusing to be mollified, the appellants went to the Lords, where their convictions were finally quashed and the sentences set aside. According to Lord Diplock, what the Withers brothers had done was not in itself a criminal offence. It was the element of conspiracy that was the subject matter of the charges. Lord Simon of Glaisdale said 'There was a time when it might have been appropriate and possible for the courts to develop the law to give greater protection for privacy, but this was now a matter for Parliament.'

At the conclusion of this controversial trial, a number of interesting facts relating to the 'spook' industry began to emerge. For example, it became apparent that a number of women were becoming skilful adepts of the trade.

Dark-haired Sheila Pattenden, a former employee of the Withers brothers, spoke very highly of her ex-bosses. In an interview with the *Daily Express* she said: 'The brothers taught me all about spying. At first they gave me simple things to do, like serving summonses and tracing people for hire purchase companies.' Mrs Pattenden then entered the world of industrial espionage: 'Ian taught me all I know, he has no nerves and would do anything for a challenge. He always emphasised that it was illegal to pose as a police officer. Very soon I found it was not necessary to pose as the police. On my first industrial espionage job I said I was a journalist.' Mrs Pattenden explained how, on an undercover job in Birmingham, she had been 'rumbled'.

Finally, after a year working with Ian and Stuart, she left to start her own agency. When asked about the availability of sensitive data, she said 'since all the publicity surrounding Ian and Stuart, things have been tightened up. But it is still possible to get such information. You just need luck.'

Apart from a brief mention in 1974 by the Reuters News Agency reporting on the arrest in Hong Kong of Ian Withers on charges of possessing and using bugging equipment to eavesdrop on the conversations of a lawyer involved in a property dispute, the Withers empire continued its clandestine operations quietly under a number of different trade names.

In 1978, Ian became once more the subject of intense publicity and controversy when the London *Evening News* and other national papers reported on a business espionage project referred to as 'Operation Unit Six.' On this occasion, the trade name used by secret agent Withers was the Nationwide Investigations Group of Crystal House, Middle Street, Brighton.

The main task of Operation Unit Six was to mount a surveillance on big time gamblers, the object of the exercise being to entice them from one group of gambling casinos to another.

The investigation began on 23rd June 1977, when the Nationwide Investigations Group in Brighton devised an impressive, and ultimately successful, plan to keep watch on affluent gamblers using prestigious London casinos. This elaborate operation was commissioned by the then marketing controller of a well known firm of bookmakers. Details from the Nationwide briefing outline were as follows:

'You, the clients, require us, the agents, to conduct simultaneous enquiries/observations at the six specified premises in a manner which is to be considered highly confidential with a view to:

'(a) Isolating the small percentage of high value clientele.
'(b) Identifying them
'(c) Reporting individually on these persons, with specific attention to their financial status, business interests and personal friends.'

Withers then described how he proposed to infiltrate undercover agents into the target organisations. Their duties would be to collect inside information that would assist the project.

An integral part of this espionage operation was the setting-up of special companies by the client to facilitate the payment of fees and the passing of information. These cover companies were conceived from a Regent Street office bureau, and the names chosen for them were The Indian Ocean Commercial Development Bank (IOCAD) and Xeno (Overseas) Ltd. These fronts were first of all set up by Mr. Christensen, who then approached Nationwide Investigations to carry out the rest of the task.

The Marketing Controller of the firm of bookmakers was responsible for the day-to-day operation of the project – until he was dismissed in October 1977.

The energetic and resourceful Withers was totally unaware of the real identity of the Marketing Controller, who had adopted the pseudonym 'Anthony Howard' for the purpose of this covert operation. According to Withers: 'I was approached by a man who said he had a highly sensitive job and that he had been given my name by a contact in Switzerland.

'Mr Howard said that he was working for a bank named

IOCAD which acted on behalf of substantial Middle East interests who wanted to buy a group of several independent London casinos. For this purpose they required detailed information and research on existing casinos and their top gamblers.'

Having hoodwinked the Nationwide organisation into believing he was acting for Middle East interests, the client accepted proposals submitted by Withers, and the assignment got under way. Within a few days of starting, undercover agents were in place and turning in fascinating details of the gambling and financial habits of famous Arab princes, as well as other prestigious individuals using London casinos. Reports also provided confidential data on a baronet businessman, a well-known newspaper publisher and a Member of Parliament.

Throughout the investigation, which lasted until October, Withers and his men provided car licence plate details to 'Anthony Howard'. This they did by mailing the registration numbers to the Regent Street accommodation address, from where they were collected and passed on, via a third party, to a 51-year-old former police officer, who was able to obtain the names and addresses of the car owners from the Police National Computer. Neither the Withers brothers, nor any member of their firm, were involved in the illegal part of this obtaining of car registration details.

Operation Unit Six came to an abrupt end with the dismissal of the Marketing Controller. Withers recalls: 'Howard just disappeared. We sent telexes to IOCAD, but there was no response. Eventually, we received a telephone call from him, and it was then that he told us of his real identity and that he had been working for Ladbrokes all along. He said we should submit our final account to them for settlement.'

The Unit Six project was probably one of the most skilfully executed private intelligence operations ever conducted in the United Kingdom. At one stage, twenty undercover operatives and surveillance vehicles were involved. At no time did Ian

Withers and his colleagues commit any criminal offence.

Regular publicity has been an invaluable marketing aid for Ian and Stuart. Their expertise has been used in hundreds of situations, notably the physical recovery of children involved in domestic disputes. In 1980, Ian's child recovery success was so well known that he appeared in a BBC television programme, 'Man Alive'. Unfortunately, not all of his recoveries went smoothly and one in particular resulted in yet another appearance in court for him, this time charged with child stealing. This happened in 1977 when, along with two fellow detectives, Christopher Austin and Leel Fieldsend, Withers was commissioned to locate and recover the two-year-old daughter of an American, Robert King.

As with most Nationwide jobs, the location and recovery of the child, Lara, went quite smoothly when, in the presence of the client, her father, she was taken from her mother whilst out walking in Hampshire. Both father and daughter immediately returned to the USA. However, complaints were made by the mother and eventually Withers and his colleagues were charged. At Winchester Crown Court they were convicted of child stealing, given a nine-month suspended sentence and fined £2,000. Appeals were submitted, but in July 1980 the Appeal Court upheld the convictions and dismissed their application.

In the United States, where there are around 25,000 children recovered by parents each year, Ian Withers is regarded as something of a folk hero. Every time he returns to US airports he is greeted by scrums of reporters and TV crews. He is regularly mentioned on radio stations, who broadcast his telephone number to enable parents to contact him. Even the powerful pressure group Childrens Rights Inc. advises it members to use the Withers Recovery Service. Ian is very open and frank, and doesn't even deny that it is a lucrative business. Ten thousand pounds would not be an unreasonable amount to pay for the military-like precision that is a feature of every Withers child recovery assignment. It was not surprising, therefore, that senior members of the United States Central Intelligence Agency (CIA) were eventually to show an interest in the activities of Ian Withers and his intelligence network. He and his men are ruthlessly efficient, planning every move with SAS-style professionalism, keeping watch and stalking their targets to ensure a clean safe lift. To date, the organisation has completed hundreds of successful reclamation operations all over the world.

The Withers 'empire' is genuinely international in scope, with Stuart in charge of the British element and Ian last heard of working as the Chief of Intelligence for the Seychelles Government.

CHAPTER 4

The Seychelles

Scattered like confetti in the Indian Ocean, the Seychelles Islands are gems of tropical beauty. However, camouflaged by this beauty lies a more sinister, less attractive side: political coups, spying and murder. On the fringe of these unsavoury activities are British private detectives who, for a decade, have engaged in secret intelligence operations carried out by the Seychelles Government. To understand just how and why British detectives came to work for the Intelligence Service of the Seychelles, it is necessary to know something about the recent history of this group of islands.

Once owned by the French, this small paradise was eventually transferred to the British who, in 1976, granted the islands independence. At this time a former London barrister, Sir James Mancham, was elected the first President of the Seychelles.

Mancham, a staunch capitalist, was known as a flamboyant individual. On election he told his citizens 'We must live for love, we must live for the moment. When I move into the Governor's residence it's going to be the swingingest State House in the world, there will be parties every night.'

There have been many suggestions that this cavalier playboy attitude was a major factor in the coup that ousted Mancham from power a few months after his appointment.

However, it is highly unlikely that this former President was entirely to blame for the actions of his Prime Minister, Albert René, a fervent Socialist and political arch enemy.

Within months of Mancham's election René began plotting a take-over. In no time at all he smuggled in Russian AK-47 rifles which he hid in his back garden. René and his left-wing Peoples United Party then set about training secretly a small loyal group of supporters in military tactics. This was done by discreetly sending a selected few to the Marxist State of Tanzania for specialist tuition in firearms and various military skills. Mancham may have spent more time partying than dealing with affairs of State so he was totally unaware of the left wing plot to oust him.

The absence of intelligence information from the British or American Secret Services leads one to suppose that they too were ignorant of the planned take-over. It is highly unlikely that they would have countenanced the Socialist take-over of such a strategically important group of islands.

The timing of the coup was perfect. It happened when President Mancham was attending the Commonwealth Leaders' Conference in London. On a tranquil Sunday morning the AK-47 rifles were retrieved from their hiding place and distributed amongst René's supporters who, accompanied by five hundred heavily armed Tanzanian soldiers, seized control of the principal government buildings in the capital, Victoria.

By Monday morning René had complete control of the islands and a curfew was in force, with tourists confined to their hotels. The coup had been a walk-over: it left the first President of the Seychelles exiled in London and three people dead, one of them a René rebel accidentally shot by his own men. In London, Mancham blamed the Russians.

President René's Marxist policies began with the withdrawal of all press freedom. News was strictly controlled by the Ministry of Information. Property was confiscated, and private enterprise was only allowed to continue under licence. Schools changed philosophy overnight, and all residents were obliged to register their personal details with the new Government.

Leaked reports suggested that young people were passing through the Soviet Aeroflot office en route for 'special training' in Moscow, and tourists spoke of poor service and the numerous restrictions typical of a Marxist régime.

René's Presidential style was completely different to Mancham's. Fully aware of the risk of a counter-coup, he took extreme precautions to ensure that he was not ousted from power. He recruited initially a small force of Tanzanian soldiers to protect the principal buildings, then, acting on the advice of his Defence Minister, he finally settled for an élite detachment of North Korean troops to provide round-the-clock protection

The Soviet Embassy increased its staff to about fifty diplomats, some of whom were KGB and GRU officers. The intelligence men monitored the military situation, passing on vital information to René and enabling him to neutralise potential counter-coups. He enjoyed total support from the Russians.

By mid-1977, Albert René was securely ensconced as President. However, the risk of a counter-coup was a serious problem and he therefore decided to develop his own secret network of intelligence agents to monitor the overseas activities of his opponents. His first move was to employ London-based private detectives to keep former President Mancham and his deposed colleagues, living in exile, under surveillance. The task of recruiting these undercover agents was entrusted to Ralph Adams, whose only qualification for the diplomatic post of High Commissioner was the fact he was President René's brother-in-law – unless his previous occupation of accounting manager was felt to qualify him for the job.

The High Commissioner's telephone call on Monday the 22nd August was made to my own firm, Euro-Tec (Private Investigators). Mr Adams explained to me that his Government required very discreet assistance for a long period, and stressed that the agency's identity would have to be top secret. At this stage in the conversation I had no idea of the nature of the assignment, and simply agreed to attend the offices of the Embassy at 2 Mill Street, London W1. At 11 am the same morning I met Adams at the Embassy, where he briefed me thoroughly.

Apart from the recent reporting of the coup, I was unfamiliar with the Seychelles political scene and so had to bring myself quickly up to date about it. Ambassador Adams stressed the need for investigations into the activities of a number of exiled former Seychelles Islands officials and residents who were suspected of planning a counter-coup to be kept secret. The suspects he named were James Mancham, David Joubert, Chammery Chetty, André Uzice, Gonzague D'Offray, E D C Camille and Jacqueline De Comarmond. In addition, a list of residents under surveillance in the Seychelles was provided, and I was asked to confirm any link between them and the London exiles.

To help maintain the anonymity of Euro-Tec, Adams insisted that all communications should be addressed c/o The Ashdown Hotel, Hereford, and that invoices should be worded: 'To services supplied to the Seychelles for various police equipment given confidentially to the President'. (*Sic.*)

Despite this obsession about secrecy, cheques were drawn openly on the National Westminster Bank Ltd, Oxford Circus Branch, 249 Regent Street, London W1, made payable to myself. These cheques were easily identifiable as being drawn on an official Seychelles Government external account, number 24954713 – a rather amateurish attempt at secrecy to say the least.

I mounted with colleagues a complex round-the-clock surveillance on the suspected counter-coup conspirators. Initially, we tried to liaise with British Special Branch officials to track down certain London-based mercenaries believed to be responsible for organising a counter-coup: unfortunately, assistance was not forthcoming. Perhaps if I had been more familiar with the general political situation concerning the Seychelles I would have realised that behind the scenes the British Government were keen unofficially that Manchan be reinstated.

However, despite the absence of Special Branch co-operation, we managed successfully to monitor meetings at top London hotels. We were also able to identify numerous plotters actually resident in the Seychelles.

The assignment generally was extremely stressful for the Euro-Tec agents. The mercenaries under observation, as well as the exiles, were alert and everything they could to conceal their activities. At times I virtually lived in my surveillance vehicle, washing and shaving in street or hotel toilets. On one occasion we clocked up thirty-nine hours of non-stop under-cover work collecting evidence.

During the course of the project, an unexpected telephone call from a polite male with a slight Russian accent asking to discuss the undercover operation was the first in a chain of events that led to the assignment being terminated. I accepted the request to meet a man who was indeed obviously Russian and who was interested in employing Euro-Tec to carry out certain local enquiries to do with the Seychelles assignments. From conversations with this man it was clear that he was in contact with Seychelles officials – and that he had an intimate knowledge of Euro-Tec activities.

After a few days seeking official advice and considering the wider implications of an Anglo-Soviet relationship, I decided to terminate the assignment. I had no wish to involve my firm in Soviet Intelligence work.

The strategic value of the Seychelles is the main reason why the government of the day will go to extreme lengths to protect its interests there. While most of the islanders are interested primarily in fishing and other traditional activities and tourism is obviously a lucrative source of income, the real value of the islands lies in their position in the Indian Ocean. Other valuable assets of the more than eighty islands are numerous coves, natural harbours and mountains that have great naval and military usefulness.

Despite his heavy Marxist leanings, Albert René maintains close links with the West. He is host to an American Air Force satellite base, leased for a cool $2.5 billion. This spy equipment is part of the Satellite Control Facility (SCF) based in Sunnyvale, California, with other branches in England and Greenland.

The SCF handles top secret electronic and photographic espionage information and is an integral part of the US official intelligence programme. As well as this American base, René also allows the operation of a World Service transmitting station, controlled by the BBC in London.

In 1977, the strategic and political importance of the Seychelles was such that dozens of foreign intelligence officers, disguised as diplomats, could be observed eavesdropping on each other at the Pirate's Arms café in Victoria every morning. Representatives of the KGB, GRU, CIA, French Security, and of course MI6, showed a continuing interest in the islands. The Russian presence was rather overwhelming, with a permanent clandestine contingent of troops and equipment. There was also the occasional display of Soviet strength by visits from warships and amphibious carriers with support vessels conveying *spetsnaz* (special forces) troops. All in all, the Soviets, along with other powers friendly to the Marxist Government, had found themselves a perfect training ground and staging post for covert military and naval operations.

This influence even extended to the main Polytechnic College, where Soviet and Cuban teachers were reported to be engaged in the indoctrination of Seychelloise students.

Now, of course, with the end of the Cold War and the old Soviet régime, things are gradually changing.

In 1979, René's overseas private intelligence service came under the control of a former London police officer-turned-private eye, Ian Withers (see Chapter 3). Moving freely round the international espionage fraternity, Ian waged a successful worldwide campaign of counter-intelligence operations for René. He was even respected by members of the CIA. The US

Ambassador to the Seychelles said of him: 'He seems to have successfully kept track of people plotting to overthrow the President – the CIA certainly seems to think so. I would really like to meet this guy, he intrigues me.'

The US Ambassador was not the only government official to praise the expertise of Ian Withers. A former senior British Special Branch officer, familiar with the private detective industry, said: 'My personal opinion, and I stress *personal* opinion, of this man is that he is an extremely competent operative.

'I agree that he has, on occasions, broken the law but let us not forget he has been punished for his crimes – and that's more than I can say for certain officials in a number of government departments who, for years, have committed identical offences and have got away scot free.'

Withers began a long-term relationship with the government of the Seychelles Islands during 1979 when President René, in desperation, turned to the British Government for help in dealing with his political enemies. A similar request to France resulted in a French Intelligence Officer, Jacques Chevalreau, being seconded to the islands to advise René on the best methods of dealing with the opposition. He also organised an armed patrol boat, along with twelve French sailors, to train the fledgling Seychelles Navy. However, this was not at all satisfactory. The serious problem was in London, where a number of determined exiles were planning a counter-coup under the leadership of Gerard Hoareau, a 31-year-old ex-immigration officer and fervent anti-socialist who had been jailed and subsequently expelled by René.

In 1979, Hoareau was the head of the London-based 'Movement pour la Resistance' (MPR) whose members were dedicated to the destruction of the René régime. Between 1979 and 1985, Hoareau and his supporters were responsible for a number of attempted counter-coups. However, our man Withers always managed to neutralise their attempts. After the refusal of Whitehall to send naval vessels to the islands, an official of the Crown Agents suggested to René that he contact Ian in London.

It is said that Withers received his initial instructions via telex, and that in a very short time a top secret scheme was devised enabling London investigators controlled by Withers to provide one of the most professional and effective private counter-intelligence services ever made available to any foreign government. There were many indications that Withers and his team had more than the tacit agreement of the British Foreign Office.

For several years, the activities of Gerard Hoareau and his fellow MPR colleagues were monitored and neutralised. Telephone calls were intercepted, even overseas visits were observed, and advance information of MPR plans obtained. Hoareau supporter Eddie Camille alleged in 1982 that his telephone was tapped by Withers, and complained to London police. However, the Director of Public Prosecutions decided not to press charges.

Having been stalked by René's spies for years, some exiles were able to recognise Withers from a considerable distance. 'We spotted him in Paris, in a hotel where we were staying', said Hoareau. 'We also saw him tailing our cars; he seemed to be everywhere.'

One attempted coup, organised by Hoareau and his MPR friends, would have succeeded had it not been for the inimitable Withers. In 1981, the legendary mercenary Mike Hoare, of Congo fame, agreed to penetrate the islands with a group of freedom fighters disguised as a rugby team. Unfortunately for Hoare and his men, telephone calls to and from the London exiles had been monitored, and Withers was able to intercept full details of the planned attack. He even sent surveillance agents to South Africa to observe the mercenaries in training. Consequently the coup was doomed from the very start.

Mike Hoare and his soldiers arrived at the airport on the main island of Mahé, posing convincingly as a South African rugby team. Instead of sports kit, though, their baggage was loaded with automatic weapons and hand grenades. The Seychelles authorities' plan was to allow the party to pass through the airport, and then for René's troops to arrest them.

However, an observant immigration or customs officer, not aware of the plan, sighted a weapon protruding from a mercenary's bag. A fierce gun battle ensued, with a few of the infiltrators escaping by hijacking an Air India aeroplane parked at the airport.

It was interesting to observe that, within twenty-four hours of the abortive coup, a number of heavily armed Russian warships arrived off the coast of the Seychelles Islands. This left no doubt about whom René could turn to in emergencies.

Withers and his private intelligence operatives continued with their covert investigations of the MPR. Their duties now extended beyond Europe to South Africa and Kenya, where it was suspected Gerard Hoareau and his determined conspirators could get aid. By 1982, the Withers organisation's detailed knowledge of MPR activity indicated that more plots were being hatched to oust René from power. The situation became so serious that a 'sting' operation was mounted by the René 'Secret Service'.

It was a simple plan depending on a pro-René agent convincing Hoareau and his followers that he would help them to reinstate the deposed President Mancham. The MPR, believing they were on the verge of a successful counter operation, organised a secret meeting with an agent at the Carlton Tower Hotel which has a reputation for high security standards. To convince their clients, the hotel publicity stated: 'You can hold the most important discussions over dinner in your luxury suite, and know that our special security service ensures complete privacy'.

The hotel staff had no idea that the occupants of Room 412 were plotting to dispatch mercenaries to the Seychelles to dispose of President René and his government. They were equally unaware that the room was bugged, and that an anonymous tip had been sent to Scotland Yard's anti-terrorist squad and to the *Sunday Times*. The bugs planted in the room were state of the art and enabled the eavesdroppers, the anti-terrorist squad and the *Sunday Times* to overhear clearly the plot hatched by Gerard Hoareau and his colleagues.

There was no doubt about the seriousness of the plotters' intentions. The conversations indicated that a coup was imminent in the Seychelles, and that it would be mounted from South Africa, preceded by violent acts of terrorism.

The coup was planned and controlled by Hoareau himself, who was present in Room 412. The money for this operation had been obtained from South African sources and was to be used to pay the mercenaries. The plot that unfolded on 30th September revealed that Hoareau intended that the coup should be carried out in two stages: firstly, a programme of destabilisation involving the use of a mercenary vanguard – this group would carry out bombings of hotels and public buildings on the islands to prepare the ground for the main force. The second stage would be for three hundred mercenaries, recruited in South Africa, to land and engage the government forces.

Unfortunately for Hoareau, he was being tailed and the hotel meeting room was bugged. So every word of the meeting was intercepted and passed to President René. In fact, the conversations in the hotel room could have been intercepted by anyone listening on an ordinary domestic VHF radio on frequency 105. The reception was crystal clear, and from the following extracts it was clear that a military operation was being planned:

> MERCENARY: 'We should hold back until we have all the arrangements and all the supplies on the spot.'
> HOAREAU: 'Yes.'
> MERCENARY: 'Tell the tour operator to take it easy until I arrive. Tell the boys to keep cool until I arrive.'
> HOAREAU: 'When will that be?'
> MERCENARY: 'Between the 16th and 21st of October.'

> HOAREAU: 'Did you get enough stuff?'
> MERCENARY: 'Five kilos, plus a few small you-know-what.'
> HOAREAU: 'Yes.'
> MERCENARY: 'And eight 25-kilo containers.'
> HOAREAU: 'That should keep you going.'
> MERCENARY: 'It's a sizeable amount.'
> HOAREAU: 'The more we have, the better it is.'
> MERCENARY: 'At this stage we must be careful on the telephone.'
> HOAREAU: 'Yes.'

Other conversations referred to the problem of uniforms for the mercenaries. It was considered very important for morale that the freedom fighters all wore the same clothing.

From this conversation it became apparent that weapons for use by the mercenaries had actually been stored at London's Heathrow Airport. On the 2nd October, men from Room 412 checked that a special consignment addressed to them had arrived on flight SAA228 and been stored in the South African Airways cargo store. Telephone calls from the mercenary recruiter, based in Durban, confirmed the arrival of the various weapons, and Hoareau was seen leaving the London hotel carrying bulging plastic bags.

The tape recorded hotel conversations revealed some sinister angles to Hoareau's plan, including a discussion about killing the Seychelles Defence Minister, Ogilvy Bertouis, who was due to return to his base at the same time that one of the mercenaries was to infiltrate the islands. Hoareau wondered whether the 'merc' might 'get at him'. The mercenary asked 'A permanent solution?' Hoareau replied 'Yes, according to our information he is very much the strength here'. The mercenary grunted 'Okay'.

At this point the *Sunday Times* realised that the plotting was serious and that lives were at risk. The Seychelles Consulate in London was warned of the imminent coup, and President René spoke personally with *Sunday Times* reporters. 'I would like to know what these people are up to in England', he said. He then revealed that a number of incidents on the islands suggested the destabilisation phase of the attack had already begun. He said 'We too have certain information about the coup. Almost every night their supporters here try to set fire to one place or another. We learned that the Foreign Office had heard about the plot earlier this month, and had alerted the Security Services'.

Now things began to gather momentum. Another plotter, Paul Chow, a former Seychelles newsagent, had found out that his London telephone was tapped; Edmond Camille discovered that he too was under surveillance and extreme concern gripped the MPR. The visitors to Room 412 carried out search after search, and eventually uncovered a bug hidden in the wall skirting. Meanwhile, the two-man vanguard successfully infiltrated the islands, only to die under mysterious circumstances when their car blew up on a lonely beach about fifteen miles from the capital, Victoria.

At three o'clock on Wednesday afternoon, Hoareau and the others heard of the deaths of their men. After a great deal of discussion, and amidst much despondency, they agreed the wording of a Press statement, which was duly phoned to Fleet Street and the BBC: 'This is another case of Seychelloises being massacred by Tanzanian soldiers', it said.

That afternoon the *Sunday Times* passed all their available information to Scotland Yard, who began a thorough investigation into the bugging of the hotel room. A stream of visitors attended Room 412, including Special Branch detectives and ex-President Jimmy Mancham.

Hoareau immediately left the room, hiding his face, and two of his colleagues refused to speak with anyone. Chow, however, admitted to being responsible for the Press statements.

Shortly after, the Seychelles police announced that the men killed in the car explosion were two South African mercenaries, Mike Asher and Simon Denousse. A police spokesman said 'We believe that the men were carrying out a sabotage campaign'. A distraught girlfriend of mercenary Mike Asher said 'I don't know why Mike should have risked his life for an island in the middle of the Indian Ocean'.

An extensive Scotland Yard enquiry into the circumstances surrounding the bugging failed to expose the culprits. President René denied being involved, and the obvious suspect, Ian Withers, also vehemently denied having anything to do with the electronic surveillance of Gerard Hoareau and his plotters. René's response to the bugging allegations was 'This has all come as a surprise. We do get information from here and there, but the facilities to listen to all this plotting we do not have'.

With his latest attempt to oust the socialist René frustrated, one would have thought that Gerard Hoareau and the MPR would have gone into hibernation for a while. But far from it: they actually stepped up their protests to include marches on the streets of London, with banners displaying the words *'KGB hors des Seychelles'*. Efforts to organise a successful coup were also stepped up.

Hoareau's continuing relentless efforts led to a massive increase in surveillance and covert operations directed against himself and his organisation. In charge of this activity was private detective Ian Withers who, in 1985, employed the freelance services of two highly skilled spooks specialising in electronics to bug and wiretap a number of exiles in London. Their primary target, Gerard Hoareau, was at that time living in the suburban area of Edgware, Middlesex.

Bugging specialists David Coughlan and former British Telecom engineer David Richards were recruited by private eye William Underwood. He had accepted the assignment from Ian Withers, who in turn was acting on behalf of the Seychelles government.

Coughlan, a former SAS electronics expert alleged to have been employed by British and foreign governments on counterespionage duties, set up what surely must be the most sophisticated private electronic eavesdropping enterprise ever conducted in the United Kingdom.

Receiving his instructions via a cut-out, Coughlan, with Richards and William Underwood, set out to bug the home telephones of Hoareau and another Seychelles exile living close by. They found it impossible to get into Hoareau's home but, not to be deterred, they managed to intercept his telephone line over half a mile away, and by installing a transmitter on the line were able to relay all conversations conducted on the tapped telephone to a nearby listening post.

Not content with successfully tapping Hoareau's phone, they also managed a similar intercept on a second exile who used a local public telephone box for his sensitive calls. This traditional method of keeping 'phone conversations secure failed: the spooks simply wired up the telephone box and transferred all calls to their listening post.

In most telephone tapping operations, the eavesdroppers normally get their intelligence data with a sound-activated tape recorder, or alternatively sit in a discreet control van and record the intercepts themselves. However, in the Seychelles case the government went to the expense of purchasing a £60,000 house located near the targets of surveillance. This proved to be such an excellent listening facility that Coughlan and his associates were able to go about their business easily without fear of detection.

For three months the electronic surveillance on Gerard Hoareau was maintained. Tapes of all telephone calls were delivered regularly by special courier to the Seychelles, and a comprehensive dossier on the activities of the MPR was compiled. Hoareau was without doubt not merely a pain in the neck for President René: he was René's most feared opponent.

On the 29th November 1985 the surveillance of Gerard Hoareau came to an abrupt end when he was shot dead by a professional hit man. Using an automatic weapon, the killer assassinated the formidable MPR leader as he left his home in Greencourt Avenue, Edgware.

The telephone intercepts for that period, dispatched to René as normal, were said to contain the sounds of the 'hit'. If this was the case, then the whole house, not just the 'phone, was bugged.

It emerged that the day Gerard Hoareau was murdered he was on his way to deliver to the *Sunday Times* a three-page dossier claiming to tell how René had tried to murder him. A major political row erupted. Coughlan, Richards and Underwood were arrested and charged for their role in the affair. They denied any knowledge of or involvement in the assassination and at their trial the Judge formally announced that he was confident they were totally unaware of any plan to kill the target of their surveillance. They were, however, sentenced to terms of imprisonment for the bugging and wiretapping offences.

The individual at the centre of the row, Ian Withers, was nowhere to be found. From his base in the Seychelles, he denied having anything to do with the killing, and indicated that all his statements would be made through his English solicitors. In the meantime, Scotland Yard issued Press releases indicating they wished to interview him.

Detectives investigating the murder seemed convinced that it was carefully planned and that the killer had a back-up team that had kept the victim under surveillance for some time before the attack. Enquiries revealed that Withers had left the country two days before the assassination.

In *The Times* on 6th January 1986 it was reported that on the date of the murder Withers was in the Seychelles Islands where, it was said, he attended the High Commission after the shooting and offered assistance to the authorities. According to solicitors acting for Withers, the police did not wish to interview him. However, his offices in Brighton and Belfast were searched, and a 21-year-old secretary was arrested under the Prevention of Terrorism Act and held for four days. Withers said of the shooting: 'As soon as I have completed my business here I shall, subject to the advice of my solicitor, come home. What I am afraid of is, they might grab me as I get off the plane.' To date, as far as is known, he has not returned to the United Kingdom and there is not a shred of evidence to connect him, or any of his men, to the assassination.

Despite the death of their leader, the MPR still carried on in the hope that one day James Mancham would replace René. Not a lot was heard of Mancham: he lived in discreet exile in London, guarded around the clock. However, this did not stop masked raiders from breaking into his house, searching it for papers – and beating him severely. Understandably, he declined to allow me to interview him. Who can blame him? After all, at one time I had kept him under surveillance.

Immediately after the assassination of Hoareau, the remaining members of the MPR went into hiding, staying underground until 1992 when René formally announced that he would restore multi-party democracy following the 1991 collapse of the Soviet Union. This encouraged Sir James Mancham to come out of hiding and plan his return to the islands to stage a come-back, but not without round the clock protection.

As expected, Mancham received an enthusiastic welcome as he went about his election campaign, protected by a crack squad of military bodyguards managed by a serving SAS soldier. According to a report in the *Sunday Express* of 17th May 1992, this soldier secretly organised a private mercenary army to guard Mancham. Another member of the team was said to be one of the Prime Minister's aides, Michael Sedgwick, and additional members of the bodyguard entourage were alleged to be other serving British soldiers. Nonetheless a Foreign Office spokesman said 'There is no form of official protection being given'.

Mancham's return to active politics is shrouded in mystery, but one thing is certain: at the time of writing he has embarked on a vigorous come-back campaign and, judging by the reaction of the islanders, he could well win the forthcoming elections. How this will affect the former René 'Secret Service' is anyone's guess. Revenge could very well be sweet.

CHAPTER 5

Electronic Eavesdropping

An interesting aspect of undercover investigation highlighted by the Seychelles affair is the use by private spies of electronic eavesdropping. Although only civilian practitioners, they could obtain and use sophisticated bugging and telephone tapping equipment with such facility that I felt compelled myself to investigate this fascinating technical world.

My research revealed that a formidable GCHQ-type of fraternity has existed within the private detective and security industry for nearly two decades, and that many of these civilians have talents equal, or even superior, to those of former MI5 agent-scientist Peter Wright, who of course caused a furore in 1987 with his book *Spycatcher*. Wright initially joined MI5 in 1955 as principal scientist and was responsible for the development of various electronic gadgets and methods of bugging and tapping.

His early work not only set the trend for other government departments to establish their own technical facilities but also led to tricks of the trade being 'inherited' by the private element of the investigation business.

Since the early 1960s, the clandestine tape recording of conversations has been for many private detectives a favourite method of collecting evidence to support cases. Journalists and other researchers have also adopted this tactic and it is now universally popular. Indeed, I have enjoyed great success with my own miniature tape recorders.

To tape record secretly other people's conversations is not actually illegal: the law is only broken when the spook resorts to breaking and/or entering to instal radio transmitters (bugs), telephone tapping equipment and other electronic surveillance items. Surprisingly, under current legislation it is not illegal to possess, manufacture or sell bugging and tapping apparatus: only if it is actually used is a criminal offence possibly committed. In general, existing regulations are vague and without any real power to deter private spies who frequently use sophisticated James Bond-style electronic equipment.

Despite an alarming increase in the number of prosecutions for bugging and telephone tapping, magistrates and judges seem to be imposing only minimal sentences in what have obviously been cases of serious espionage.

In 1988, two private detectives were sentenced under the Interception of Communications Act for tapping the telephone of a former Dixons executive working for the rival firm Comet. Their sentence was a mere six months, despite the fact that they were engaged in industrial espionage involving large amounts of money. The remarks of the Judge at this trial raised a number of eyebrows. He said 'Companies and individuals are entitled to engage in industrial espionage, such as under-cover surveillance and electronic eavesdropping.'

This toothless legislation, along with court officials who do not understand how serious civilian espionage activity is, has encouraged spies to adopt an almost blasé attitude to eavesdropping assignments. Also, the availability today of cheap, sophisticated high-tech electronic devices means that any private eye willing to undertake bugging commissions can now earn vast amounts of money. If the perpetrators are caught they face a sentence of only six months' imprisonment with perhaps a token fine. Frankly, the fees offered are big enough to tempt even the most ethical individual onto the eavesdropping trail.

The tapping of the 'phone of the Comet executive already mentioned, Peter Hopper, resulted not only in the prosecution of two private detectives but also exposed a nationwide corporate spy ring operated by eavesdroppers working on the behalf of a big business institute in the City of London. According to *Today* newspaper, up to fifty separate wiretaps had been installed by private detectives engaged in industrial spying. The scandal was said to date back several years, and involved an Essex police officer from the Technical Support Unit who was suspended from duty for revealing to the private eyes confidential information held on the Police National Computer.

This espionage network would never have been discovered had Mr Hopper not begun to have trouble with his telephone. He contacted British Telecom, whose engineers detected a small tape recorder connected to the external phone line. Police enquiries led to the organiser of the ring, a former police officer operating a detective agency in Stratford-upon-Avon.

According to reporter Quentin Cowdrey of the *Sunday Telegraph*, a private investigator employed by a firm with 20 offices in Britain, admitted to having eavesdropped for three months on the London headquarters of a major company involved in a one million pound take-over. The *Sunday Telegraph* reported that this detective had bugged the firm three years ago, and had also placed taps on nine of the company's phone lines, eighteen months before the 1989 revelation. It was reported that the fee for this service was £110,000. 'There is in the City now a very cold, calculating element which is quite prepared to hire private detectives to get information', said the perpetrator. He denied breaking the law, despite the fact that according to recent legislation telephone tapping had been declared a criminal offence and radio transmitters had to be licensed by the Department of Trade and Industry. It is not my intention to examine the complicated legislation covering electronic surveillance, except to say that the overall situation is ludicrous in that numerous private spies have for years escaped just punishment for their espionage activities. A major contribution to this situation has been that relevant legislation, even the most recent, is totally inadequate.

Electronic detective Terry Rowe, one of the defendants jailed for his part in the Comet tapping case, has turned his expertise to counter-surveillance. According to a *Times* report compiled by journalist Tony Dawe, Rowe, described as the 'Barnes Wallis' of bugging, has developed equipment that will assist potential victims to counter or detect bugs and telephone taps. Mr Rowe is adamant that he will stick to debugging (checking offices and telephone lines for eavesdropping equipment) and that his days of climbing telegraph poles to tap phones are over. He says that his services are in great demand, and amongst his clients are businessmen and a Water Board. He has also installed secret cameras aboard the QE2.

Professor Michael Beesley of the London Business School claims his research indicates that over 2,000 bugs a week are being sold in the United Kingdom. Another research programme, carried out by the *Independent* in 1988, revealed that numerous firms of private eyes were willing to supply and instal eavesdropping equipment. The *Observer* went so far as to investigate the methods of operation of one Middlesex detective who accepted a request to monitor telephone conversations using a bug. This detective, a former senior officer from New Scotland Yard, was exposed for this offence.

To the lay person, expressions such as 'telephone tapping' and 'bugging' conjure up complicated technical images of electronic wizardry. Put simply, *bugging* means the use of any form of radio transmitter for the purpose of intercepting conversations.

Transmitters ('bugs') vary in size and can be planted in any room or building, in a vehicle, or even attached to a telephone handset or the actual line. In order to listen in, the eavesdropper must possess a receiver, which can also vary in size.

The spy simply tunes the receiver to the frequency programmed into the bug and listens to conversations, which can easily be recorded. The dangers involved in the use of illegal transmitters are few, but it is quite possible for police and aircraft frequencies to be interrupted by unauthorized intercepts. Such a situation could lead to the detection of the eavesdropper. But more serious than that, vitally important police or aircraft messages could be distorted by illegal communications traffic with potentially disastrous results. For example, in the case of passenger aircraft over flying congested areas it goes without saying that interrupted radio messages could have horrific consequences.

Tapping is an expression used to describe the attaching of a hardwire link anywhere along a telephone line. Usually, the 'tap' is connected to a tape recorder or listening device, and the conversations are recorded by the listener. In cases where a bug is attached, the phone is then not tapped, but bugged.

In many such cases, telephone bugs are very sophisticated and manufactured to automatically switch on and off at the beginning and end of telephone conversations.

With suitable equipment, the determined spook can easily plant his bug or tap. All he needs is to get into the target premises: the rest is easy. Some equipment can be installed in a few minutes, and is quite often undetectable by the naked eye. Everyone in the United Kingdom is a potential victim, but obviously some people are more at risk than others. For instance, high profile company directors are often targeted by private detectives and security agents, as are executives engaged in takeover transactions. Pre-takeover investigations are regularly passed to private investigators who, for substantial fees, will undertake electronic eavesdropping for their clients.

Any industrial or commercial firm involved in the development of new processes or products should beware. Industrial spies, operating in most major cities, regularly take on espionage assignments for business consultants and

advertising agencies anxious to steal new ideas. These operators have access to the latest technology, and in some cases
have spied for years without being caught.

They often masquerade as public relations or management
consultants, or even journalists, but in all cases their intention
is to steal secret data. It is not uncommon for a professional
spy to receive £50,000 or more for a one-page document detail-
ing the advertising plans for a new product. Expansion plans
are also vitally important to competitors.

In 1987, a London private eye, working as a business espionage agent, was paid £100,000 in cash for the expansion
plans of a top British company engaged in takeover negotiations. Six months later, the same detective received a £250,000
fee for placing a transmitter in the offices of another company.
His brief on the second occasion was to intercept plans for a
redundancy programme being considered by the firm.

Cellular telephone advertisements bedazzle users with electronic jargon like ETACS, DUAL NAM FACILITY, ALPHA
NUMERIC STORE, MULTIPLE LEVEL CALL RESTRICTION,
and a host of other technical terms that are difficult, if not
impossible, for the ordinary user to understand. Despite this
high-tech marketing approach, the actual equipment and cellular communication system, although a miraculous techno-
logical creation, has serious security problems. One very
serious technical flaw that appears to have gone unannounced
by the manufacturers and service suppliers is that conversations conducted on cellular telephones can be intercepted – as
embarrassed members of the Royal Family have discovered
recently.

The truth about the British cellphone system is that all calls
are at risk, and there is no built-in safeguard to protect the confidentiality of customers' conversations. Users appear quite
unaware of this problem, and openly discuss very delicate
business matters, without realising that anyone possessing a
simple piece of equipment known as a scanner can listen in.
Once in operation, the scanner automatically searches for

active calls. On detecting communications traffic it locks on, thus enabling the eavesdropper to listen and, if necessary, tape record the conversation. British Telecom land line calls connected to the cellular system can also be intercepted and there are few, if any, indications for the caller that a call is being monitored. In any event, the ordinary cellphone user will simply assume any change in conversation quality is due to one of a number of normal factors affecting reception within the cellular system.

Scanning equipment is readily available at numerous specialist electronic outlets all over the country. One popular High Street chain, Tandy, admits to having sold over ten thousand scanning devices. Despite the fact that it is illegal to intercept radio communications without an official licence, brochures and instructional leaflets describe, in simple detail, how to detect and listen in to cellphone conversations. But it is impossible to assess precisely how many customers have been intercepted. However, a study of the sales figures of scanning equipment suggests that there must be over 30,000 such devices in the United Kingdom. If all these were used regularly, then the number of eavesdroppings would run into over a quarter of a million each week.

While researching this book, I acquired a simple scanning device to demonstrate just how easy it is to intercept 'phone calls. The victims were astounded to hear tapes of themselves discussing very confidential business matters.

> VICTIM (1) – Famous showbusiness manager Tony Cartwright, responsible for the affairs of internationally known singing star Engelbert Humperdinck, was overheard discussing highly sensitive financial matters with an accountant. The identity of the star was mentioned several times.
> When presented with a tape recording of his conversation, Cartwright said 'I am absolutely dumbfounded. I always assumed my calls were secure. This is terrible, it should not be allowed.'

VICTIM (2) – A Kent businessman speaking with his cell-phone airtime supplier reacted strongly when informed of the intimate details of his conversation. 'The sale of these devices is appalling: they are of no use to the public and should be banned. This must be exposed', he said.

As well as the above conversations, I also monitored a number of obviously confidential-bordering-on-secret discussions between foreign Embassy staff discussing diplomatic security, and sub-contractors to the Electricity Board arguing over a nuclear power problem. Even bank staff were overheard passing balances to customers. Another conversation between hotel guests giving details of their credit cards exposed a great potential for postal fraud.

By far the most serious breach of telephone security was the conversation between VIP bodyguards, discussing on their cellphones the movements of a famous industrialist.

Private detectives and security consultants use scanning devices to steal industrial secrets, and London-based industrial spooks openly advertise receiving equipment in their company brochures and eagerly respond to enquiries from clients looking for espionage services. One established private security agent admitted to numerous cellular telephone intercepts for industrial clients: 'I have been listening in to cellphones for years. The system is a piece of cake. Once I've confirmed the target's frequency, I simply sit up the road or follow his car, and tape record all his conversations. I've even been paid to spy on a politician who uses a mobile phone', he said.

Without doubt, the cellphone is the most popular method of mobile communication. Businessmen, civil servants, journalists, law enforcement agencies, and even – as we know – members of the Royal family are potential victims of the eavesdropper. Buckingham Palace declined to discuss what security precautions were in force, but did say 'Several members of the Royal family use cellular telephones in their cars. We are unable to comment on anything to do with security of calls'.

A firm involved in high-risk security operations is Executive Security, based in Virginia Water. This firm is responsible for the safety of many houses on the prestigious Wentworth Estate, including property adjacent to a new temporary home of HRH Duchess of York. Managing Director Colin Halsey described how his company uses cellular communications for delicate security operations: 'Our staff use cellphones, and I assumed that our calls were secure. Only a few days ago one of our clients mentioned a secret code we use, in a telephone conversation'. He went on to say 'It concerns me that our calls are vulnerable. Many large London security firms also use this equipment. The sale of these scanning devices must be banned. I am now very apprehensive about using cellphones. There is great potential for armed robbers and terrorists to use this equipment'.

There are two organisations currently providing the cellular telephone service in the United Kingdom, Cellnet and Vodaphone. Although these organisations operate independently of one another, technically scanning devices are capable of intercepting either service. Bruce McCormack of Cellnet said 'There is nothing built in to the current system to protect calls. Eventually there will be the new Pan European equipment operating on 900mz, this should make eavesdropping initially more difficult'.

Mr James Malcolm of the Federation of Communication Services in London was very concerned at the use of scanning devices for eavesdropping purposes: 'We frown on the availability of scanners: this is an invasion of privacy of the highest possible order. It is also an open invitation to all kinds of espionage. This is very disturbing indeed', he said.

With the sale of scanners increasing, the problem of eavesdropping is bound to grow. According to a spokesman for the sales department of a major supplier of this equipment, there are two models 'selling like hot cakes.' It is estimated that by the end of 1993 there will be almost one hundred thousand scanners in the United Kingdom, so escalating the number of illegal intercepts. Unfortunately, the cellphone user can do very little to protect the confidentiality of calls apart from adopting one or two commonsense precautions:

Be guarded in general conversation
Refrain from imparting sensitive data on the air
Never identify names, addresses, or ex-directory numbers
Remember – eavesdropping criminals can use such data
for the purpose of planning robberies and kidnapping
If possible, adopt some kind of code
Investigate the possibility of a scrambling device

Private detectives have little or no difficulty in getting hold of covert surveillance equipment. A number of London agencies, especially those engaged in confidential security assignments, have experts on staff whose sole job is to maintain high-tech bugging and telephone-tapping equipment. However, in the main, detectives usually buy in special devices for particular assignments. The substantial retainer paid by the client usually finances the purchase of the necessary gadgets.

There are many specialist electronics firms operating throughout Britain, and some of them have brazen advertisements running in national magazines. The equipment available from these organisations is of high quality and capable of performing most electronic intelligence functions. Other more discreet companies adopt a personal marketing approach in selling their wares, and quite often have government agencies as clients – the Home Office or Ministry of Defence, for example. Their products are manufactured to the highest specification and are only used by official departments on approved frequencies. To put it simply, they are legal, although perhaps unethical.

A firm called Security Specialists Ltd was found operating from a Post Office box number in Essex. According to their brochure, the various sophisticated items for sale included a Data Bug. This interesting but frightening piece of equipment was demonstrated by director Mark Williams in an industrial espionage mock-up for Channel 4's *Network 7* programme. He demonstrated how, sitting in his car in London and with the use of a lap-top computer, the Data Bug could divert information from other computers onto the screen, and he was able to retrieve it. This kind of computer espionage has horrific implications.

Security Specialists' 32-page catalogue also advertises numerous impressive devices, from the small PPTX FM micro transmitter with a battery life of 250 hours to the more cumbersome Bionic Ear. This equipment is described as being used by law enforcement and private detective agencies in the USA. It is said to use sensitive microphones and to be capable of amplifying sounds thousands of times. Security Specialists Ltd also sell transmitters disguised as fountain pens, and even calculators. On page 17 of the brochure is the AR2001, a radio receiver scanner suitable for intercepting – that's right – cellular telephone calls, plus a number of services they say 'cannot be mentioned.'

The AR2001 comes complete with a car adaptor and confidential listening guide. This guide includes the private frequencies of cellular telephones, official law enforcement agencies such as the police and military, British Telecom car 'phones, and even those of the Ministry of Defence and nuclear safety teams.

Without doubt, the most impressive supplier of covert equipment is the firm Lorraine Electronics of East London, a trade name used by Ruby Electronics Ltd. The Lorraine brochure describes in professional detail the many items available to the adept spy, including the recording briefcase which is constructed so that its carrier can easily activate a hidden switch, the briefcase then tape recording all conversations in the immediate vicinity. An excellent tool for espionage agents, or even researchers and journalists, it is not illegal to use and provides very clear recordings. More unorthodox equipment includes the notorious telephone infinity transmitter that can be used to eavesdrop on conversations from any location, even another country. This gadget has been popular within the industry for nearly twenty years.

Also described in the Lorraine brochure are other kinds of bugging devices suitable for many applications or situations, such as deceptively innocent 13-amp twin adaptors, wall contact amplifiers, voice-activated amplifiers, room transmitters, and telephone transmitters. In particular, the 13-amp twin adaptor is a most useful listening device. Disguised as an ordinary adaptor, it actually functions as such – and at the same time transmits conversations to a simple receiver operated by the eavesdropper. Also, for £750 one can purchase a UHF room transmitter built in to a 13-amp socket: this device is simple to instal and blends in immediately with the surroundings.

Bugging is such big business that suppliers can afford the services of public relations and advertising consultants. On 26th July 1988 the firm of Smedley McAlpine, advertising and marketing consultants, wrote to a Channel 4 independent TV production company offering to arrange a bugging demonstration by their clients, Lorraine Electronics. Smedley McAlpine offered to set up the demonstration in any way that suited Channel 4, and suggested that they (Smedley McApline) should bug their own office and relay the conversation to the office of the production company.

Private detectives and security agents now have easy access to supplies of bugging and tapping equipment from firms like Lorraine Electronics, Security Specialists Ltd, and many other organisations scattered over the country. One former private detective, now serving a prison sentence, said: 'I worked in the detective business for ten years. When I get out of prison I will start up again. I often used bugs, and used to purchase them from firms advertising in *Exchange and Mart*. I remember getting one piece of kit from Lorraine Electronics: it was superb and did what I wanted it to do. Bugging is big business in the City – bankers, politicians, they're all at it.'

Another firm of private investigators and security specialists advertise on their letterheads 'British Investigation and Security Service, authorised distributors of surveillance equipment for Lorraine Electronics.' Prices for bugging and special tape recording equipment can vary from a few pounds for a small fountain pen transmitter to hundreds or even thousands of pounds for complex eavesdropping equipment. Special tape recorders can cost as much as £275, and the recording briefcase sells at £399, including the built-in micro cassette tape recorder.

There are a number of gadgets that can be used in the fight against espionage. In some cases this equipment is very expensive, sometimes in excess of £3,000, and can quite often be so complicated to use that a specialist has to be hired at a rate of £300 per hour or room. To complicate matters further, eavesdropping equipment currently being used by private spies is so complex and sophisticated that quite often a device can be remotely controlled, so that when carrying out an electronic sweep the expensive de-bugger can quite often fail to detect the dormant bug. Fortunately, there are a number of simple-to-operate radio frequency detectors on the market that, for approximately £180, perform a reasonable job of de-bugging. The only other method of protection open to the potential victim is to take commonsense precautions. For example:

> Never reveal the location of confidential meetings. Wait until the last moment before announcing a venue.
> Never leave secret documents unattended.
> Vet all staff employed by the company. Ensure that confidential data is only released to those with a need to know.
> Do not discuss sensitive matters on the telephone, or in suspect situations.
> Do not become a slave to telecommunications, especially cellular phones. *All* telephone equipment is vulnerable.

If it is suspected that telephones or offices are bugged, carry out a physical search. Include in this search an examination of the outside of the target premises: it is possible a surveillance vehicle will be parked near the building.

If a discreet counter-surveillance service is required, do not under any circumstances approach a firm that sells *offensive* bugging equipment. Many suppliers provide both bugging and de-bugging equipment, and it is quite easy for an unwitting client to approach a de-bugging company that has in fact also supplied the bugs already installed in their premises. When choosing a de-bugging expert, make sure that the firm approached specialises in that kind of service.

One London security agency working only in counter-surveillance has achieved regular success against the electronic buggists. 'We have uncovered hundreds of eavesdropping incidents for clients over the years. We do not rely on complicated, expensive equipment. We use our experience and ability physically to detect an eavesdropping situation. Our countermeasures programme is the best in Britain,' said a spokesman.

It is not uncommon for intelligence and police departments to turn occasionally to the private sector for discreet, unofficial electronic assistance.

For instance, in October 1976 a police detective working on the (now famous) Operation Julie drug case was keen to intercept the telephone conversations of one of the principal suspects. Instead of officially applying to the Home Office for a tapping warrant, he approached a private security and detective agency who carried out the operation illegally. The detective's excuse for this unorthodox method was that he believed police corruption was such that any mention on paper of a telephone tap would have come to the notice of the drugs gang.

One of several interesting features of this incident is the detective knew where to contact a private spy who was willing to engage in illegal espionage. It also raises the question of how many other illegal surveillance operations have been carried out in this manner.

As long as toothless legislation allows the sale of bugging equipment, and as long as the criminal courts fail to discourage espionage activity, then private spies will continue to act for rich clients who are willing to expend large sums of money. However, if some official system could be devised to regulate both the activities of detective agencies and the use of transmitting devices, then industrial espionage in this country could be contained.

Whilst such legislation would obviously inhibit private practitioners engaged in covert intelligence operations, it is highly unlikely that the work of the Security Services (MI5 and MI6) and other secret government units will ever be controlled, despite the fact that much of this work is immoral and at times actually illegal.

CHAPTER 6

Security Services

A secretive and controversial organisation within the official spy fraternity, MI5 is responsible for intelligence operations within the United Kingdom. Controlled by the Ministry of Defence (MOD), the structure of 'Five' is such that different sections carry out a variety of duties, e.g. monitoring the activities of foreign diplomats, vetting defence companies' employees, surveillance of suspected enemy agents, and so forth. It is not my intention here to delve deeply into the work of these departments, except to point out that there *is* a specialist department concerned with the breaking and entering of premises for the purpose of searching, bugging and other covert activity. Occasionally, this kind of work is subcontracted to freelance civilian agents.

Formed on 28th August 1909 by an asthmatic Captain (later Sir) Vernon Kell, MI5 has expanded from a small office with one clerk into a massive secretive cloak and dagger organisation, with a reputation for being unorthodox and quite often less than legal in its activities.

In recent years, the public has been treated to an endless series of shock revelations about MI5, from the discovery of staff working as foreign agents to allegations that the actual Director General of the Service between 1956 and 1965 was himself a Russian 'mole'. More recent damaging confessions from two former fulltime employees reveal in candid detail how MI5 operatives have for years burgled and bugged their way around the country, not investigating enemies of the State as one would expect but invading the privacy of ordinary citizens simply exercising their democratic right to speak out. Victims of this illegal activity have included the Campaign for Nuclear Disarmament (CND), Greenpeace, the National Council for Civil Liberties, journalists and politicians – in fact, just about anyone who is considered to be a threat not so much to the State as to a small diehard faction's view of the status quo.

In most of these cases there was little, if any, evidence of espionage and subversion as described in the historically evolved functions of MI5, which are 'to foil the spying efforts of enemy countries (counter espionage), to detect perpetrators of sabotage (counter sabotage), and to pre-empt any revolutionary potential which may arise in the country (counter subversion)'. (Sources: the 1952 directive issued by the then Home Secretary, Sir David Maxwell-Fyfe. The Security Services Charter.) This divergence from the official line has caused serious dissent within the Service, so much so that career officers are now going public with their own accounts.

Two MI5 'whistle blowers' who have recently exposed embarrassing facts about their work are Cathy Massiter and, perhaps the most controversial of all, Peter Wright, author of *Spycatcher*. Officially, the MOD will not comment on the problems associated with MI5. However, unofficially some officers are perturbed over recent events and current trends:

'We've had serious problems for years', said one officer. 'It is now manifestly obvious that we have lost track of our true identity and rôle. We waste a considerable amount of our time investigating people who are in no way associated with espionage or subversion. To make matters worse, we have our own subversive clique within the Service, who are a law unto themselves. Hopefully things will improve in the future,' he said.

This decline in morale is not restricted exclusively to MI5 career operatives. It also extends to the freelance arena, where unofficial spies are also becoming concerned about their work.

On the 31st July 1981, a private investigator attended the Ashford, Middlesex, offices of W L Booth, a Solicitor and Commissioner for Oaths. Holding a copy of the New Testament in his right hand, the detective attested as follows:

> 'I swear by Almighty God that this is my name and handwriting and the contents of this my affidavit are true'.

The document was then notarised by William Booth and duly signed by him in the presence of the detective. The affidavit, omitting the usual formal introductory preamble, read as follows:

> 'During November 1979 in the normal course of business activities I found it necessary to submit a written report to the Security Services. This I did via a friend employed in the Foreign Office, London.
>
> 'As a result of my report I had a number of meetings with officials of the Security Services (MI5) and eventually during March of 1980 I was recruited to act as a freelance agent, concentrating on a specific project.
>
> 'Since March 1980 until the present time I have been involved in a very intense investigation dealing with several officials from MI5.
>
> 'Throughout the assignment I have kept duplicates of all reports submitted and where possible I have obtained tape recordings of my dealings with MI5 officials, as well as other persons involved in the investigation. This evidence is now lodged in a secure place.
>
> 'During my relationship with the Security Service, I have frequently found myself in situations that could have caused me considerable professional and personal harm had any mishap occurred and I now find it necessary to put on record the fact I am acting for the Security Service.'

The affidavit was then annotated as having been sworn at 2 Station Approach, Ashford, Middlesex, on the 31st day of July 1981, and signed by Commissioner of Oaths W L Booth.

The person making this affidavit was a detective from a Middlesex-based agency who had been recruited to spy for MI5. However, like many of his official counterparts, he became disillusioned at what he was expected to do. But what drove him to tape record his conversations with his handlers, why did he find it necessary to lodge duplicate reports in a 'secure place', and what did he mean by 'considerable professional and personal harm'? Before examining this man's story, I think it is important first of all to explore briefly the use of civilian secret agents by the Security Service.

An integral part of security and intelligence operations is the spotting, recruiting and handling of informants. Civilian men and women from all walks of life have, for years, been used by MI5 to supply information of interest to the Security Service, and providing they are strictly controlled, then there is no better way to conduct intelligence operations. An early recorded example of this kind of official 'domestic' spying occurred in 1950 when MI5 successfully recruited a man working at a Vickers Armstrong aircraft factory. For fourteen years Fred, operating under the code-name George, passed on useful data from inside the Communist Party. At one stage he even became a shop steward, which greatly aided his undercover work. He received several hundred pounds for his services.

It is relatively easy to spot many of these potential agents. After all, there are thousands of private detectives and security consultants operating in Great Britain, many of whom are themselves former Special Branch employees or erstwhile members of Armed Forces Intelligence. These people are, in effect, ready-made for undercover assignments and, if they are not already enjoying a relationship with government contacts of their own, to approach and cultivate such a freelance is a reasonably straightforward business.

An examination of the 1984 register of the Institute of Professional Investigators (IPI) and the 1987 Year Book for the International Professional Security Association (IPSA) clearly shows individuals from all branches of the official Security and Intelligence Services, as well as from the police, sharing membership with private detectives and security consultants. For example, on pages 53 and 57 of the IPSA Year Book, serving officers in the Royal Air Force, the Ministry of Defence and the Nuclear Security Department are listed alongside civilian members. The ranks held by these government servants vary from junior NCO to senior commissioned officers holding the rank of Squadron Leader and above, all sharing membership with private practitioners.

Also listed in the 1984 IPI Register are private investigators and officers from all branches of the Armed Forces, the Ministry of Defence, the police and Military Intelligence. Even two Foreign Office officials are listed as being members. I must stress that there is nothing illegal or unethical about private and government officials enjoying membership of the same organisation. Having said that, my personal opinion is that such cosy relationships can create a great potential for impropriety.

My own recruitment as an unofficial secret agent occurred about a year after joining the IPI (March 1979). On admission to the Institute I was unaware of the numbers, or types, registered as professional investigators, although I did assume incorrectly that the organisation was made up only of private operators. When I discovered that among the four hundred or so members there were representatives of virtually every branch of the police, Security and Intelligence services, I must say I was a little surprised, to say the least. My own experience of relationships between government and private agencies was such that I had always made every effort to maintain a degree of discretion and correctness, even with operatives I considered my closest friends.

Throughout 1979 it became all too clear to me that some members of the Institute were working for secret intelligence units and that civilians had unauthorised access to information supposedly protected under the Official Secrets Act. I also discovered that one particular detective agency, based in London, was undertaking regular covert assignments which could only have been commissioned by either the Security Services or other government departments. Although I was not overly concerned, I was gradually becoming apprehensive about the carefree and at times downright blasé attitude being displayed both by my private colleagues and official servants of the Crown. I will elaborate further on this in due course.

Surprisingly, my own induction to MI5 did not result from my association with the IPI. By 1979 I had cultivated numerous contacts of my own, particularly a former Intelligence Corps Staff Sergeant who had progressed to the Foreign Office where he was working as an operative for the Secret Intelligence Service (MI6). We were such close friends that it was not unusual for 'Sparky' (I am obliged to use his nickname for security reasons) to spend his off-duty hours working for my detective agency. Our friendship spanned nearly a decade and I eventually became godfather to his son.

On the 26th February 1980 I received a telephone call from Foxtrot Bravo (name changed to protect identity). He identified himself as a Ministry of Defence official and mentioned the name of my MI6 friend 'Sparky'. After a brief conversation, it was agreed that I should report to a Whitehall address on 28th February.

At 11.10am, dressed in a smart pinstriped suit and carrying the obligatory umbrella, I strutted along Whitehall, curious but enthusiastic about joining what I had been led to believe was an élite spy service. At precisely the appointed time, 11.15am, I entered the old War Office building and reported to the security receptionist. I had taken my first step into the shadowy world of counterintelligence. After working privately for over a decade, with an occasional quasi-government assignment, I was about to become official. This was my fantasy at any rate as I announced my name to the steely-eyed security staff who issued me with a temporary pass. After a cursory search I was escorted by a smartly dressed secretary to Room 055.

Room 055 was in fact a small suite of two or three mini-rooms, tidily but sparsely furnished. From the atmosphere and general appearance, I sensed that this was not an operational intelligence office but probably nothing more than a hospitality suite or occasional meeting place for Ministry Intelligence officers. After being politely relieved of my umbrella and invited to take coffee, I was introduced to two officials from MI5: Delta Whisky and Alpha Hotel (I am obliged to adopt codenames for these individuals: it is, after all, possible that they were using their correct names). For a few minutes we chatted about the weather and how long I had known 'Sparky' my MI6 friend. Delta Whisky gave an impression of animosity towards MI6: this was to become more apparent in the following months. Eventually, we got down to the nitty gritty of my visit.

My ability as an investigator was checked. 'Do you have access to people's credit ratings?' was one question put to me by Alpha Hotel. Great interest was also shown in my experience as a civilian pilot, types of aircraft on which I was rated and how many hours I had accumulated as a captain in command. The area of my work that attracted by far the most interest was the recent change of direction in my professional career which meant I was now undertaking assignments for television programmes and national newspapers. This frequently brought me into contact with investigative journalists, CND protesters and other radical types, with whom I would eventually come to share an affinity.

I remained in Room 055 for just over an hour, during which time I was asked if I would undertake freelance work investigating people suspected of espionage or subversion. I was given a pep talk on how some people working in the media were very dangerous, and was told that their subversive attitudes were a threat to the security of the nation. I did not agree entirely with this statement but accepted that it was possible some irresponsible types might fit into this category. Excited at the thought of becoming an MI5 agent dedicated to hunting down enemies of the State, I enthusiastically accepted the offer without realising that during the coming months I would discover that the most dangerous enemy of all was not to be found in the media or anti-nuclear fraternity. It was a bit closer to home.

At the conclusion of this meeting, it was agreed that I should return at a later date to finalise operational arrangements. I assumed this to mean that some kind of contract would be signed to formalise our association. How wrong I was.

I returned to Room 055 on 10th March 1980 at 11am and was introduced to 'Golf Romeo' (once again I am obliged to adopt a codename) who was to be my operational controller or, as they are sometimes called, 'handler'. Discussions on this occasion were confined solely to general aspects of my future work, whom I would be investigating, the fact that no debriefings would ever be held at Ministry locations, and so forth. It was stressed that I was to concentrate on collecting evidence of espionage and/or subversion. Targets of investigation were agreed and special telephone numbers were provided.

Subsequent enquiries through a British Telecom contact eventually confirmed that these numbers were registered to the Ministry of Defence at Curzon Street, the headquarters of MI5. Despite my repeated requests for a written agreement that would set out guidelines, my hosts dodged and weaved skilfully in conversation, using flowery academic talk which, while sounding impressive, ultimately led nowhere. I finally accepted their profound assurances of a future contract and agreed to start work immediately.

I left the old War Office building with my handler and we walked across the river to the National Theatre where, over lunch, he set out the various ground rules for the freelance spy. No records were to be kept, even my wife was to be kept ignorant of what I was engaged in, and of course under no circumstances was I to discuss my work with *anyone*.

I explained politely that I did not have a photographic memory and that it would be necessary for me to compile reports for analysis by his department. He eventually agreed to such reports, without realising I would be keeping copies – which of course I did, my trade training and general craftsmanship being such that I was not about to leave myself open to being compromised. Arrangements were made to meet at regular intervals outside London: Richmond, Windsor and Guildford became favourite rendezvous points. There were also a number of debriefings held at London Airport terminal buildings, Bracknell, Amersham, and Cobham. On these occasions I was always treated to a meal, during which various aspects of my work would be discussed. My reports were then handed over in exchange for my regular retainer plus expenses.

My first operational controller did not impress me. He had a formidable capacity for drink and some of our evening meetings often ended with him staggering off into the night with his Ministry briefcase full of who knows what sensitive material.

It was not uncommon for him to flourish a ten by eight surveillance photograph and ask me if I could identify someone, all this taking place in restaurants or bars, sometimes full of drunken customers. This behaviour sat oddly with his paranoia for secrecy which was, in my opinion, almost a sickness. At every meeting he would ask me 'Are you sure you weren't followed?' Sometimes he would look around furtively and say 'I hope you've done your counter surveillance'. I lost count of the number of occasions he voiced his concern about the possibility I was tape recording our telephone conversations.

In addition to his professional shortcomings as a counter intelligence operative, he also left a lot to be desired on the personal level. After a few drinks he had a habit of talking about himself: I considered this to be unbelievably amateurish and found myself interrogating him indirectly about his background and personal circumstances. Over a couple of days I was able to extract from him the fact that he was born in

Lancaster and had a brother aged about 39 years serving in the Royal Signals who was due to retire from the Army to live in Yorkshire. Before joining MI5, it would appear my handler had served in the RAF as a National Serviceman. He then did a three-year engagement in the Signals Branch, during which time he learned Russian. I presume this must have been a valuable asset to the Security Service.

I was very surprised at just how easy it was to extract such personal details out of this man. He even described some of his experiences during basic training for MI5, and how he had served for twelve years in the London area. He also imparted information about his hobbies, his family, children and the area in which he lived. If the very unusual name he was using had been his true name – and I believe it may well have been – it would have been relatively easy to track him down to his home address. I remember thinking when he was posted to Ireland later that year 'Poor bastard, if he doesn't keep his mouth shut and watch the drink he's a dead man'.

Despite my dogged attempts to conduct myself in a professional and security-conscious manner, I found it impossible to instil a similar sense of responsibility in my operational controller. Here we were, supposedly engaged in a top secret investigation in the interests of State security, and he couldn't even arrange a meeting with me so that I could deliver reports and documents concerning suspected Russian agents. After telephoning my MI5 'hot line' on the morning of 29th July 1980, I was informed by a female officer that my handler was unavailable. This infuriated me. I was in possession of two urgent reports plus important documents I had managed to get from a major intelligence target – and I had no way of contacting my controller. After only a few weeks I was already becoming seriously disillusioned.

At 9.15 the same evening, I finally received a telephone call from my intoxicated handler. He was deaf to my frustration and just tried to placate me. 'I'll contact you tomorrow and we'll arrange to meet', he promised. However, it was not until

Saturday 2nd August 1980 that he condescended to make himself available for a debriefing, which took place sitting on a
park bench in the middle of Richmond Green. At this point in
time I was involved in a difficult investigation and needed
as much back-up and guidance as possible. My chief worries
were that I was expected to obtain information that appeared
to have nothing to do with espionage or subversion, and
that I had urgent reports and documents to deliver to the
Department.

Following another exasperated telephone call to Curzon
Street, I rendezvoused with my handler on 6th August 1980,
again in the open air and in full view of the public, this time
on Kew Green. On this occasion he really surpassed himself:
he was an hour late and eventually, when he did arrive, he discovered that the hands of his watch had fallen off. To add to
my vexation, he gave off a stale odour of alcohol, and to cap it
all he informed me nonchalantly that he would be unavailable
for a month.

I left that meeting determined to improve my MI5 situation.
I had now become embroiled in complicated investigations
that depended on personal and business relationships which
had to be nurtured and handled with the utmost discretion.
My first move was to contact 'Sparky', my close friend in the
Secret Intelligence Service, MI6.

After lengthy discussions, he agreed to speak with his own
Section Head, who he was confident would liaise with his
opposite number in MI5. It was also suggested that in the
meantime I should tape record all my conversations with anyone and everyone from Curzon Street. This, Sparky assured
me, would provide some protection should I ever find that any
of my subjects of investigation had been arrested. This was a
very important consideration throughout the two years I spent
working for the 'Wombles of Curzon Street', as they had now
been nicknamed by myself and Sparky. One target in particular obsessed my masters who were determined to get him one
way or another. I lived from day to day fully expecting him to

be arrested and dreading that I would be drawn into the prosecution case by mistake.

Having discussed my problems with Sparky, I was confident that MI6 would see me all right with their counterparts on the other side of the river. I was therefore quite cheerful at the next meeting that took place on 4th September 1980, in a small pub in Amersham. After I'd passed over my latest report and received expenses of £90, the conversation turned to MI6 and my relationship with Sparky. Why had I spoken to him about my work? The mood of the meeting changed: now I could see the obvious rivalry between the two Services. It was certainly not a healthy competitive spirit such as can encourage different teams who are essentially on the same side to strive as friendly rivals towards a common goal. What I was witnessing was a mutual hostility between our principal Security and Intelligence Departments that was definitely not in the best interests of national security. I did not like what I heard at this meeting: highly critical and at times downright abusive remarks about the ability not only of MI6 but also the Special Branch were made by my handler. Finally, the meeting ended with him directing me in no uncertain terms to sever all contact with my friends in MI6, Special Branch and all other official departments.

This was the last straw. I decided that in the continued absence of a formal contract it would be foolhardy for me to carry on working for MI5, so in an attempt to create a satisfactory professional safe relationship I decided to send a letter to the Head of Section responsible for overseeing my operational controller.

On the 2nd September 1980, I sent an eight-paragraph letter which, on the advice of my MI6 friend, made no complaints about my controller's conduct. He felt that it would not be in my own interests to expose this man's behaviour. 'After all, there are other ways to deal with such a person', hinted Sparky. I often wondered if my handler's transfer to Belfast later that year was anything to do with his conduct, or whether it was a bit of subtle back-stabbing by the Foreign and Commonwealth Office who 'control' MI6.

My letter of 2nd September was straightforward and to the point. It read as follows:

'I have given great thought to our relationship during the last few weeks and I now find myself in a position of having to apply concentrated thought to a number of situations in which I could find myself involved. Three important examples are:

'1. Classified and/or stolen documents being found in my possession while in transit to your Department.

'2. Becoming greatly involved with the subject (on your instructions) in particular projects that could be considered illegal.

'3. Possible eventual arrest of the subject and finding myself pinpointed by him and the Press as the person leading to his downfall, the end result being a complete Press hammering and misrepresentation of my actual status and involvement. I could be presented not only as an informer or grass but an actual fellow conspirator.

'You yourself have stated many times under no circumstances will my identity ever be revealed. – This is fine from the operational point of view but in any of the mentioned situations, that could make life a little awkward for me.

'I consider it a great honour to assist your Department in my limited amateur way and am more than willing to continue for as long as is required, but I do feel completely out on a limb operating in this very informal manner. When one examines my position I am nothing more than an informant. Your Department of course has a different and more glamorous description, but my position remains the same. I have no professional protection or guarantees when acting on your behalf.

'If you feel our relationship has been successful to date and is worthwhile continuing, then I do feel obliged to put my feelings to you and respectfully suggest that I do require a more formal relationship with your Department.

'My normal method of operation is to have a contract or letter of instruction but in our case this I assume would

not be even considered. Perhaps we can discuss this matter in more detail and reach some mutual agreement.'

Having sent off my letter and conditioned myself to with-
drawing from the assignment, I went about the normal every-
day routine of running my detective agency, Euro-Tec. This
ready-made cover had been excellent camouflage for cultivat-
ing my targets of investigation for the Security Service, as
well as being my primary source of income. It would have
been foolish of me to neglect the agency's general work and
progress.

After two or three weeks of normality and working in the
real world, I received a telephone call from my controller.
'How are things? Have you anything for us?' he asked. 'I need
to discuss something with you, when can we meet?' There was
no mention of my letter or a formal agreement. I was irritated
but agreed nevertheless to meet him that evening. For once he
was sober and we managed to have a reasonable conversation,
but there was still no reference to my urgent requirement. It
was obvious he was simply being polite: perhaps his Section
Head had reprimanded him.

It turned out that this meeting was important to my handler.
His Chief urgently wanted the people involved in a certain
television programme investigated, in particular a journalist
who was suspected of passing on restricted documents to
CND. MI5 considered me the ideal person to infiltrate the programme.

Because I was now committed to the many relationships I
had cultivated over the preceding months, and was still hoping for some kind of formal agreement with MI5, I decided to
persevere with my 'official' undercover work. However, by
now I had taken further action to safeguard my personal interests. Realising that it was essential to my wellbeing for me to
have on record full details of my Security Service work, I
contacted a firm of solicitors who agreed to retain copies of all
my MI5 reports. Immediately on completion of an investigation, my wife would prepare three copies, one for the Service,

the remaining two copies for the solicitors and our own files respectively.

For over two years I served MI5, investigating the business and personal lifestyles of journalists and TV producers. My reports contained details of Members of Parliament, British Telecom officers, former RAF officers – I even extended my research to the friends and relatives of targets of investigation.

Quite often I would be steered to specific areas of activity and asked to watch out for individuals of interest to MI5 surveillance teams. Car registration and telephone numbers were always gratefully received by my information-hungry controller. The telephone interception unit must have had a field day with the information I provided.

On one occasion, when investigating a television project on nuclear bases, I used my skill (on the instructions of MI5) as a helicopter pilot to fly a television camera crew around secret bases in the South of England. Having been assured by my illustrious controller that all would be well and that there was no chance of me being implicated in any breach of security committed by the TV company, I managed to worm my way into the position of second pilot on a Jet Ranger helicopter based at Blackbushe Airport, near Camberley. I knew very little about the project, except that it was sensitive and concerned nuclear bombs. Having been convinced that the television people involved were a threat to national security, I agreed to discover the intimate details of their project. I now know, of course, that there was no such threat to the security of the State, and, having since watched the programme, I feel ashamed that I undertook this assignment.

Not surprisingly, this mission did not go without incident: I should have had the foresight to realise that we would not be allowed to fly over secret nuclear units with a camera-man hanging on to the outside of the helicopter without the security authorities guarding these establishments taking some kind of action.

On the 21st September 1981 at 11.35am, we took off from

Blackbushe and flew north. Captain Snape was sitting in the first pilot's seat and I occupied the P2 seat. In the rear of the aircraft was a well known film director and the camera operator was sitting in the open doorway with his feet hanging out of the machine, controlling a specially adapted aerial TV camera. Using the intercom system we were able to discuss the best approach to our objectives, the first of which was a top secret nuclear storage base. This unit is so secret it has now been removed from all general maps. I am therefore reluctant to reveal its precise location.

Approaching our target from the south initially at 1100 feet, we were guided by Farnborough radar. Descending to 900 feet, we flew around the site two and a half times, filming what appeared to be a central core in the centre of the base.

It was not until later, when I was visited and questioned by the Civil Aviation Authority Investigation Branch, that I became aware this site was considered to be one of the most secret in the country. To make my predicament worse, security personnel on the ground had observed the registration number of our aircraft, and their enquiries had revealed that it was registered in Ireland of all places. During my interrogation by the CAA investigator, I learned that Captain Snape had vanished abroad to work, and as second pilot I was the only remaining member of the crew who could be pursued.

Anticipating prosecution and perhaps loss of my licence and a heavy fine, I immediately contacted my MI5 handler who took advice from his superiors. After receiving bland assurances that all would be well, I decided to make a formal statement to the CAA, omitting any mention of the Security Service involvement. The matter died a natural death and no further action was taken by the Civil Aviation Authority. What did emerge from this aviation adventure was the disclosure by the CAA investigator that the guards at the nuclear site thought that the helicopter was actually engaged in terrorist activity, and they were preparing to retaliate with missiles and firearms when one of their observers fortunately realised that it was a camera pointing out of the side of the aircraft and not a weapon.

At the outset of and throughout my affair with MI5, I was worried at the lack of control and back-up. The frequently requested contract never did materialise, despite a lengthy meeting with John, an elderly Section Head who attended a debriefing on the 11th May 1981 at the Skyline Hotel, Bath Road, Heathrow. On this occasion I did manage to convince him that, should I ever be involved in a motor accident when the contents of my report and associated items might fall into the hands of police or ambulance officers, a very embarrassing situation could well develop. 'There's always the possibility of the Press getting to know,' I teased.

Finally they were convinced and gave me a document case with a secret compartment. This was a very useful item that enabled me to carry my reports around with some degree of security. For the occasions when my controllers were unavailable, I was instructed to post my reports to a civilian firm operating from what I understood to be a Security Service Post Office box number. Not knowing the current status of this facility, I am reluctant to reveal the full address.

By the end of 1981 I had suffered at the hands of several controllers. It was also becoming evident that I was not engaged in work of national security. I was nothing more than an informer, helping the Security Service to monitor the activities of ordinary citizens voicing their opinions on nuclear weapons, the police and Security Service secrecy and inefficiency. By now, I had established dozens of relationships and people trusted me. As a private detective with numerous broadcasting credits to my name I was becoming well known in television. I had failed to uncover any evidence of criminal espionage or subversion and was now of the opinion that innocent people, especially those engaged in sincere anti-nuclear protests, were being hounded. I not only found this distasteful, but I sympathised and agreed with the majority of the protesters I had investigated. This new emotionally charged state of mind had turned me into ideal double agent material.

For months I dodged and weaved away from requests by my many media contacts to use my expertise as a private detective. Criminal records information was a popular request, as were checks on car registrations, especially from certain journalists who found themselves under surveillance by Special Branch. By far the most common plea was for me to penetrate SB files for details of Russian illegals operating in London. Rather than disappoint my media friends (who failed to appreciate the seriousness of stealing government data), I sat for hours in Companies House collecting names and addresses of directors affiliated to Soviet firms trading in England.

It was relatively easy to get their names and addresses, and with a little applied imagination I was able to convince my media friends that the information had been obtained from official files. In actual fact, the chances were that most if not all of these Russians *were* engaged in covert operations of one kind or another.

When I was on the last lap of my Security Service work I operated a similar deception in reverse. When asked by my controller to report on any Soviet interest being shown by a particular journalist, I simply provided MI5 with names and addresses of Russian directors obtained from Companies House rather than deceive my target any longer.

A successful spy has to gain credibility with his targets of investigation, and he can only do this by impressing them in some way. In undercover criminal work, police officers are forced to adopt the lifestyle of the people they are investigating and this usually leads to situations where the undercover agent is tempted to commit criminal offences in order to achieve his aim and on occasion has no choice but to do so. This was something I was determined to avoid.

Throughout my freelance service with Curzon Street, I was regularly exposed to situations that required me to assume a long-term false front. Consequently I found myself journeying along that very narrow path reserved exclusively for double agents. The stress of this journey, accompanied by the associated difficulties I had with MI5, eventually led to my resignation on the 26th February 1982 at 10.30am. The final showdown occurred at the Cunard Hotel, Hammersmith, when I informed my latest operation controller, Sierra Mike, of my decision. After a weak attempt to blackmail me, he let me go about my business. Perhaps mention of tape recordings, duplicate reports, and solicitors being aware of my activities encouraged him to let me off the hook. There was also the additional fail-safe I had established: that was the affidavit I had lodged with Solicitor and Commissioner for Oaths W L Booth on 31st July 1981.

On reflection, from a personal point of view working for the Security Services was a grave mistake. Having said that, I now realise that the chance to familiarise myself with what really goes on behind the scenes in British Intelligence was a once-in-a-lifetime opportunity that has enabled me to appreciate the problems of innocent men and women attempting to expose situations they consider contrary to the public interest.

I now have many friends in the media and on the anti-nuclear scene, and I regularly give these people my help. I now genuinely believe that members of our so-called élite services are capable of any illegal act, including blackmail, telephone and mail interception, burglary – and even assassination. More of this later.

Assassination is of special interest to me, for the simple reason that at one stage in my relationship with MI5 it was suggested that I take a subject of investigation, who was described as 'a menace', for a ride in my private aircraft and drop him out over the North Sea! I have no doubt in my mind that this was an attempt to expand my function from spy to assassin. Some time after this suggestion, the person referred to was involved in a mysterious road accident.

Having cut the umbilical cord, so to speak, I found myself in a state of confused euphoria, so much so that it took several days before I was able to settle back into my routine. Whilst I was able to return gradually to the criminal and other general investigations of my detective agency, I found that I was developing an unhealthy habit of reading through my old MI5 reports. Furthermore, I was spending hours listening to the numerous tape recordings of my conversations with security service handlers. I doubted the usefulness of (and motive behind) this apparently time-wasting exercise, but after a lot of thought it dawned on me that I was angry at the conduct of my former masters, illicit and contrary to the true public interest as it was. Somehow it had to be stopped. Stimulated by the idea of exposing the duplicitous cloak and dagger agents of British Intelligence, I therefore began what I realised could well be a very lengthy investigation fraught with danger.

Having added a new string (media work) to my professional bow, I decided that my detective agency would join forces with the serious Press to examine past and present information about the illegal activities of the security and intelligence services. In addition to my own research, I also planned to make my investigatory skills and expert knowledge available to established authors and journalists to assist security and intelligence service exposés that I thought were in the public interest because of the serious abuses that would be brought to light.

Following my 'divorce' from MI5, many (if not all) of my Security Service contacts abandoned me. However, Special Branch and other contacts remained in place, so fortunately I was able to confirm from independent sources something I had known personally for a long time – that both MI5 and MI6 used established private detective firms for covert operations at home and abroad. Of course, it would have been foolish to assume that all such firms were engaged in work against the public interest, so, as a responsible investigator, I decided to target only detective agencies or solo operators who appeared to be acting illegally or outside proper guidelines. Much of my research was helped along by my work for national news-papers and magazines, as well as on major television docu-mentaries. Assignments with Duncan Campbell and other best-selling authors led to valuable sources of information which confirmed my belief that our so-called democratic society was in the vice-like grip of a faceless clique who were unable to understand what damage they were doing to the social fabric.

The mystery of MI5 permanent-staff recruitment was unravelled by Sandy, a university graduate with a degree in Russian who was asked by her Careers Adviser if she would be interested in doing research work for a department that was not normally advertised. 'I can't tell you what the work is', said the Careers woman. According to Sandy, the intake now is socially broader than in the old days when one simply 'knew a chap', or was a personal friend of the founder, Kell. In those days, too, one had to be much older.

Sandy's opinion is that the Service is short of suitable can-didates because spying is becoming less glamorous. 'They get you to join straight from University. In my intake there were quite a few people from redbrick universities, but the overall tone is still right wing. The people I know who were approached at Durham were all middle class and public school. What they are looking for is someone from a stable background who is conservative, they don't like people who are politically active left or right', she said.

The cloak and dagger world of Curzon Street did not impress Sandy who thought some of her colleagues were odd-balls and social misfits. 'The people I was working with had obscure degrees, they were lacklustre pedants who couldn't fit in anywhere else and could not earn a living in competitive circumstances. They were inadequate, failed people who com-pensate for their own shortcomings by working for the Secret Service, eavesdropping or sneaking a look at private mail', she said.

Applicants find the selection programme for MI5 long-winded and time-consuming. Members of the Civil Service Commission oversee applicants while they tackle IQ tests and write reports. The selection process includes the applicant pretending to be a member of a committee discussing various projects. There are also numerous question and discussion groups which are usually followed by a not very searching session with a psychologist, who asks lots of banal questions about the applicant's childhood. The final hurdle for the budding spy is a committee of ten people from MI5 who question the candidates to ensure they really are suitable.

It took a year from when Sandy was first approached to the day she joined the Security Service, during which time the Positive Vetting (PV) squad visited various friends and referees listed on the lengthy PV form. One of the questions Sandy was asked was whether or not she was promiscuous (as though she would tell them if she was). The squad hunted for skeletons in the cupboard such as bankruptcy, drug abuse, criminal convictions, membership of undesirable organisations, and, of course, any offbeat sexual predilections likely to leave her open to blackmail. The first four months were devoted to a training stint around various departments, followed by a posting to the section dealing with Russian agents and political extremists in Britain.

'It sounds thrilling and sometimes it was', Sandy said. 'On a typical day you would be going through transcripts of telephone-tapped material. Occasionally you would pick up something, but your real subversives are intelligent enough not to talk on the phone. Sometimes you have a surveillance on someone because you think he is suspicious. He may do something near a nuclear site'.

Like myself, Sandy began to question the morality of her work – listening to people's private conversations, snooping on their mail, and ruining the careers of fellow citizens when she discovered something about them. She also found the job stressful, and that in turn affected her private life. The most interesting facet of Sandy's story is that neither she nor her colleagues were ever provided with a cover story. She would go to a party and avoid asking anyone what they did for a living, for fear of being asked the same question.

Sandy found the system not only dull and inefficient but also stifling. There was no room for initiative, no space for independent thought at all. Finally, after a year, she left the service, and still feels marked by that time, which has affected her promotion prospects. It is impossible to include her MOD work on her CV, and she feels that if people ever find out what she did they will mistrust her, thinking that she is still working as a spy.

These experiences were not unlike those of another Curzon Street permanent staff officer, Cathy Massiter, who also began to question the morality of her work. However, in contrast to Sandy, rather than just resigning and settling down to a more normal lifestyle, Cathy decided to go public: she became a whistle blower, and a brave one at that. How she got away with her television interview for *20/20 Vision*, we will never know. Apart from Peter Wright, who decided to write a book as his method of going public, there has never been a more revealing inside story unmasking the undemocratic and illegal activities of MI5.

In 1970, Miss Massiter decided to seek a change of employment from what was, for her, a boring job as a librarian. She returned to her University Careers Department who put her in contact with the Ministry of Defence, from where B Branch of MI5 wrote, requesting she attend for interview. After the usual vetting, she was eventually employed as a counter-intelligence officer and worked in this capacity until resigning in 1984, after completing fourteen years of loyal service. Her resignation was not as straightforward as one would expect. She said 'I think it is totally unjust and immoral to direct surveillance techniques against decent law-abiding citizens and members of political organisations like CND. We were violating our own rules, it seemed to be getting out of control, not because CND justified this, but because of political pressure. The heat was there for information, and we had to have it'.

Cathy's decision to speak out was encouraged by the fact that the various rules which exist to control what MI5 and Special Branch may or may not do in carrying out surveillance were constantly being broken, seemingly for political and commercial reasons which had nothing to do with the defence of the realm. There were also certain duties that she was told to carry out that she found distasteful – spying on political parties, trade unions and groups like CND, whose views, while different from those of the Establishment, are not illegal or subversive.

During her many years of work with F Branch, much information about the activities of left wing types was supplied by Special Branch who, although supposed to be independent of MI5 and reporting to their own Chief Constables, were functioning as the arms and legs of the Security Service. Victims of F Branch include *New Statesman* journalist Duncan Campbell and two officers of the National Council for Civil Liberties, Patricia Hewitt and Harriet Harman. Even the Fire Brigade Union had their telephones tapped during the 1978 strike.

Trade union infiltration appears to have been a popular area of undercover operations for MI5. According to a woman lecturer bragging to trainee agents 'We have moles so deep in trade unions even their own wives and families don't know what they are up to'.

During the 1978 Ford Motors pay dispute, MI5 tapped the telephone of a shop steward, Sid Harrow. The agent responsible for transcribing the tapes was specifically instructed to listen out for economic information, to which the Service had no right. 'This could only have been requested by the Department of Employment', said Cathy Massiter.

In 1981, Cathy was placed in charge of investigations into CND, her brief being to analyse the potential left-wing subversive influence within that organisation. While she accepted that a limited study of CND for these reasons could be considered legitimate, she did in fact find herself, because of political pressure, involved in a full scale investigation of the whole CND organization. This, she says, led to MI5 again breaking their own rules. One facet of the investigation that Miss Massiter found particularly disturbing was that although CND had been declared a non-subversive organisation (as it was in the 1960s) the treatment dished out to them by MI5 was more appropriate to a threat to State security.

It goes without saying that any nuclear matter is potentially relevant to the defence of the realm, but does it mean groups like CND should automatically be treated as subversive? The events of 1983 during the period leading up to the general election appear to answer this question.

In March of 1983, Defence Secretary Michael Heseltine considered anything nuclear of paramount importance, both as a defence and political issue, so much so that he formed a Special Information Unit Defence Secretariat, known as DS19. Cathy Massister became very concerned when a senior officer from DS19 approached her boss for information on CND. It appeared that what was being requested was data about any subversive political affiliations of leading members of CND. This request came just before the general election, and Miss Massiter believed that the information was being sought for party political reasons. It transpired that, because of this increasing political pressure, surveillance on CND had become so intense that telephones were being tapped, including that of its Vice President, John Cox.

Shortly before the election Michael Heseltine said, in a speech in April 1983, 'CND are led and dominated by left-wing activists, ranging through the Labour Party to the Communist Party. Behind the carefully turned phrases of peace, lies the calculating professionalism of full-time Socialists and Communists.' Nothing could have been further from the truth, and this upset Cathy Massister so much, she complained to her boss that they were in breach of the 1952 Maxwell Fyfe directive. This Order, introduced by the then

Prime Minister, clearly sets out guidelines for MI5 officers: 'No enquiry is to be carried out on behalf of any government department unless you are satisfied that an important public interest bearing on the defence of the realm is at stake'. Her complaint was ignored.

An eminent Judge, Lord Denning, reiterated back in 1963 that 'the Security Services are to be used for one purpose, and one purpose only, the defence of the realm. Most people in this country would, I am sure, wholeheartedly support this principle, for it would be intolerable to us to have anything in the nature of a gestapo or secret police to snoop into all that we do, even at the behest of a Minister or government department'.

Perturbed at the continued breaking of Security Services guidelines which, after all, were – and for that matter still are – very specific, Cathy eventually resigned her position in 1984. Since her departure there have been numerous operational changes, some caused by the unexpected end of the Cold War, plus new legislation which will mean that both MI5 and MI6 become more accountable. And for the first time in the history of both branches of the Service, it is now officially acknowledged that they actually exist: even the identities of the respective Director Generals have been announced. This formal acknowledgement by statute, accompanied by the Prime Minister's promise of a general shake-up of the Intelligence Services, is thought by many to herald a cleaner, more ethical and more legal approach to Intelligence and Security operations. I for one hope so. However, for many officers still serving in both MI5 and MI6 these recent sanitising gestures are nothing more than a public relations exercise conducted by the Government in a desperate attempt to deflect criticism.

According to one former MI5 officer: 'Absolute nonsense. The operational role will of course change now that the Cold War is ended, but other than that it will be business as usual.

'Priority is now given to terrorists, especially the IRA, and quite rightly so, but you can take it from me the green brigade, along with all anti-nuclear protesters, will still be investigated. Nuclear energy is a major priority, and anyone upsetting the apple cart will be dealt with accordingly'.

Throughout my own service with MI5, my controllers referred regularly to information gleaned through telephone monitoring and mail interception. Cathy Massiter and other informants also mention the electronic skulduggery of their organisations. So, not surprisingly, I have always been fascinated by the technical facilities available to the Security Services. It wasn't until late 1983 that I fully appreciated the scope of their special units. On a budget of more than £200 million a year, MI5 has an extraordinary armoury of high-tech devices enabling them to spy on the 600,000 or so citizens entered in their central registry, which is housed in the heart of the red light district of Mayfair. Agents have the authority, and even when they haven't they still manage, to obtain information from virtually anywhere. They bluff and double deal in order to collect data from local police, tax officers, medical records, customs, and passport offices. These snoopers pull every trick in the book to build up what they refer to as a 'still-life portrait' of their targets.

Surveillance victims are monitored by the Watchers Unit (A4) who operate from various secret locations in London. These men and women (50 per cent of M15 staff are said to be women) have at their disposal cars, vans, motorcycles and scooters, taxis, ordinary bicycles, and a wardrobe of disguises that would do the BBC or any other television company proud. Fake identity passes, all part and parcel of the watcher's work, are used to gain access to any building in the country. When access by pretext is not possible, then the 'heavy mob' from Al(A) or Al(D) – the burglars, locksmiths and carpenters who are so skilled at their job they can strip a room down during a search and return it to its original condition – move in. Normally after such an operation, sophisticated bugging devices are planted in the premises. These are often capable of transmitting conversations direct into MI5 listening posts.

Another important unit is based in a large British Telecom building in southwest London from where telephone calls can be tapped and relayed direct to Curzon Street for tape recording. The Tinkerbell Squad, staffed by specialist British Telecom engineers who have no contact with regular telephone staff, is just one of a number of telephone monitoring facilities used by MI5, MI6 and Special Branch. Other law enforcement agencies also have access to these services. In some instances, GCHQ (Government Communications Headquarters) also intercept telephone calls, especially overseas conversations.

For assignments where the information required cannot be obtained from tapping phones or bugging premises, the Rat Catchers are used to intercept and photocopy a suspect's mail. Letters posted by spy targets are sneaked out of mail boxes, letters arriving are simply intercepted and opened before delivery. The days of painstakingly steaming letters open are over: now there is a simple, speedy process for opening and reading hundreds of letters at a go.

Assassination is a topic regularly mentioned when discussing the spy business, and over the years there have been a number of mysterious deaths said to be attributed to MI5, including that of Sir Maurice Oldfield, the former boss of MI6. Oldfield, a close friend of former MI6 officer-turned-businessman Anthony Cavendish, is alleged to have said to Cavendish when dying 'I think they've got me'. By this he meant that rogue MI5 men he considered his enemies had poisoned him with a special potion acquired from the top secret research station at Porton Down. This lethal toxin is said to be undetectable in humans. Sir Maurice was one of thirty top people supposed to be on a dirty tricks 'hit list' drawn up by rebel MI5 agents who wanted a change of government. These outlaws used sex, forgery and drugs in what became a seriously bungled campaign.

One of the key figures in the plot was brought out of retirement in 1987 to act as an adviser to the services. He was previously a member of the section which drew up secret files on MPs, trade unionists and journalists. This officer was the chief to whom all my own reports were delivered by my handler: no wonder I was asked to take one of my targets of investigation for a no-return flight over the North Sea. Names from the abovementioned hit list make interesting reading: Edward Heath, Reginald Maudling, Francis Pym, Norman St John Stevas, Harold Wilson, Tony Benn, David Owen, along with numerous other well-known MPs and trade unionists, were listed for special attention.

Despite the tremendous amount of circumstantial evidence that exists to support these allegations, there is no first-hand evidence to bring a *prima facie* case against MI5 for any illegal act, especially not for murder. If acts of assassination have been carried out, then they must have been unofficial and nothing more than a private enterprise operation master-minded by what I have been told is called 'The IP' (Inner Policy Club) that is said to have direct contact with an outside unit operated by private detectives and security consultants who undertake covert operations on their behalf.

This so-called IP Club is alleged to consist of a group of staunch traditionalists who believe that it is their God-given right to use MI5 facilities to advance their own political aims. In the armed forces, such conduct would more than likely be classified as 'mutiny'.

My general detective agency work, interspersed with research into the Security Services, carried on through 1982. During this time I was also developing my relationship with the Institute of Professional Investigators (IPI). I didn't realise it at the time, but the IPI and my friendship with a senior officer, Barrie Peachman, were to have far-reaching effects on my personal and business life through corruption and mysterious deaths. I was also maintaining my links with the Secret Intelligence Service via my friend 'Sparky' who, apart from a few brief conversations, very rarely mentioned my fiasco with the opposition north of the river.

On the face of it, I was enjoying a steady routine of general detective agency work, varied by the occasional media assignment or broadcast. I had managed to establish relationships with many Press folk and instead of spying on them I was now developing some worthwhile rapports.

However, despite this apparently stable existence, there was something missing: I was inexplicably frustrated. Like most undercover agents, I needed to experience regularly the uncertainty and, at times, danger of covert intelligence operations. In effect, I was an espionage junkie. This craving was satisfied on the 14th January 1983, when I attended the offices of Chubb & Sons (Lock & Safe Co Ltd) at 51 Whitfield Street, London W1, after a telephone conversation with my longtime MI6 friend Sparky, in which I agreed to undertake an assignment on behalf of Chubb & Sons.

From the general tone of the discussion, this was obviously an MI6 job that, for whatever reason, had to be 'laundered' through a civilian company. I was aware of the very strong link between the Secret Intelligence Service and Chubb, who I understood supplied training facilities and equipment, so I didn't hesitate when it was suggested I contact Hotel Whisky (code name), the son of a former high-ranking Intelligence chief. Present at the 14th January meeting was another officer of the company, who I shall simply call November Charlie. I was told by these gentlemen that the Chubb organisation was experiencing a problem with a certain individual who had acted as some kind of agent for them over contracts with the Nigerian Ministry of Defence.

I was also told that Nigerian security officers were present in England, and that the suspect would possibly try to sabotage a current contract between Chubb and the Nigerian authorities for the provision of ballot boxes for the forthcoming Nigerian elections. This sounded like a joint British-Nigerian special operation.

The story as presented was very disjointed and my contacts were not specific with their presentations or request.

I gathered they wanted some kind of investigation into the activities of the suspect, who was allegedly trying to extort money from Chubb. Blackmail was indicated and great concern was voiced at what damage the suspect could do to the Nigerian ballot box contract.

Having agreed to investigate the activities and background of the suspect, I discussed my fees with November Charlie who described to me a complicated system he would be using to settle my charges. He referred to a 'special fund' which he regularly used, and informed me I would be paid by this method and could well receive a cheque from a source other than Chubb. However, I must say he was very unclear in his description of this fund and at this point I began to feel slightly uneasy. Nevertheless, despite the rather peculiar aspects of the assignment, I accepted it.

I produced a formal certificate of instruction, which November Charlie signed in his own name, also giving his own address. However, immediately afterwards he suddenly stated that he did not wish his address to be used in this transaction, and then inserted the home address of Hotel Whisky, who did not have time to agree or disagree. I accepted a retainer of £1,000 (paid by a Chubb cheque), which I collected the following week.

The investigation began and I eventually submitted an interim report and account on 7th February 1983. My account was a correctly issued invoice, number 2024, for a total of £2,205 inclusive of VAT. I attended a further meeting at the offices of Chubb on Friday, 11th February 1983. On this occasion, Hotel Whisky (my Foreign Office contact) said very little. He appeared to be dissatisfied with his associate and ill at ease. November Charlie discussed the report and case generally, and we talked about how best to proceed with the suspect. It was suggested by November Charlie that he should be taken to the other side of the world on a pretext business project, until the Nigerian elections and ballot box contract had been concluded in October.

I suggested other kinds of covert approaches to the problem, and it was eventually agreed to set up an undercover operation that included monitoring the suspect's movements and at the same time collecting information about his activities, with special attention to any illegal or compromising act that he was committing in this country or abroad. No mention was made of fees on this occasion as I assumed my invoice would be paid within a few days, in accordance with our agreement.

I continued with the assignment throughout the month of February but did not actually set the agreed undercover operation in motion. I completed all the necessary planning and kept a very cursory watch on the subject, but did not fully commit myself to the operation. My reasons were simple: I was very uneasy about November Charlie's motives, especially in view of his suggestion that maybe an 'accident' could be arranged. There was also the question of my fee: five weeks had elapsed and I had still not received payment of the initial account for £2,205. After a number of discussions regarding the outstanding account, I realised that November Charlie had misled me about the financial aspect of our relationship. He gave excuse after excuse for the non-payment of the account and I was by now extremely suspicious of his reasons for employing me.

I became very worried at the possibility of something happening to the target. Eventually, on 10th March 1983 I prepared a detailed report of my activities and an account for my services to date and attended the offices of Chubb on Friday 11th March 1983 at 10.30am.

After a lot of argument, I eventually received a Chubb cheque for the outstanding amount of £2,205. We talked about various aspects of the assignment and from the general tone I could not help but feel that the target of investigation was about to come to some physical harm. Although it had been made to look as though he was engaged in criminal activity, my own investigations had failed to uncover anything to suggest he was engaged in sabotage of a Nigerian Ministry of

Defence contract with the Chubb organisation. The target of investigation was a 65-year-old Austrian Jew who lived in Pursers Cross Road, London SW6, and who was said to be a European agent for the Nigerian Government. My job was to provide specific information about him which ultimately found its way to the offices of MI6 in Westminster Bridge Road, near Waterloo.

Although the assignment was potentially an interesting and exciting intelligence operation, my enthusiasm for it was extinguished not only by the confusion over the settlement of my fees, but also by the unprofessional operational approach to the investigation. There was also the question of the target's safety: I had no desire to be involved in some kind of illegal act. As far as settlement of my charges was concerned, had I not been tenacious in pressing for payment it's anybody's guess when I would have been paid. As it was I was forced to accept payment by way of two cheques, one for £2,205, issued by Chubb on a Lloyds Bank cheque dated 11th March, the second issued on another Lloyds cheque in the name of a Channel Islands-based company, FDC Jersey Ltd, and dated 23rd March. To complicate matters further, the letter accompanying the Jersey cheque was from an address in Tunbridge Wells, in the name of yet another firm, Roderland International Ltd.

I decided that this was the end of my relationship with any agency within or even associated with British Intelligence. The obvious inability of MI6 itself to organise an efficient freelance operation had totally extinguished my confidence in the Service.

I am not the only person to have experienced difficulty with MI6. Another interesting case of a spy shoddily treated over expenses concerns Tony Divall, a private intelligence agent who for most of his adult life operated under risky and often potentially lethal conditions for his SIS spy masters. Anthony Stephen Divall, now aged 65, initially served his country in the Royal Marines. He drifted into Secret Service work at the end of the Second World War, and until 1988 bravely worked undercover investigating all manner of cases in his country's interests.

His cover identity and occupation was that of a gunrunner, although he prefers to describe himself as an entrepreneur. His work landed him in many high-risk situations, including arrest by the German police. Masterminding several MI6 successes, including the capture of an IRA gunrunning ship, he also devised a successful 'sting' operation which sabotaged an Argentine Exocet-buying mission during the 1982 Falklands War. Divall is also credited with preventing an Argentine attack on the ship carrying Prince Andrew during that conflict.

Private intelligence work from MI6 quickly dried up for Tony Divall when he was investigated and arrested by the West German Federal Office of Criminal Investigation for his part in the shipment to South Korea of Soviet-made surface-to-air missiles. Acting for MI6 did not make him immune from the German FOCI but his Secret Service controllers were able to placate them and Divall was eventually freed.

Despite working for nearly forty years as a freelance unofficial arm of the Secret Intelligence Service, Divall is very bitter, and feels he has been left out in the cold. He was last heard of in 1988 claiming what he described as 'unpaid expenses' from his former spy masters.

It is common knowledge that the Secret Intelligence Service (MI6), like MI5, have a few skeletons in their cupboard, including a number of well-known traitors. In 1963 Harold 'Kim' Philby, a high-level British diplomat and senior intelligence officer, defected to Russia. Prior to that, two other British agents, Guy Francis Demoncy Burgess and Donald Maclean, had changed sides. There was also the embarrassment of frogman/spy 'Buster' Crabbe who, on the instructions an MI6 officer got himself involved in a botched operation underneath the Russian battleship *Ordzhonikidze*.

There have been many theories about what happened to Crabbe, the most feasible being that he was in fact a dedicated

Communist and traitor who defected to the Soviet Union. This theory is supported by his former diving partner, Sidney Knowles, now living in Spain. These defections, and the seeming general inability of MI6 to keep their house in order, contributed greatly to the longstanding rift between MI5 and the Foreign Office. One would have thought that over the years relations between the Services might have improved, but according to a currently serving Army Intelligence officer who has worked with MI6 this is not so. 'The rift is irreparable, there is always something to drive the wedge deeper. Look at what happened in the 1970s with the Littlejohn brothers.'

Without doubt the most controversial covert mission involving private detectives was the strange case of these brothers. The saga of Kenneth and Keith Littlejohn began in 1972, with the arrest in Ireland of John Wyman of Chelsea, London. Along with a serving Dublin police officer, Wyman was charged with a number of espionage offences. Running in parallel, and seemingly independent of the Wyman case, were the bank-robbing activities of the Littlejohns.

Initially, the two cases appeared totally unconnected, until solicitors acting for the bank robbers informed the court that their clients had been acting under the control of the British Secret Intelligence Service (MI6). Following the revelation that the robbers were secret agents working in Ireland through London-based contacts, the media and political worlds rang with hysterical cries for a thorough investigation by Government.

At first it appeared that the Littlejohns were simply attempting to avoid conviction for their criminal offences. However, as the plot unfolded substantial corroborative evidence was produced to support their claim. Full details of their London contacts and the events leading to their recruitment were revealed, along with the identities of the government and intelligence officials dealing with them. By far the most explosive revelation to come out of the affair was not only that British Intelligence had been employing bank robbers as freelance secret agents but that their activities were being operationally controlled by a private detective John Wyman, who turned out to be working undercover for MI6 through an Oxford detective agency. The firm, run by a former Detective Chief Inspector of police, was traced to the picturesque village of Longhanborough in Oxfordshire.

To date this man has refused to be interviewed, and the firm ceased trading shortly after the Littlejohn/Wyman affair blew up so spectacularly.

It transpired that private eye Wyman, alias Michael Teviot alias Douglas Smythe, was in fact part of the Security Service espionage network, feeding information to British agents in the Republic of Ireland. The Littlejohns had been recruited following meetings in London with a number of Intelligence officials. The Ministry of Defence took the unusual step of issuing a full statement, which confirmed the allegations that Kenneth Littlejohn had in fact met with Mr Geoffrey Johnson-Smith, at that time Under Secretary for the Army.

At his trial, the Judge said that Wyman had admitted he was an agent of a British Ministry and that he had visited Eire seeking information about IRA activities and the source of arms being smuggled into Northern Ireland. Wyman was eventually acquitted of the charges, and released from custody. On leaving Court, he went to great lengths to hide his identity by wearing dark glasses plus a heavy beard he had grown whilst in custody. The Littlejohns, however, despite strong arguments from their lawyers, both received twenty-year sentences.

Mr John Lovatt, who represented them at the trial, said 'I am not at all satisfied: the British Government appears to draw a distinction between the crime it wanted them to commit (that of spying) and the crime it did not want them to commit'.

As for the private detective and government spy John Wyman and the Oxfordshire detective agency – they vanished into obscurity, presumably to create new identities so they could carry on with their covert intelligence operations.

It is difficult, if not impossible, to comprehend why armed robbers should be recruited as intelligence agents. According to Captain (retired) Fred Holroyd, a former Military Intelligence Office (MIO) and MI6 agent, some members of the Security Services are little better than criminals, operating as they do with flagrant disregard for any legislation and security guide lines. His own experience of unlawful intelligence work is highlighted in subsequent chapters.

CHAPTER 7

Nuclear Counter Espionage

During and after the Chubb investigation what little spare time I had was spent working on the affairs of the Institute of Professional Investigators (IPI). Having graduated from ordinary member to Board Director, I became jointly responsible for the day-to-day running of the Institute whose motto was 'Honour, Integrity and Learning.' What I discovered horrified me: some members (not of the Board of Directors) with criminal records, others – ostensibly reputable professionals – employing convicted felons, some Directors of the Board illegally obtaining confidential information from official sources, and mismanagement at the highest level by unscrupulous private spies fraternising with serving police, military and security intelligence officers. One security company, whose managing director was an IPI member (although not on the Board) had direct contact with the highest echelons of British Intelligence and Whitehall, including Number 10, Downing Street.

Despite my concern at this state of affairs, certain other even more serious factors became alarmingly apparent. I discovered that a top secret surveillance of anti-nuclear protesters had been launched by one of the most prominent private detectives in the business, and to make matters worse he was one of my closest friends, the President of the IPI.

Barrie Charles Peachman entered the world of private spying in 1963 when he formed the Sapphire Investigation Bureau. Initially, with the assistance of his wife Jean, he worked from a spare room in his house, gradually expanding over the years to purpose-built premises in Long Stratton, a small village on the outskirts of Norwich. Apart from his passionate desire to become a private detective, Peachman had no qualifications in police, security or investigations work. But he still managed to develop his agency into a thriving and successful company known throughout the world.

From the outset, Barrie and I knew that we were kindred spirits. We joined forces to create a formidable team that played havoc with IPI Board meetings. Together we attacked the web of corruption that was destroying the profession.

An example of the seriousness of the battles we fought can be seen in a letter dated 21st November 1983 from another Director, Les Kirkham from Carlisle:

> 'Dear Mr Principal
> I regret to inform you in writing of my decision that I now submit my resignation from the Board of the Institute of Professional Investigators with effect from Friday the 18th of November 1983. Under no circumstances whatsoever will I allow my name to be put forward for re-election. I am of the opinion that there is turbulence being steered from a central force with ulterior motives in mind as far as the Institute of Professional Investigators is concerned and I do not wish to be involved in this in any way whatsoever.
>
> Yours sincerely, L Kirkham'

Throughout 1982 I worked closely with Peachman, both on problems associated with the IPI and on special investigations handled by our respective agencies. We visited each other's homes, and our families were also friendly. During this period I had no idea that he was working for my former spymasters (MI5) as a sub-contractor controlled by a London-based security company.

As a result of a request from one of my media contacts,

Duncan Campbell of the *New Statesman*, to investigate rumours of a suspected undercover operation against protesters demonstrating at the Sizewell nuclear power station, I decided to have a casual chat with Barrie Peachman. After all, his was the leading detective agency in Norfolk and Suffolk and if anyone knew what was going on locally it was likely to be him. You can imagine my astonishment when it turned out that he was one of the principal organisers of the operation, which had apparently been launched by MI5, not the power industry.

After much discussion, during which Peachman explained that for reasons of personal morality he was very unhappy about the assignment, I decided to take him into my confidence about my own work for the Security Service. I explained to him in no uncertain terms the risks he was taking working for badly run, morally bankrupt spy departments. He agreed with me, but revealed that he was so deeply involved he could not back out. He spoke of mysterious things that had happened to him and to other directors of his firm, and on one occasion, nearly in tears, said 'I don't know what to do, I've got my back to the wall.'

Shortly after that remark, he wrote to me that he was very worried at the number of Intelligence officers affiliated to the IPI.

Without doubt, the nuclear industry is one of the most powerful and dangerous organisations in the world. Like a giant octopus, it spreads its tentacles over the globe, generating power and depositing highly toxic radioactive waste into the environment. The result – hundreds of deaths by cancer every year, and for those who are lucky to survive exposure to radiation, a pathetic, painful lifestyle for the rest of their days. Shrouded in secrecy and protected in the UK by a formidable security apparatus provided by the Atomic Energy Authority Constabulary, MI5 and Special Branch, this industrial monster affects the lives of every single citizen in the United Kingdom 24 hours a day, seven days a week, 365 days a year.

According to official company documents, the Sapphire Investigation Bureau Ltd was recruited to spy on anti-nuclear protesters on the 21st January 1983 at 7.13pm, when the Managing Director, Barrie Peachman, received a telephone call from former Intelligence officer Peter Hamilton of Zeus Security Consultants Ltd, London.

Peachman was asked specifically to ascertain the identities of principal objectors at the Sizewell Atomic Power Station public hearing being convened at Snape Maltings in Suffolk. If possible, he was to obtain a list of those objectors, their connections with the media, their political leanings and so on. He was told by Hamilton that locals should be targeted, as they could well be more than front men. Arrangements were made to telephone reports to Hamilton on his home ex-directory number. In his absence messages were be left with his wife, Patricia Hamilton.

Immediately after this conversation, Peachman telephoned convicted felon Victor Norris, alias Adrian Hampson, who traded as Contingency Services from 433 Ipswich Road, Colchester. Norris was a freelance undercover investigator regularly used by Sapphire. Like Peachman, he had no formal training in security or intelligence work. He simply drifted into the business and, by his own admission, undertook dirty work for the Home Office. On the occasion of the above-mentioned telephone conversation, Norris agreed to investigate as a freelance.

Raring to go, Norris got stuck in to what was (although he didn't know it) probably the largest and most complex private intelligence operation ever mounted in this country. Controlled by Peter Hamilton of Zeus Security, the Sizewell surveillance involved undercover investigators with experience in all aspects of covert spying, including bugging and telephone tapping. Norris's method of operation was simple: he carried out the sensitive enquiries and reported to Sapphire Investigations (Barrie Peachman) who in turn re-vamped the reports for transmission to Zeus Security. From conversations

I had with Peachman, there is no doubt in my mind that this was an officially sponsored intelligence mission. In any event, the information requested was in no way similar to that sought in the standard commercial or industrial type of enquiry.

From the numerous entries on the Sapphire Investigation reports, it can be seen that a Shirley Smith was also involved in the general administration of the assignment. Miss Smith, I learned, was not only a co-director in the firm, she was also Peachman's mistress, with a nine-year-old boy as living evidence of their relationship. This was another secret that Barrie had managed to conceal for nearly a decade.

The intelligence data collected by Norris was impressive. His reports indicated that he had formed dummy peace groups for the purpose of infiltrating the different anti-nuclear organisations protesting at Sizewell. One sinister entry on the file read: 'Vic Norris phoned, claims he can put a stop on CND if required. Will send further report.'

Further reports indicated strongly that he had achieved a very deep level of penetration with his investigation. For example, his report of 14th February 1983 read:

'I will enlarge on something which I mentioned to Shirley when she telephoned. As a preliminary measure and with a feeling that it might be extremely useful to us later on, I have set up three dummy organisations apparently sympathetic to CND, all three run by trusted friends of mine. One is in Lancashire (Accrington), one in Kirkcaldy, Scotland, and the third in Ipswich. The one in Lancashire has already made contact with peace groups, and is accepted as a bona fide peace group itself, and the one in Ipswich has established contact with some of the people mentioned in my report. This initial groundwork may later prove invaluable or may not, but I have gone ahead on the instinct that it may be.

'The main point being that, if the principals for whom you are acting lose interest, we must consider that there are other (wealthy) sources who have a vested interest in seeing CND discredited and perhaps we could look elsewhere for potential clients?? However, for the time being, I will just do a little steady digging and nosing about and await your further instructions.'

Not only was Norris capable of infiltrating the protest groups, but he was also able to see that there was a lot of money to be made from discrediting the Sizewell protesters. From the general tone of this report I would say that Peachman was losing interest in the assignment and was attempting to withdraw, thus spurring Norris's attempts to inject enthusiasm into the proceedings with the mention of 'wealthy' clients and money. According to Sapphire company records, the investigation ceased at the end of February 1983. However, from a note by Peachman dated the 21st April 1983, the project was obviously still active. This information was to play a vital part in a murder investigation the following year.

The memo of 21st April referred to a telephone call from a local journalist, Jennifer Armstrong, at 4.49pm to Peachman's office. She enquired about his involvement in the Sizewell enquiry, but was fobbed off with remarks about cheaper electricity. From the contents of this memo, it is apparent that Peachman denied all knowledge of the Sizewell investigation.

The reports compiled by Peachman, which contained much data that would have been invaluable to an intelligence department such as MI5, were posted to Peter Hamilton, Driftway, Badwell Ash, Bury St Edmunds, Suffolk. Dozens of organisations and individuals were listed by Norris, who suggested at one stage that company searches be carried out on Greenpeace and Friends of the Earth, emphasis being placed on a Mr Graham Searle and the obtaining of his home address. The only possible reason for acquiring the home address of such an individual would have been for the purpose of entering his premises, mail interception, telephone tapping, and/or bugging the house.

In addition to Greenpeace and Friends of the Earth, the following organisations and individuals were targeted for investigation:

Campaign for Nuclear Disarmament
Stop Sizewell B Association
Anti-Nuclear Campaign
Anti-Nuclear Campaign, Sheffield
Cornish Anti-Nuclear Alliance
Welsh Anti-Nuclear Alliance
East Anglian Alliance
Town & Country Planning Association
Council for the Protection of Rural England
East Anglia Trade Union Campaign
Ecology Party
European Group for Ecological Action (ECOROPA)
National Union of Mineworkers
Socialist Environmental Resources Association
Suffolk Preservation Society

Mr P Medhurst – Mr G Searle – Mr P Bunyard
The Chief Executive, South Yorkshire County Council
Mrs M Sierakowski, Ipswich Constituency Labour Party
Mrs I M Webb, Ipswich & District Friends of the Earth
Mr M Blackmore, Socialist Environmental Resources
    Association
Mr R Jarrett, Campaign for Nuclear Disarmament
Mr R R Grey, Wansbeck District Council
Mr L Daly, National Union of Mineworkers
Mr D Somervell, SCRAM
Mr C Sweet, Centre for Energy Studies, South Bank
    Polytechnic
Mr M Barnes, Electricity Consumers Council
Professor J W Jeffery, Department of Crystallography,
    Birkbeck College
Mr D Lowry, Energy Research Group, Open University
Mr G Stoner
Mr D Hall, Town & Country Planning Association
Mr G Hancock, Portskewett Action Group
Mr J Popham, Suffolk Preservation Society
Mrs K Miller, Scottish Conservation Society
Mr C Conroy, Friends of the Earth
Mr R Grove-White, Council for the Protection of Rural
    England
Mr H Richards, Welsh Anti-Nuclear Alliance
Mr G Pritchard, Cornish Anti-Nuclear Alliance

Mr Birch, National Union of Public Employees
Mr J E Lodge, Northumberland County Council

Running in parallel, but independent of the Sapphire-Norris undercover investigation, Zeus Security of London had arranged to use a number of additional freelance spies.

One of these agents was David Coughlan, an electronics wizard experienced in all manner of covert electronic surveillance including telephone tapping, bugging and clandestine tape recording, to name but a few of this extraordinary man's skills. By his own admission, Coughlan has carried out clandestine electronic spying assignments for a number of years for foreign and British Government departments, including the Security Services, MI5. In 1987, along with other private detectives, he was jailed for tapping the telephone of Gerard Hoareau, the former leader of the Seychelles resistance movement who was assassinated in 1985.

In a taped interview, Coughlan admitted supplying covert tape recording equipment for use in the controversial Sizewell surveillance. According to his statement, this equipment was supplied to Zeus, the security firm controlling the operation, and included tape recorders designed for concealment about the body and similar equipment. Coughlan stated that the whole surveillance was a long affair which lasted throughout 1983, and involved 'all kinds of people'. In a lengthy statement to Yorkshire Television's *First Tuesday*, he elaborated on his affiliations with covert government departments and how he actually went about tapping phones and bugging targets of surveillance.

First Tuesday described Coughlan's background as a former military technical expert seconded to the Special Air Service Electronics Unit where he had acquired his clandestine skills. He revealed how he was recruited by Zeus Security to fit out undercover agents with secret tape recorders to spy on the hundreds of Sizewell protesters. When questioned as to who he believed was the client behind the scenes of this surveillance project, Coughlan stated that as far as he was aware the investigation was mounted by the British Security Service, MI5, and that they had employed Zeus who in turn had sub-contracted out to a number of other private detectives, Sapphire Investigations and Barrie Peachman being among them. Coughlan also stated he and his associates had been informed by their masters that the investigation had been mounted to detect 'sinister subversives' who had infiltrated the various anti-nuclear groups.

The reason for the Sizewell surveillance, presumably given by the organiser, Peter Hamilton, is very interesting and tends to confirm that Coughlan is speaking the truth. If one studies the *Handbook of Security*, section 5.21, which deals with the security of nuclear installations, it can clearly be seen that great emphasis has been placed on intrusion by anti-nuclear groups:

'The determined intruder will gain access to a nuclear power station site regardless of any obstacles put in his way, and it is completely impossible to prevent such intrusion. It must also be appreciated that the operator of a nuclear power station must not only be aware of possible intrusion by terrorists but, following publicity arising from minor radioactive leaks and especially from more serious incidents such as occurred at the Three Mile Island plant in the USA in 1979, of the activities of the various anti-nuclear power groups which have been established on a world-wide basis. These groups try to infiltrate such sites in order to prove that it is possible to effect such infiltration and to highlight the risks of terrorist activity. It must not be overlooked that these groups, however genuine, peaceful and dedicated they may be, will inevitably become infiltrated by activists holding extreme views.'

The *Handbook of Security* is a private publication, edited by Peter Hamilton.

David Coughlan is another disaffected freelance spy. His statements to the *Yorkshire Telegraph* about freelance spying contradict the soothing assurances made by the Government that it has firm control of its Security Services.

Coughlan is an expert technician rather than an information assessor or investigator. Over the years, he has invaded the privacy of a whole range of British citizens, from anti-nuclear protesters to the Militant faction in Liverpool's Labour party during the 1980s.

Coughlan's career as a 'buggist' started in the Army twenty years ago, when his electronics skills were employed by the Intelligence Corps as well as the SAS. After his discharge from the military he decided to set up in private practice as an electronics specialist, and since then appears to have had the tacit consent of Special Branch and MI5 to engage in all manner of clandestine projects, in addition to his official work. Enquiries by the *Observer* revealed that he was so well trusted in official circles that he was asked to supply monitoring equipment for Margaret Thatcher's old flat in Flood Street, London. The most unsettling aspect of the use of freelances like Coughlan is that they are being used as 'cut-outs'. In other words, if they get into trouble the government can deny all knowledge of them, which of course happened when he bugged the home of assassination victim Gerard Hoareau in 1985. (See Chapter 4.)

An interesting aspect of surveillance directed against anti-nuclear campaigners emerges from Coughlan's statement. It would appear the agency primarily responsible for investigating nuclear matters is in fact MI5, and not, as many have assumed, the Atomic Energy Police or other security agencies of the power industry. For it goes without saying that there has to be a strong link between MI5 and the atomic energy industry over such matters as the vetting of staff, breaches of security at plants, and, of course, infiltration of protest groups by terrorists or other undesirables.

Despite the statements of Barrie Peachman and David Coughlan, there is no hard evidence to confirm that the instigator of the Sizewell surveillance/investigation project was in fact a government department. But it is obvious that the information sought would have been invaluable to a counter intelligence unit such as MI5, and expecting us to believe that no action whatsoever was being taken by the Security Services over anti-nuclear protesters would be unreasonable, to say the least. There is, of course, the additional testimony of Victor Norris, alias Adrian Hampson, which tends to strengthen the MI5 theory.

To pursue this line of investigation, I adopted a fictitious identity and cover story to throw some light on the 'pedigree' and general *modus operandi* of this convicted criminal. Believing me to be a potential client, he told me 'I work for the Home Office, doing the dirty work they don't want to be associated with.' He then went on to elaborate how he would be prepared to get into people's homes and if necessary, in cases where homosexuals were involved, how he would be prepared to infiltrate agents into the lives of subjects under investigation. He claimed that his men would, if required, be prepared to engage in sexual acts to get information.

Generally speaking, Norris gave me the impression that he was prepared to do whatever was necessary to complete a mission. 'We've got a couple of very good imitation lefties who are extremely convincing. They know the patois that these people use, they can drop names, and have connections.

'We can infiltrate, all right. We can also take care of trouble makers by unexplained methods. The best thing is that you did not know, we have our own methods but the less you know about them the better, in your own interests', he boasted. In later statements made to the *Daily Star*, he again mentioned his Government work by revealing that both he and Peachman had worked as 'temps' for the Security Services. 'A temp is someone who isn't on their books, but does things on the quiet for them. The temp does the dirty work, and if anything goes wrong they make it quite clear you are on your own', said Norris. He also elaborated on how Peachman was proficient at electronic surveillance, and how he (Norris) was the expert in getting into places without trace.

On the 25th January 1989, the Right Hon Paddy Ashdown MP, Head of the Social and Liberal Democrat Party, wrote to the then Prime Minister, Margaret Thatcher. According to Mark Payne of the SLDP, the questions contained in Ashdown's letter caused Mrs Thatcher to become incandescent with rage. The general content concerned the appointment of Lord Chalfont as Deputy Chairman of the IBA and his close connection to a number of privately run firms operating in the twilight world of security and intelligence.

Two of the organisations named were Zeus Security Consultants Ltd and Peter Hamilton Security Consultants Ltd. Mr Ashdown elaborated on Lord Chalfont's business association with directors of Zeus.

This letter revealed, with utmost clarity, the quality and pedigrees of directors responsible for the Zeus operation. It also highlighted other firms set up by Zeus directors to carry out assignments connected with government espionage, along with their affiliations to the nuclear industry. To my mind, the most sensational revelation in this letter was the implication that prominent Tories were involved in a firm dumping nuclear waste. The business connection from this waste company led all the way to Zeus Security and Peter Hamilton.

To appreciate fully the seriousness of what Mr Ashdown was alleging, I believe it is vital to examine the complete text of the 25th January communication. So here is a verbatim transcript of this letter:

> Rt. Hon Margaret Thatcher MP, Prime Minister
> House of Commons
> London SW1A 0AA   25 January 1989
>
> Dear Prime Minister,
> You will recall that I raised with you at PMQs last week the subject of your appointment of Lord Chalfont as Deputy Chairman of the IBA. You expressed surprise that I should even ask.
> I do not want now to raise again the widespread concern that has been expressed about Lord Chalfont's views on television, although I share that concern; nor the more general concern that is felt at the way the Government uses

its powers of executive appointment in relation to those who can be considered to be supporters of its own views.

There are other very serious matters that are of public interest in Lord Chalfont's appointment, which I believe bring into serious question the decision that the Government has taken. I am seeking to raise these today, on the first day of the Committee Stage of the Official Secrets Bill, for the simple reason that the bill would make it unlawful in future to discuss or write about them.

You will see from this speech that this concerns, in part, Zeus Security Consultants Ltd, which changed its name to Peter Hamilton (Security Consultants) Ltd on 28 September 1983.

It is a matter of public record that Zeus were engaged by an unknown client for the investigation and surveillance of the objectors at the inquiry into the Sizewell B proposal. Zeus contracted the work to Sapphire Investigations Bureau Ltd.

I have looked at the objects of Zeus which are stated, in the Articles of Association, as including: "To carry on business, as security experts and agents of all kinds and to provide advisory and consultancy services to Government and other Authorities and to encourage the adoption of security and precautionary measures and devices against industrial and other espionage."

There is also well documented and public evidence that, at the time of the Sizewell Inquiry, Zeus, or one of the companies which is in the Zeus group, was subcontracting such work to agents who had criminal records to engage in this work.

I raise these matters in some detail because at the time of the instigation of the Sizewell operation, Lord Chalfont was Chairman of Zeus Security Consultants Limited. As at April 1988 he is named as a Consultant on the headed note paper of Peter Hamilton (Security Consultants) Limited.

There is other evidence relating to those connected with Zeus and Government Departments which I would be happy to disclose to you should you wish it.

Lord Chalfont has since joined a number of other directors of Zeus as a director of Securipol Limited, incorporated on 16 January 1986. Securipol shares a registered office and directors with Ensec Limited whose purpose is the undersea dumping of nuclear waste. Some prominent Conservatives are Directors of Ensec. The objects of Securipol, as stated in the Articles of Association, are almost identical to those of Zeus.

According to the latest information at Companies House, Lord Chalfont has never resigned from the office of director at Securipol Limited. Against this background there are a number of questions which I would now like to put to you.

Did you know of Lord Chalfont's involvement in Zeus Security Consultants and Securipol when he was appointed to the Independent Broadcasting Authority? If not, will you now reconsider this appointment?

If you did know of Lord Chalfont's past and present connections, do you consider that it is appropriate for someone with these long standing and close links to be charged, as Deputy Chairman of the IBA, with the task of effectively mediating between commercial broadcasters and the Government of the day?

I ask you especially to bear in mind conflicts which could involve on the one hand national or citizen security and on the other the freedom of broadcasting.

Let me be clear. It is your judgement I am questioning in this affair – not Lord Chalfont's past or present activities.

The Official Secrets Bill would allow Ministers to designate all these matters – now on the public record – as protected by the secrecy of Clause 1. Will you now agree to amend that Section so that information of this nature can be revealed?

There are matters connected to this case that will no doubt interest others. For some the security methods employed by the Electricity Industry in the light of privatisation are a matter of current debate.

Others will be concerned about the use by the state of private security companies and the surveillance methods that are employed.

Yours sincerely
Rt Hon Paddy Ashdown MP

The above letter clearly indicates that Peter Hamilton, via a number of companies, including one in his own name, was professionally connected with titled individuals. As well as Lord Chalfont, other prestigious types as described on his company notepaper and records were: Major General Sir Philip Ward KCVO CBE, a former Army officer who sports an impeccable military pedigree, including service as Commanding Officer at the Royal Military Academy, Sandhurst. Lord Chalfont's own accomplishments grace 26 lines in *Who's Who?* where there is mention of his relationship with Zeus Security, along with a brief resumé of his military record and the fact he held various staff and intelligence appointments. On Hamilton's notepaper, dated 1988, Lord Chalfont is listed as a 'General Consultant', while Major General Ward is described as 'Chairman of the Board'. Another notable member of the Hamilton clan is Sir Dallas Bernard, described as managing Peter Hamilton (Security Consultants) Ltd.

As a leading City banker, Bernard has contacts at the very highest level in Whitehall. Indeed, these contacts were so close that Sir Robert Armstrong, the one-time head of the Civil Service and Cabinet Secretary, was godfather to Sir Bernard's daughter at her christening at the Royal Chapel, Windsor, on 11th July 1981. As Cabinet Secretary, Sir Robert's authority extended to the Joint Intelligence Committee, the top secret clearing house for all government intelligence matters – including the operations of MI5. The Zeus/Hamilton-Whitehall link is further strengthened by the fact that Lord Chalfont and Sir Robert Armstrong worked together as officers of the Royal National Institute of the Deaf, whose headquarters, ironically, are in Gower Street, a stone's throw from a major MI5 establishment.

But what about Peter Hamilton, the individual who, according to the files of Sapphire Investigations, initiated the Sizewell surveillance? According to *The Handbook of Security* published by Kluwer Publishing Ltd, Hamilton is a former Director of Chubb Security Services and has spent most of his working life in security and intelligence. His first appointment of this nature was in China in 1943, when he was appointed to the British Military Mission, Chung King, after which he served in Malaya, both in combat and in the intelligence field.

After serving three years as Security Officer to the Cyprus Government and two years in Rhodesia as Security Adviser to the then Prime Minister, Sir Edgar Whitehead, Hamilton returned to England to take up a position with the Chubb organisation. In 1979, he was elected Chairman of the European Chapter of the American Society for Industrial Security. During his work with Zeus and Peter Hamilton (Security) Consultants Ltd, he admits to having undertaken confidential assignments for the much publicised and notorious Economic League, an organisation known to collect data for private and government subscribers. Much of the 'information' they have collected has resulted in the blacklisting of totally innocent workers who have been unable to obtain or maintain jobs because of the inaccuracy of the League's data. It is now a matter of public record that the League was set up by former intelligence agents, and that since its inception it has maintained official links with MI5 and Special Branch. After all, how else would they be able to obtain details of peoples' criminal and political affiliations?

In addition to his 'quality' contacts and associates, Mr Hamilton has also been known to associate with, and/or employ, characters who can only be described as having questionable reputations.

We have already discussed the background of Victor Norris, alias Adrian Hampson, the undercover agent working on the Sizewell operation, and David Coughlan, the telephone tapper and buggist who was convicted for his part in the Seychelles Islands fiasco. Another interesting unorthodox spy-associate of Hamilton is one Nick 'the Greek' Vafiadis, who has been accused in the newspapers of dirty tricks directed against businessmen. According to official company records, Nick the Greek purchased 500 shares in Hamilton's company in 1984, and also undertook covert investigations of a sensitive nature.

Operating under the trade name Tempest Consultants, Vafiadis described himself as an 'international investigator,' operating from a Post Office box number in Great Malvern, Worcester, as well as from a London ex-directory telephone number permanently hooked up to an answering machine. Vafiadis has always been a man of mystery, skulking around the shadowy corridors of fringe intelligence operations. Some of his sleazy work has been publicised, but somehow he has always managed to escape the net. He has never actually been tracked down to a permanent address and no one has been able to examine his work or involvement with Hamilton beyond his modest shareholding in Hamilton's company.

In 1985, quite by accident, I came across a sales letter advertising the various services of Tempest Consultants among which was an on-line computer service providing nuclear science and technology data. This was a most unusual and unique service for an international investigator to be selling, so much so one wonders where such a person would acquire this kind of information.

An example of Mr Vafiadis's private espionage work was exposed in a 1986 edition of *Today* reporting on a City of London scandal centred around Argyle Chairman James Gulliver. According to witnesses, Nick the Greek offered several thousand pounds in exchange for any information that would help to discredit Mr Gulliver. Immediately following this exposé, Vafiadis vanished from his home address, leaving a trail of unanswered questions ranging from the Gulliver affair to the Sizewell surveillance and his connections with Hamilton. According to local witnesses, Nick was a likeable rogue who had operated a number of companies, some of which were working for various Ministries. At one stage he is said to have produced antiterrorist and espionage equipment from a laboratory in Malvern, and by his own admission 'there is a lot more spying going on than people think'.

As well as employing the services of Norris, Coughlan and

Nick the Greek, Peter Hamilton also had a longterm relationship with freelance electronic expert Hassan Assali who, in 1984 was arrested and subsequently jailed for nine years – for manufacturing bomb timers. At the time of his arrest, Assali was vetted by MI5 for work with the Ministry of Defence. I will report in more detail on the activities of Assali, his criminal convictions and his work for Hamilton in Chapter 11.

A study of Barrie Peachman and his family-run firm, Sapphire Investigations Ltd, reveals a lifestyle completely different from that of Peter Hamilton and his colleagues. Whereas Hamilton was an experienced intelligence investigator surrounded by associates of similar expertise with high-level connections, Peachman was just an ordinary type of person who as a young man had an urge to work as a private eye. He satisfied this ambition by forming the family company that by 1984 was highly successful. Unlike Hamilton, he was not surrounded by 'pedigree' spies: his associates were his immediate family who helped in the running of the business.

His wife, Jean, assisted by their two sons Mark and Paul and daughter Sandra, played an integral part in the day to day affairs of Sapphire Investigations Ltd, as did Shirley Smith, co-director and, as we have seen, mistress. However, when it came to covert operations the only two people in the firm who knew the intimate details of any special investigation were Peachman and Shirley Smith. Although financially sound and impressive compared to other detective agencies, by Hamilton's standards the Sapphire Investigation organisation was small fry. Be that as it may, Peachman and his firm were considered useful enough to play a part in what was the most complex private spy operation ever conducted in the United Kingdom.

The closing months of 1983 were not kind to Barrie Peachman. In addition to the stress of the various political problems he was having with the IPI, he discovered that he himself was under some kind of surveillance. I lost count of the number of telephone calls I had from him, describing bizarre incidents involving his private car and the car used by Shirley Smith. To make matters worse, for some unknown reason his relationship with Shirley appeared to be in turmoil. Despite our close personal and working association Peachman would not go into detail about what was causing him to be, at times, erratic and quite unstable. All I could get out of him was 'I've got my back to the wall, there's nothing I can do'.

Conversations about the Sizewell surveillance were taboo, apart from occasional cryptic comments like 'It's not my job any more, Norris is going it alone'.

During the Christmas of 1983 he seemed to stabilise slightly, and even booked a round-the-world cruise in the New Year for his wedding anniversary. However, by late winter he was in a frame of mind that I can only describe as suicidal. His problems with Shirley had escalated to a point where the relationship had completely collapsed, despite the responsibility they shared for their nine-year-old son. I found this most strange: Shirley was in secure, well-paid employment and as a director had many privileges and financial advantages over the ordinary employee. Maybe she had become frustrated with her 'unofficial' status as Peach-man's mistress and mother of their son. (As it turned out, she was apparently quite happy with the arrangement, especially since the whole family and the locals were aware of, and accepted, the situation.) What, then, drove her to resign abruptly from the company on 2nd April 1984?

There were also a number of other unexplained and more tragic events around the same period. A few days previously, on 24th March, the body of an elderly woman was discovered on the outskirts of Shrewsbury.

The deceased, 78-year-old Hilda Murrell, had suffered knife wounds and had died of hypothermia after being abducted in broad daylight, bundled into her car, and driven to the copse where her body was eventually found. Hilda was a high-profile anti-nuclear campaigner, waging her own private war against the Government's plans for the installation of the Pressurised Water Reactor (PWR) at . . . Sizewell.

Approximately three weeks after Miss Murrell's murder, another death occurred, this time a few miles from the offices of Sapphire Investigations Ltd. On Tuesday 17th April 1984, Barrie Peachman visited London where we had planned to meet to discuss the various problems that were upsetting him. Regrettably, I was unable to keep the appointment and Barrie returned to Norwich, arriving at his headquarters at approximately 6.30pm. He made a number of calls, one of which was to Shirley Smith. At the conclusion of that call he wrote on a piece of paper the words 'Shirl refused to help me'. Immediately after this conversation, he loaded a .410 shotgun, walked to his car and drove to the home address of his mistress in nearby Newton Flotman. A local resident saw Peachman sitting in the car speaking to Smith who, after a few moments, left the stationary vehicle and entered her bungalow.

After sitting alone for a few moments, Peachman took the .410, placed the barrel in his mouth and squeezed the trigger. According to the one and only witness, there was a loud explosion, accompanied by a puff of smoke.

I first heard the sad news of Peachman's death thirty minutes after the event, when his son Mark telephoned me. It goes without saying that I was stunned. My immediate reaction was to wonder what had driven him to such despair that he had found it necessary to end his problems so violently. At this point in time my knowledge of Hilda Murrell was limited and I was not even aware that she had been one of the Sizewell campaigners. The mystery deepened when Victor Norris revealed that shortly before his suicide, Peachman had contacted him and was quite distressed. 'He was virtually incoherent', said Norris. 'His girlfriend, who I knew well as the one I always spoke to about Sizewell, never came into the conversation. He was incredibly upset, claiming his back was against the wall and saying that people were out to get him'.

It is highly unlikely that the truth about the Sizewell surveillance, Hamilton and Zeus Security will ever be known – unless, of course, Mr Hamilton, in the public interest, decides to open his records for examination.

One thing is certain: Hamilton and his group of companies have probably the most influential security contacts ever used by a supposedly private practitioner. Despite what he might insist concerning official employment, one of his companies *was* employed by the Foreign & Commonwealth Office (who control MI6) on two occasions during 1983, and on another in 1982. This can be seen from written answers given in the House of Commons by David Mellor to questions put down by Ken Livingstone MP on the 23rd May 1988 about the Zeus and Lynx private security companies.

CHAPTER 8

Hilda Murrell

At first, there appeared to be no connection between the death of Hilda Murrell and Peachman's suicide and for months police and media investigations were focused on the death of Hilda, without anyone realising that there was in fact a common denominator: the Sizewell nuclear power station.

Miss Murrell had been an outspoken anti-nuclear campaigner, hell-bent on her own private investigation into the Government's plans to instal a Pressurised Water Reactor (PWR) at Sizewell. Her research appeared to have uncovered a number of flaws in the design of PWRs and problems with the disposal of waste, so she had decided to present a damning report at a public hearing convened at Snape Maltings in Suffolk. Barrie Peachman, on the other hand, as we now know, according to his official company records had been recruited to 'ascertain the identities of the principal objectors at the Sizewell Atomic Power Station public hearing being held at Snape Maltings. If possible, to obtain a list of objectors, their connections with the media, political leanings, etc.'

Immediately following the murder, media activity escalated to a very high level. The case was compared with that of Karen Silkwood, a nuclear analyst in the United States who, ten years previously, had died in mysterious circumstances while attempting to reveal flaws in a nuclear fuel processing plant in Oklahoma. International publicity and a major feature film starring Meryl Streep highlighted the death of this young woman. The Murrell murder precipitated similar media excitement with excited politicians accusing the Security Service, Government and nuclear industry of all manner of misdeeds, including murder.

Hilda, born in Shrewsbury on 3rd February 1906, was an extraordinary person of many talents. She won a scholarship to the local High School where she eventually became Head Girl. Despite the handicap of having been born blind in one eye, she attained good results in her exams and later went up to Newnham College, Cambridge, from where she graduated in 1928 in English, Medieval Languages and French.

After the excitement of undergraduate life at Cambridge, things changed dramatically for Hilda. Although keen to follow an academic career, she found herself obliged to help the struggling family business Murrells Nurseries where she worked for the next thirty years. She became such an acknowledged expert at growing roses that even Buckingham Palace became clients of the firm. However, despite her tremendous loyalty and dedication, Hilda often felt trapped. During the war, she diverted her energies to charity work for Czechoslovakian Jewish refugees, even finding homes for some of them in Shropshire.

By 1962, Hilda had sold the original family business and opened a new one, Portland Nurseries, on the A5 by-pass just outside Shrewsbury. At about the same time she helped to launch the Shropshire Conservation Trust. In 1970, at the age of 64, she finally sold her business and retired. This was a retirement in name only for this woman of strong beliefs and great determination. Hilda now directed her formidable energies into conservation and the welfare of the community by setting out to challenge the authorities over what she saw as the danger of nuclear war and the menace of those industries that polluted the countryside she loved. Little did she realise that she had set out on a journey that would eventually lead to her abduction and end in a slow, undignified death.

Hilda was greatly respected in the local community by all who came into contact with her. On the surface she might have seemed rather unsociable, perhaps even a bit of a loner (and indeed she did rather shun the usual round of social life in Shrewsbury) but nothing could have been further from the truth. Once you got to know her, Hilda was revealed as a warm human being with a keen sense of humour and an infectious laugh. Although at times impatient and prickly, exacting in her demands on herself and others, she was nonetheless a woman of tremendous integrity and had many friends. She appeared not to have an enemy in the world – until the 21st March 1984.

Despite her quiet, private lifestyle, Hilda, as we have seen, was very strong minded and capable of tenacious, articulate debate on matters close to her heart. She would plan her strategy during her walks and leisure time at Llanymynech near Oswestry, where she had a chalet and would tend her garden and take delight in the local wildlife. It was at her chalet that Hilda composed letters to *The Times* and the *Guardian* newspapers, voicing her concern and criticising government policy about various matters, in particular their plans to instal a PWR at the Sizewell nuclear power station.

Not content with letters to the editor, Hilda began lobbying politicians, and even wrote directly to the Prime Minister, trying to draw their attention to what she thought of as the 'madness of nuclear power'. These attempts to get the Government to change its policies were totally ignored so she decided to present her own scrupulously researched case to a public hearing being held at Sizewell in Suffolk.

According to former Military Intelligence Officer Captain Fred Holroyd, this is something that would undoubtedly have been brought to the notice of the Security Service. 'Any person writing to the Prime Minister or the newspapers voicing their anti-nuclear or anti-Government views would have, without doubt, been investigated by MI5'. Holroyd and other impeccable sources have revealed that this would have been done initially by local Special Branch officers, who would have submitted a preliminary report to MI5. Then, depending on the profile of and potential threat posed by the subject of investigation, further courses of action would have been considered, including telephone tapping, mail intercepts – and covert investigation using undercover agents.

Unaware that she had become of interest to the Security Service, Hilda became involved during the 1970s with several established peace groups. By 1979 she was actively supporting the Campaign for Nuclear Disarmament (CND), Greenpeace, the European Disarmament Group and the Nuclear Weapons Freeze Advertising Campaign, to name but a few. Hilda's enthusiasm for her work was such that she even travelled to London to take part in a huge CND demonstration protesting against Cruise missiles. Her interests by now clearly extended to nuclear weapons.

According to former Ministry of Defence MI5 officer Cathy Massiter, around this time there was a massive expansion of surveillance directed against CND and other peace groups, and anyone involved in or associated with these organisations was potentially in line for special investigation. Targets of the Security Service included solicitors, barristers, journalists and ordinary members of the public simply exercising their democratic rights. Examples of such surveillance can be found in my own work and, of course, in the Zeus/Sapphire investigation into the Sizewell protesters. The Atomic Energy Constabulary (AEC) also played a small part in these covert operations by infiltrating Police Constable Mike Steel into the CND protesters demonstrating at Capenhurst. Steele eventually went public, admitting that he penetrated Operation Snowball, a fence cutting protest planned by CND, posing as a freelance photographer. He claimed that the AEC was concerned that terrorist groups might take advantage of the demos to gain entry to nuclear plants.

Holroyd is adamant that by 1983 Hilda would have been a priority investigation target for the Security Services, long before her formal announcement that she wished to present her anti-nuclear paper at the Sizewell public hearing. If the truth is ever revealed, we will probably learn that Miss Murrell was under investigation for over ten years prior to her anti-Sizewell campaign. This speculation gains credibility when we examine other aspects of her life that would have attracted the attention of the Security Service. First, nephew Rob Green, a Commander in the Royal Navy: throughout his 20 year service career, he maintained regular contact with her and was aware in the 1970s of her interest in what she saw as the unacceptable hazard of nuclear power generation. In his introductory statement, prior to reading his aunt's paper at the Sizewell public hearing, Commander Green (by then retired) said 'Besides being her nephew, I knew her well and agreed with her views on the civil nuclear industry. She therefore kept me informed on the progress of her paper'.

To fully appreciate why Commander Green would have been an additional reason for surveillance on Hilda, we must recall the events of the 3rd April 1982 at a special sitting of the House of Commons. This was when it was decided to send a Task Force to recapture the Falklands Islands. At this stage in the dispute, MPs were hoping for a diplomatic solution to the confrontation with Argentina. However, this was not to be and by the 30th April the conflict had escalated to such a level that Mrs Thatcher, the then Prime Minister, with the backing of her War Cabinet, authorised an attack on the Argentine cruiser *General Belgrano*, which at that point was said to have been closing in on the Task Force. This, it turned out later, was not so: the *Belgrano* was in fact sailing *away* from the Task Force, heading for home.

The order to attack the Argentine cruiser was transmitted from Fleet Headquarters at Northwood, Middlesex, to the nuclear submarine HMS *Conqueror* which carried out the orders on 2nd May 1982. The *General Belgrano* sank, and 368

Argentine crewmen lost their lives. In the closely guarded world of top secret coded signals, one of only a few naval officers who knew the intimate details of the Prime Minister's message to HMS *Conqueror* was a senior Naval Intelligence Officer (IO): Commander Rob Green.

Green, a graduate of the Joint Services School of Intelligence, was subject, like all servicemen employed on secret duties, to the Official Secrets Act (OSA) and regular positive vetting (PV).

His work during the Falklands war was vital to the defence of the realm, and he was one of the few Intelligence Officers who had access to top secret defence information, as well as the intimate details of official signals. Throughout his service career, Green complied to the letter with every requirement of the OSA, and during his frequent PV screening properly disclosed anything and everything which affected his status as an IO. This would certainly have included frank details about the campaigning activities of his aunt, Hilda Murrell.

The normal routine of positive vetting in the Navy involves a simple but probing investigation by security staff to check regularly the reliability of servicemen employed on secret duties. Investigators look into the background, habits and sympathies of all those related to the subject of vetting. During the screening, which can in the first instance last three or four months or even longer, depending on what is discovered, naval investigators liaise with other agencies, including MI5 and Special Branch. Criminal records, political affiliations and anti-nuclear sympathies all become part of what can turn into a lengthy scrutiny. The vetting procedure is usually updated every few years, depending on the post held by the candidate.

In the case of Hilda's nephew, his work gave him continuing access to much secret material that could have proved highly embarrassing to the Government had it been leaked to peace groups such as CND. However, the fact that he was employed in such a sensitive post throughout the Falklands War is an indication that Naval Security considered him stable enough to hold such a position. His positive vetting would have been regularly updated, with relatives and associates frequently coming under the security microscope. Hilda would have been investigated regularly as well as casually, not just because of her background but also because of the nature of the Intelligence work carried out by her nephew. This investigation and monitoring is not carried out because officers are under suspicion or distrusted: it is simply standard practice during positive vetting procedures.

During the vetting of Commander Green, Naval Security Investigators would have liaised with Special Branch (SB) and MI5 to check if anything was known about Miss Murrell. Her anti-nuclear activities would have been noted, and her nephew's Navy file duly annotated.

Further field enquiries by the SB unit based nearest to Hilda's home in Sutton Road, Shrewsbury, may well have been requested. It is also highly likely that naval researchers carried out their own enquiries. Whatever method was adopted, there is no doubt that before her anti-Sizewell campaign Hilda Murrell was the subject of continuing investigation, both by the Security Services (for their own reasons) and the Royal Navy. According to Captain Holroyd 'During their casual investigations on behalf of Naval Security, MI5 would have shown their own personal interest in the fact that Commander Green was a serving Intelligence Officer and related to Hilda Murrell. Completely independent of any Navy vetting requirements, MI5 would more than likely have increased their own interest in Hilda Murrell because of her anti-nuclear work, the result being that surveillance on her would have been intensified.'

Throughout the Falklands War, Commander Green held a senior Intelligence Officer's post at the naval base in Northwood, Middlesex. This gave him access to classified signals and intelligence data emanating from Government Communications Headquarters (GCHQ). He was also privy to sensitive signals from the then Prime Minister, Margaret Thatcher, who was later to be criticised for her general handling of the Falklands issue.

Green's own philosophy was such that he became very anxious at the direction the war was taking and the decisions that were being made. His worries, frustrations and disillusionment with the Service increased to such a level that he resigned his commission and left the Navy in December 1982 to live with his wife in Dorset where he began work as (ironically enough) a thatcher. He now runs his own anti-nuclear campaign.

The resignation of Rob Green came at a particularly awkward time. Controversy was raging over the Falklands War and in particular the sinking of the *Belgrano*, with all kinds of allegations circulating around Parliament and the media. Green's position in all of this was central in that he had personal knowledge of official activity and decisions that took place behind the scenes and his own personal views differed from Government policy. The fact that he was a disaffected Officer who had in effect 'jumped ship' must have caused increased blood pressure in some parts of Whitehall.

In December 1983, a year after Green's resignation from the Navy, Sir Robert Armstrong, the then Cabinet Secretary, commenced an investigation into the *Belgrano* affair.

Running parallel to this enquiry, Detective Chief Superintendent David Cole of the West Mercia Constabulary CID was put in charge of an investigation into the case of the GCHQ spy Geoffrey Prime. The main concern of the Armstrong enquiry was leakages of information about GCHQ and *Belgrano* matters, among other things. Anybody and everybody connected with Signals Intelligence or GCHQ was targeted for investigation. This included Commander Green and his aunt Hilda Murrell, who by 1983 was well and truly committed to the preparation of her anti-Sizewell paper. In 1983 there was also another development in Hilda's life that attracted the attention of government spies, namely her relationship with a young man, Malcolm, and his girl-friend, Trina.

For some time, Hilda had enjoyed the company of Malcolm and his intelligent lady friend who both lived in Shrewsbury. The relationship of the two women was such that Trina would refer to herself as Hilda's unofficial niece, and Malcolm, who was at that time living with Trina, also became friendly with Hilda. The three, being close friends, occasionally spent week-ends and holidays together. On these occasions, Hilda's work, in particular her anti-Sizewell paper, would be discussed. Malcolm and especially Trina were, naturally, supportive, not just verbally so.

At this time, only a few of her nearest associates knew that Hilda was working closely with the European Group for Ecological Action (ECOROPA), a Welsh-based, highly pro-fessional and committed organisation, well known on the Continent for its campaigns on environmental and nuclear issues. In 1985 an insider with the Central Electricity Generating Board (CEGB) described ECOROPA as a force to be reckoned with.

ECOROPA's reputation was such that it was reckoned to be one of the five most openly political groups among the Sizewell protesters. As an equal partner to the Stop Sizewell B Association (SSBA) it provided most of the technical and scientific support for the campaign.

It was in association with ECOROPA that Hilda had been preparing her paper. She was to be a second string to their campaign bow, and to ensure maximum impact their relation-ship had to be kept secret.

Hilda had first come into contact with Gerard Morgan-Grenville of ECOROPA in 1979. There was a regular exchange of news and views about her research, and Morgan-Grenville put her in touch with experts within the ECOROPA network who were able to supply the technical expertise she needed.

Mr Morgan-Grenville said 'It was felt that Hilda would have more impact on her own — as an apparently independent witness – because she was a celebrity rose-grower. Now I feel responsible for her death: had I not persuaded her to do this I believe she would be alive to-day.'

Hilda's work with ECOROPA was not confined to the preparation of her paper. She (and Trina) also assisted in the organisation's general operations by distributing thousands of highly critical leaflets highlighting many sensitive nuclear issues which the authorities are never keen to discuss such as contamination, deaths of plant workers, and accidents.

Mr Morgan-Grenville explained in a matter-of-fact way that ECOROPA is a regular target for Security Services surveillance, and was certainly being monitored over its Sizewell B activities. 'It is important to understand that this was not just any old planning enquiry. Sizewell B is a matter of national importance which could decide the direction of the nuclear industry for many years. That was why it was so important to the powers that be to keep tabs on the situation', he said.

Readers might well ask 'Why would Hilda's relationship with Trina and Malcolm attract the attention of officials investigating leakages of information about the *Belgrano* and GCHQ?' Well, had police and media investigators dug deep enough they would have discovered that Malcolm was in fact the son of a senior Signals Intelligence officer employed by the Ministry of Defence. Like Rob Green, he was engaged in top secret Signals Intelligence work to do with the defence of the realm. He is still so employed, and regularly vetted, with the usual particular emphasis on his next of kin and their leanings. According to a former Signals Intelligence Officer with thirty years' service: 'All Signals Intelligence staff are vetted to the highest possible level. 1983 was a particularly embarrassing time for the Government, with paranoia stalking the corridors of Whitehall over GCHQ and the Geoffrey Prime spy case; there was also the *Belgrano* affair. A massive purge was started on Signals staff and other Intelligence departments, with everyone being considered a potential whistle blower', he said.

Hilda was drawn into the *Belgrano*/GCHQ inquiry firstly because of her nephew, secondly through her relationship with Malcolm, and thirdly on account of the other work she was doing for ECOROPA – distributing contentious and inflammatory leaflets purporting to describe the disturbing truth of the Falklands War.* There was also the fact that for two years before her murder she had broadened the scope of her campaign to cover nuclear weapons and possible usage of 'civilian' plutonium for military purposes.

As part of her involvement with ECOROPA, Hilda circulated thousands of leaflets around Shrewsbury, including one which revealed a Government decision to send nuclear weapons to the South Atlantic.* Question 10 of the leaflet reads: 'Is it true that nuclear weapons were taken to the South Atlantic?' Answer: 'Yes, both from Gibraltar and the RFA (Royal Fleet Air Arm) Fort Austin, on carriers, destroyers and frigates, and from Portsmouth, though after a major row some, not all, of the nuclear weapons were withdrawn before the fleet reached Ascension Island. Efforts to retrieve nuclear depth bombs from the graves of *Sheffield* and *Coventry* have been only partially successful, and attempts to find nuclear bombs from two downed Sea King helicopters have been unsuccessful.'

According to Morgan-Grenville, one of his leaflets contained information known to Rob Green during his official Naval Intelligence service, but none of the information contained in the ECOROPA publications actually came from Commander Green. However, Hilda was his aunt, and here she was, probing (very thoroughly) into nuclear weapons and their links to 'civilian' plutonium.

There can no real doubt that Hilda was officially targeted for investigation. It is inconceivable that no action was taken to investigate her ECOROPA activities and her relationship with the son of a Signals Intelligence officer. There is also the

* See Appendix.

question of her nephew Commander Rob Green, ex-Naval Intelligence, who supported her anti-nuclear views and who knew the intimate secrets of the Falklands War, especially those relating to the sinking of the *Belgrano*.

Setting aside the matter of any interest they might have had in her nephew, the Security Services and local Special Branch would in any case have been aware of Malcolm's father who at that time was employed by the Ministry of Defence in a Shrewsbury signals unit, where his work involved handling Intelligence traffic between GCHQ and the Falklands. The trail would undoubtedly have led to Hilda, whose activities throughout 1982 and 1983 made her many new contacts within the peace fraternity, several of them affiliated to CND, Greenpeace and other high-profile groups under surveillance by government agencies.

Her anti-Sizewell research led to contact with experts in various scientific fields who were known to the Security Services. Many of them had been under surveillance for years, especially those holding membership in the Communist Party or similar organisations.

From an examination of letters written by Hilda between 1979 until just before she was murdered, it is clear that she had an open and straightforward way of communicating with her numerous contacts and friends. How easy it must have been to intercept her mail and analyse her materials.

An examination of the reports compiled by Vic Norris for Zeus Security confirms that many of the organisations and individuals in contact with Hilda were listed for investigation. These highly qualified engineers and scientists were all sympathetic to her cause, so she got invaluable assistance from expert sources. This helped her to complete an early nineteen-page draft, which she forwarded to her 'niece' Trina for her opinion. That document was never found by police investigators, and to date Trina and her boyfriend have not been interviewed. So the document remained undiscovered until the research for this book.

Sadly, Hilda's dossier, despite being full of impressively researched material accusing the nuclear industry of unnecessary secrecy and of failing to keep the public informed of the true dangers of nuclear waste, does not introduce anything that has not been exposed before.

It simply recapitulates the contents of the Department of the Environment's July 1982 White Paper, CMND 8607, reporting on the management of radioactive waste. She does attack the Government for their siting of a new PWR at Sizewell and also lambasts the then Central Electricity Generating Board (CEGB) and British Nuclear Fuels (BNF). She goes on to cite occasions when unstable nuclear compounds had been transported on railway lines used by public railway services but, once again, this was public knowledge.

Although some of the material Hilda used to back up her arguments was out of date, it must be said that the main points in her report are still relevant to-day, especially those about decaying radioactive waste. Paragraphs 6 and 7 refer to the White Paper's discussion on decaying waste: 'WP paragraph 7 and figure 1 – One basic characteristic of radioactivity which actually assists waste management is that it decays over time.' Hilda's expertly presented reminder is that it was precisely the decay of unstable elements which was causing many of the dangerous problems. 'To say that decaying actually assists in waste management is to stand the whole situation on its head and is unbelievably fatuous', wrote Hilda.

In contrast to the Murrell paper, a recent British Nuclear Fuels report in the *Mail on Sunday*, on 24th November 1991, states we should not over-react to the problems associated with waste management. 'Nuclear waste should be put in context with other, often more hazardous, materials. Highly infectious hospital waste and some industrial waste containing mercury for instance, may remain hazardous forever. Radio active waste decays with time', it said. Once again, the inference here is that decaying active waste is easier to deal with. Hilda's argument, of course, was that it was completely the opposite.

In 1983/84, the nuclear industry comprised the Central Electricity Generating Board (CEGB), now known as Powergen, the Atomic Energy Authority (UKAEA), and British Nuclear Fuels Ltd. The overall primary responsibility for nuclear security and investigations on behalf of the industry is vested in the UK Atomic Energy Authority Constabulary whose official role is said to be 'to police UKAEA and British Nuclear Fuel establishments in the United Kingdom.'

Technically, this force is a private organisation but with constabulary powers of arrest similar to those of other police forces. The nuclear police have their own dog section and responsibility for escort duties. They also undertake a minimal amount of undercover work which is carried out by a special investigation unit of which very little is known.

Many of its officers are armed, and the annual financial budget is top secret. Although they work independently of all other police forces and the Security Services, the nuclear police do liaise with the various official agencies, and there is an exchange of intelligence information, especially with MI5 and Special Branch who are the principal investigation agencies responsible for nuclear matters.

The months from November 1983 to March 1984 must have been extremely active for MI5, Special Branch, and the nuclear police, what with investigations into GCHQ, the *Belgrano* affair and, of course, the Sizewell atomic power station public hearing. Security Service agents must have been spread thin during this period. It is therefore not surprising that private detectives were recruited to infiltrate the Sizewell protesters. Captain Holroyd said 'this poor woman's name must have been top of the list in the *Belgrano* investigation and, of course, the Sizewell operation because of her intended paper. MI5, pressured by Whitehall, must have been in a bit of a tizzy over her.'

A currently serving Special Branch officer, who does not wish to be named, suggests that by 1984 Hilda was the subject of several intensive investigations by official agencies who were frantically stumbling over each other in their respective attempts to obtain details of her activities. In such situations it is common knowledge in the spy fraternity that the dominant organisation is always MI5.

For Hilda, the months November to March were very active. She kept in touch with her 'niece' and many other close acquaintances as she sought last-minute advice before making formal application to read her paper at Sizewell. A number of these contacts detected an air of uneasiness in Hilda's manner. It appeared that she was now becoming worried about her safety. This was hardly surprising, since her telephone was tapped, her home bugged, her mail intercepted, and a mysterious van often seen parked opposite her house.

Hilda's overall concern for her safety was such that she sent to her nephew, Rob Green, a copy of her paper, asking him to read it at the Sizewell hearing should anything happen to her.

This was out of character, as it was not Hilda's nature as a rule to discuss her personal life, even with close friends. One thing is sure: during the last few weeks leading to her murder something specific occurred which led her to believe she was in danger.

The countdown, as it were, to Hilda's abduction appears to have started on 18th February 1984 when she attended what has been described as a 'very subversive meeting of the Medical Campaign Against Nuclear Weapons (MCANW).' This was held by a local group at Shrewsbury Hospital, where the subject of the talk given by Dr Don Arnott was 'How to make a nuclear bomb'. Dr Arnott, formerly with the Vienna-based International Atomic Energy Agency, spent hours explaining the technical intricacies of nuclear physics to Hilda, and gave her invaluable support. He was well known to the Security Services.

The meeting of the Shrewsbury branch of the MCANW was attended by highly qualified professional medical people, whose opinions could have far reaching effects.

Hilda's presence on this occasion would almost certainly have been noted by local Special Branch agents monitoring the activities of the group. It is also highly likely that MI5 agents were operating in the area independently of Special Branch.

This meeting was very important to Hilda. One of the organisers, Dr Harry Bury, who had been friends with her for nearly ten years, had invited Hilda to attend so that she could learn more about the potential for 'civilian' plutonium to be diverted for use in military weapons. Dr Bury was in contact with Hilda until a few days before her death. He described her as being 'frightened, and of late very secretive.'

It seems that for two years before her murder Hilda had also investigated aspects of nuclear weaponry, in particular how these devices are made and exactly how 'civilian' plutonium can be used in their manufacture. As well as liaising secretly with experts, she also visited the local library to read up on all available information on nuclear weapons and their construction. According to Dr Bury 'she kept well-documented files on this subject in her house.'

Two questions arise from all this. Where are these files? And had Hilda discovered something to justify a break-in and abduction? The contents of Hilda's nuclear paper most certainly did not warrant a burglary, let alone murder. In any event, as will be seen in due course, neither the nuclear industry nor MI5 had any need to steal her paper for the simple reason that she submitted a copy with her application to appear at the Sizewell hearing.

On the 25th February 1984, Hilda telephoned her friend Gerard Morgan-Grenville of ECOROPA. This call was the first obvious sign of a change in her demeanour: she sounded so agitated and worried that he felt he had to drag himself out of the bath to concentrate fully on what she had to say. The conversation lasted about thirty minutes, during which time Morgan-Grenville was sitting draped only in a bath towel. Despite speaking with Hilda for such a long time, he could not persuade her to elaborate on what was worrying her. She eventually rang off, saying something which, again, was totally out of character. 'If they don't get me first, I want the world to know that one old woman has seen through their lies'. Morgan-Grenville is adamant that in all the time of his acquaintance with Hilda he had never before heard her say anything remotely like that.

Immediately following the murder, Mr Morgan-Grenville contacted the police to inform them that he had a lot of correspondence and other information that might be relevant, particularly concerning her fears. In an interview with the *Daily Star* he said 'they came to see me, but frankly didn't seem too interested. I offered them my files with all the details of Hilda's involvement with ECOROPA, but they refused it. I find that extraordinary, and still do.'

A former Metropolitan Police murder investigator, now in retirement in the south of England, was amazed to hear this. 'I am an experienced murder investigator and can categorically state that during enquiries relating to such a crime, it is proper and correct, and sensible, to examine all documents and information in anyone's possession that might be relevant to the activities of the deceased. After all, there is no telling what clues can be obtained from these sources'.

It is important to note that the experiences of other active anti-nuclear campaigners (which I will deal with in due course) included difficulties with telephones, anonymous 'phone calls, and surveillance vehicles observed outside the house. It is therefore more than possible that, some time before the telephone call to Morgan-Grenville, Hilda Murrell received some form of anonymous threat and was worried about a mysterious motor vehicle parked opposite her house.

From letters passing between Hilda and the Editor of the *Ecologist*, Peter Bunyard (a colleague of Morgan-Grenville), it can be surmised that Hilda made formal written application, between the 6th and 19th March, to appear at the Sizewell public hearing to present her paper. It is also vitally important to realise that, having been advised by Mr Bunyard on the 1st March 1984 that she should apply in writing to speak at the Sizewell hearing, Hilda forwarded a copy of her proof of evidence, which contained all her research information. This then effectively eliminates the long-held opinion that Hilda died solely because of her Sizewell anti-nuclear paper. It is inconceivable that MI5 or the nuclear industry would have gone to the trouble of burglary, abduction and murder for a report they already possessed.

Other interesting information gleaned from the Murrell-Bunyard letters confirms that Hilda had in fact requested to attend London, not Sizewell itself, to present her paper, and that on 19th March, two days before her murder, she was still awaiting official acknowledgment that she would be allowed to attend. Concerning the actual content of Hilda's report, in a February communication to Bunyard she wrote 'I do not flatter myself that there are any new ideas in my paper, though it does fit neatly into the slot in answer to the DOE's opening statement, which was based entirely on the White Paper.' In other words, there was absolutely nothing for the authorities to worry about. Mr Bunyard readily agrees that Hilda's contribution, although thoroughly researched, consisted of nothing more than already published material.

On 12th March 1984, Ian Campbell, who lives in Borth, Dyfed (Wales), spoke at a meeting in Llangollen during the European election campaign. Following the meeting he contacted Tam Dalyell MP to inform him that he had been told by a Labour MP that Hilda Murrell (whom he knew) was very worried about her safety. At this stage, Hilda was in a continuous state of agitation about this matter.

On Sunday, 18th March 1984, Hilda travelled to her cottage in Wales to meet with one of her many contacts, a nuclear physicist who had been helping with the final preparation of her paper.

The following day, Monday 19th March, Hilda telephoned another friend and arranged to meet her the next day, for breakfast and a chat. At this meeting Hilda mentioned that her paper was complete. On the same day, an unusual incident occurred in the home of an old friend, Constance Purcer. (Miss Purcer lives alone in the White House, which is in a secluded location up a track a quarter of a mile from the village of Aston Munslow.)

85-year-old Constance informed Rob Green that Hilda had visited her for the last time on the afternoon of the 19th March, two days before she was abducted. On this occasion Hilda attempted to leave some papers with her, but Constance sensed something very threatening and declined to take them. It seems Hilda did not press her, and simply put them back inside a brown paper envelope which she placed in the bottom of her basket, under some plants. Constance assumed that the papers were to do with Sizewell.

Apparently, Hilda was very tense and trembling. According to Miss Purcer, she told her that she had taken her papers to London 'to show some people, who were very pleased with them.' Hilda also said that between Christmas 1983 and March 1984 she had been worried about the security of her house in Sutton Road, and that a new neighbour had called on her and said if she ever felt nervous about anything she should let him know. Constance felt that this was some kind of psychological intimidation. Despite Rob Green's attempts to persuade the police to record Constance Purcer's evidence, they did not take her seriously, presumably for their own operational reasons.

About a month after the murder, Constance was in her kitchen at approximately 7.30pm when her dog started to bark in the adjoining buttery at the back door. Someone was clearly outside the door, trying to open it. After a few moments, the intruder seemed to go away and the dog calmed down. Next morning, Constance opened the back door and found that the wooden plug had been prised out of an old finger hole through which it was possible to lift the door latch. The plug was lying on the ground outside the door. She immediately arranged for new locks and chains to be fitted. Miss Purcer is convinced that this was a blatant attempt to intimidate her following her stubborn insistence on passing her information to the police.

On the fateful day, Wednesday, 21st March 1984, Hilda did some routine domestic tasks before leaving for a 12.30pm lunchtime appointment with two Welsh friends, Doctors John and Alicia Symondson. At about 10.15am she left her home in Sutton Road, Shrewsbury, in her small white Renault car, registration number LNT 917W, and drove to the town centre. Here she visited a local bank to withdraw £50, after which she did a little shopping at a local Safeway.

What is alleged to have happened next has been the subject of much discussion and controversy. Despite the fact that other unrelated incidents appear to corroborate the witness's statement, official investigators refuse to seriously consider it as being relevant to the Murrell murder. It would be true to say that, for reasons they are not revealing, the police refuse to believe that Mr Laurens Otter is telling the truth.

During the morning of her visit to the local shops, Hilda (according to Mr Otter) telephoned him some time between 11 and 11.30am to ask if he would travel to Shrewsbury from Wellington where he lived to collect a pile of papers she had with her in the 'phone box. 'Not just Sizewell', Hilda said.

During the course of the conversation, Hilda said that she was being watched, had received threats by 'phone and that her mail was being opened. She also asked Mr Otter where he would publish something that the Government would not want published. They then discussed the train journey which Otter would have to make, with Hilda stressing that she did not have time to wait for the train because she was expecting a visit at midday from an Inspector or Chief Inspector Davies or Davy who was 'coming up from London.' She didn't know what it was about, but she did not think it was about Sizewell.

Because of their respective circumstances that morning it was impossible for Mr Otter and Hilda to meet. The conversation ended with Hilda suggesting that perhaps she would see him at an Alliance meeting that evening. The evidence of this telephone call, which was supposed to have been placed from a local call box, is vitally important. However, CID officers have never really taken Mr Otter seriously and have failed to pursue this line of enquiry.

In any event, it is clear that Hilda completed her shopping and, after meeting a local neighbour, George Lowe (who by coincidence followed her home in his own car), returned to her house in Sutton Road where Mr Lowe saw her turn into her driveway just before noon. After arriving home, Hilda walked across the road to the residence of Mrs O'Connor, who earlier that morning had seen a mysterious pipe-smoking male, dressed in jeans and with short curly hair, hanging around the pavement opposite Hilda's house. (From Mrs O'Connor's description, this man had a rather military look about him.) He was also capable of jumping a fence easily when she approached for a closer look. After paying Mrs O'Connor sixteen pence for a raffle ticket, Hilda left, walked across the road into her own drive, and entered the house. That was the last time she was seen alive.

At approximately 10.25am on Saturday, 25th March, Hilda's body was found in a small coppice known locally as The Moat, in an area of Shrewsbury called Hunkington. Her white Renault car was found abandoned in a roadside ditch a few hundred yards away. Inside the vehicle was a Hamlet cigar wrapper, and a small tent peg with wire attached in such a way it could have been used as a poacher's snare. Hilda, as we now know, was a non-smoker, and she was certainly not familiar with the art of poaching. The tent peg and wire could have been used to hold her wrists or ankles. I understand that this poacher's snare-gadget could have been an improvised implement, similar to that used by various Special Forces for immobilising prisoners.

Hilda's activities during her final months, and the fact she submitted her paper to the Sizewell enquiry along with her application, raise questions that to date remain unanswered. For instance, why was she so agitated over something that she readily admitted was 'nothing new'? And why would she frantically ask friends and associates to hold documents we can only assume were to do with her Sizewell project? There were also her remarks to Morgan-Grenville about seeing through 'their' lies and 'if they don't get me first'!

Whatever was worrying Hilda could not have been to do with her Sizewell paper. It must therefore have had some connection with the additional research she was doing into the relationship between the civil side of the nuclear industry and military weapons, or with the Falklands War. It was well known that she was a CND supporter and, Hilda being Hilda, knowing full well that her nephew Rob was in a precarious position because of his Falklands-related Naval Intelligence post, she could have been too terrified to use what she had discovered, both because of the threats she had received and the fact that her work could well compromise her nephew.

Assuming for the sake of argument that what she had discovered involved either the use of 'civilian' plutonium in nuclear weapons or the Falklands campaign, the *Belgrano*, or the intended use of nuclear weapons in the South Atlantic, then it is not surprising that Hilda was nervous to the point of paranoia and living in fear.

CHAPTER 9

Who Killed Hilda?

The Conservative Prime Minister during 1970–74, Sir Edward Heath, who was responsible for the expulsion of Russian diplomats in 1971, stated 'I met people in the security services who talked the most ridiculous nonsense and whose whole philosophy was a ridiculous nonsense. If some of them were on an underground train and saw someone reading the *Daily Mirror*, they would say "that is dangerous, get after him and find out where he bought it".' Another ex-MI5 officer remarked 'Some officers live a very sheltered life and never work in the real world and the overall tone is right wing. Some of them thought people who wore jeans were potentially subversive'.

If MI5 officers can seriously consider *Daily Mirror* readers and people who wear jeans subversive, then it is easy to imagine how they might regard people like Hilda Murrell, who had for several years been active anti-nuclear campaigners questioning the Government's every move and policy concerning nuclear power and weapons.

Reports of the sequence of events during the period Wednesday, 21st March (the day Hilda was last seen alive) and Saturday, 24th March (the day her body was discovered) were initially beset by contradictions. However, with the co-operation of reliable witnesses it has now been possible to construct a likely scenario for those three days:

Wednesday 21st March 1984

(a) At approximately 12.30pm Hilda's white Renault car was seen by no fewer than sixty-nine witnesses being driven in an erratic manner. In the driving seat was a man aged about 30. He had a white narrow face and darkish collar-length hair. He was possibly wearing a grey jacket. Witnesses also reported that they saw a woman thought to be Hilda 'slumped' in the passenger seat. For reasons best known to himself the driver, instead of turning right on leaving Hilda's house, which would have taken him (and his cargo) to open country in less than a mile, turned left, driving towards the centre of Shrewsbury. He then took another surprising course of action by heading for the Newport road, driving right past the West Mercia Divisional Police Headquarters.

It is unlikely that these were the actions of a local man, who would surely have known the whereabouts of the police headquarters and the fact that a right turn out of Hilda's drive would have taken him quickly to a deserted area suitable for dumping his victim (assuming it was his intention to dump her there and then).

(b) Earlier in the morning a neighbour, Brian George, who lived near Hilda, saw what he described as two 'suspicious' people walking along Sutton Road close to Hilda's property. A man aged about thirty or forty with longish hair and, possibly, a moustache, was with a woman dressed in a cloak. Mr George described the male as wearing a suit, open-neck shirt and trainer boots, and, according to this witness, he looked like an off-duty policeman.

(c) At 1.20pm on the same date, Hilda's car was seen by farmer John Marsh who had been working in the area of the copse in Hunkington. The empty vehicle was parked in such a manner it appeared to have been abandoned, a few hundred yards from the copse where Hilda's body was discovered on the Saturday. Mr Marsh examined the car, but could see nothing obviously amiss, even though it was unlocked.

It was not until after his lunch, when he noticed the car was still in the same position, that he began to feel uneasy, to such an extent he telephoned his local policeman, PC Paul Davies.

Statements of the various witnesses show that Hilda's car must have been dumped, or driven off the road and abandoned, between 1pm and 1.20pm. A running man was seen in the area between 2pm and 2.20pm on the same day.

(d) During the afternoon, two telephone calls were made to Hilda's house by Dr Alicia Symondson, who was of course expecting Hilda to visit in accordance with their earlier arrangements. On both occasions Hilda's phone was heard to ring normally but, not surprisingly, there was no reply. The evidence of the normal ringing tone was to play an important part in the subsequent investigation.

(e) Some time during the morning, a red Ford Escort car was seen close to Hilda's address.

Thursday 22nd March 1984

(a) Hilda's car remained in its abandoned state without any immediate efforts from the local policeman to enquire why it was still there.

It was later said that a police national computer check had given incorrect information about the registered owner.

(b) Some time in the morning, at approximately 10am, a Mrs Reekie was in the vicinity of Hilda's house: the curtains were closed and the lights switched on. Mrs Reekie was subsequently visited by police officers, who did not ask for a written statement. This witness found the officers oddly relaxed, and thought that they appeared not to be pursuing a murder investigation. Her husband, Mr Reekie, revealed that police officers had been drafted in from outside the area for the investigations and that they lacked local knowledge.

(c) Mr Scott, the owner of the land adjoining and including the copse, spent some time examining his trees with a view to doing some felling. His evidence shows that he examined every inch of the copse as he counted the trees: as it was so early in the year there was very little undergrowth. Scott is adamant that there was no sign of a body in the copse on that Thursday afternoon. He said 'I examined the place so thoroughly I would have seen a dead rabbit, let alone a person'. The time at this point was approximately 3pm.

(d) Another incident on that Thursday involved a local tractor driver, working in a field nearby, who saw a dark car drive up the lane. It parked in the gateway to a field and a man was seen to leave the vehicle, walk over to the copse where he remained for about twenty minutes, then return to the car and drive away. To this date, car and driver have not been traced.

(e) Finally, later in the evening, a resident living near the copse observed what they described as 'lights and movement' there.

Friday 24th March 1984

(a) A number of unexplained events happened on this day. Various friends attempted to reach Hilda by telephone: all were frustrated by the continuous ringing sound on both her Shrewsbury and Welsh cottage numbers. They too assumed both telephones were in working order and that there was simply no reply.

(b) Brian George, neighbour and part-time gardener, passed Hilda's house in Sutton Road and noticed the kitchen door was open. He was not suspicious and as he was not due to work on Hilda's garden until the following day just went about his own business.

(c) At 10.30am, John Marsh, the farmer who had originally reported the abandoned white Renault to PC Paul Davies, rang

Hilda Murrell – abducted and murdered 21 March 1984.
(Press Association)

Hilda Murrell and Malcolm – son of Ministry of Defence Signals
Intelligence Officer 1983 (Trina Paskell)

Trina – close friend of Hilda Murrell and undiscovered witness.
(Gary Murray)

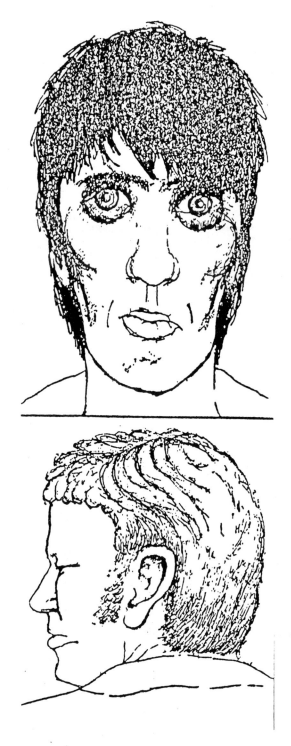

Two police artist impressions of suspect in the Murrell case.
(Shropshire Star)

Hassan Assali – electronics expert, convicted in 1985 of manufacturing bomb timers. (Gary Murray)

Surveillance of dockers in the 1972 National Dock Strike.
(Gary Murray)

Sabotaged fuel injection nut from author's vehicle.(Gary Murray)

MI5's Gower Street, London, complex. (Gary Murray)

MI5's proposed new £350 million HQ on London's Embankment. (Gary Murray)

Current MI5 office in Curzon Street, a minute's walk from the vice dens of Shepherds Market. (Gary Murray)

Rivals across the river, in Vauxhall. Proposed new HQ of Secret Intelligence Service (MI6). (Gary Murray)

Current MI6 HQ, Century House, close to Waterloo railway station. (Gary Murray)

Davies again to inform him that the car was still in the same position. Mr Marsh was informed that the matter had been reported to Shrewsbury Police.

(d) Mid-afternoon, a red Escort car was seen again, this time driving slowly past the field where the copse was located. It passed three times during the space of an hour and a half.

(e) Later in the evening Shrewsbury Police, now in possession of the correct identity of the registered owner of the Renault, attended Hilda's house but could find nothing unusual and, after knocking on the door and failing to obtain a reply, left.

(f) By far the most unusual incident on this date occurred at the home of a local man working as a counsellor to people with sexual problems. In a statement to Member of Parliament Tam Dalyell in the presence of journalist Judith Cook the man, said to have an excellent relationship with the police, was visited at about 6.30pm by two senior officers from Shrewsbury police headquarters.

The counsellor was asked if he could think of anybody who might have a sexual hang-up about elderly ladies. Could he think of a loner, a man with sexual problems who would be turned on by going into a woman's bedroom and interfering with her clothing? The type of man these officers were seeking needed to have or be rumoured to have a violent disposition. After discussion the police went away, leaving the counsellor completely confused as to what the visit had been about. He told Judith Cook and Tam Dalyell 'I realised when I read the first reports in the paper the next evening of the finding of Hilda Murrell's body that it seemed as if the police had been describing the murder, but I am at a loss to understand why they came to me on *Friday* night, when she wasn't supposed to have been found until the next day'.

If this evidence is correct, and there is no reason whatsoever to doubt the integrity of the witness, it means that Hilda's body must have been found *before* the 'official' discovery. If this was so then where and, more importantly, *why* was her corpse being held when it is common knowledge among experienced murder investigators that an autopsy as soon as possible after discovery makes it that much easier for the pathologist to determine accurately cause of death. As we now know, the first autopsy was carried out on the Saturday evening, when the body had allegedly been lying in the copse for three days.

I will deal with the medical aspects of the case in due course. In the meantime we should look at the credibility of the sex therapist. It would be very convenient simply to dismiss this witness as a 'crank': after all, such people do come out of the woodwork from time to time with all manner of allegations. However, before we do that we should ask what could have been his motive for making such a statement – money or publicity, perhaps? That was definitely not so with this witness. He travelled from Shrewsbury to the House of Commons to speak with Tam Dalyell and Miss Cook, a crucial part of the deal being that his identity should not be revealed: hardly the action of someone seeking some form of publicity or financial advantage. Then there are the unimpeachable reputations of the two people who heard and recorded this man's testimony, Tam Dalyell MP and journalist Judith Cook, two highly intelligent individuals who would not give the time of day to an impostor.

Saturday 24th March 1984

(a) Brian George arrived at Hilda's house at about 8.45am to carry out his usual gardening duties to find that the police had again visited the property where, according to a constable, the premises appeared a bit untidy, with the kitchen curtains drawn and the lights switched on.

Mr George found it a little odd that, despite having been at the property for two hours, the PC had failed to confirm (or so it appeared) that Hilda was missing. After locating a nearby relative he (the PC) had borrowed a key, locked Hilda's house and returned to the police station.

(b) At nine o'clock a second gardener, David Williams, arrived and the two men set about their work. Much to their surprise, they found the kitchen door still open and on the table they saw Hilda's handbags and some of her Sizewell papers. The general state of the kitchen worried the two men, so they attempted to telephone Hilda at her Welsh cottage. Their first call was frustrated by the line appearing to be out of order so they made a second call from Mr George's home telephone, only to hear a prolonged ringing tone. They then contacted the police.

(c) As the morning progressed, activity increased with the arrival of various police officers, including a Superintendent Needham who initially took charge of the search which rapidly expanded to include the area around the abandoned Renault. Eventually, at 10.30am, Hilda's body was found in the copse. According to a Mrs Randall who, with her two dogs, had assisted the police in the search of the copse, Hilda's body was lying face up with her knees scratched and bloody, suggesting that she was either dragged or had been crawling.

(d) Poor Hilda was in a sorry state, with stab wounds and other injuries to the body, including large bruises on her face. She was partially clothed, wearing only a coat, pullover and a skirt, but no underwear. The keys to the Renault were in her pocket. Police searches uncovered her driving licence and other personal items lying in a hedge close to the road, and her shoes were in a nearby field. A knife was also found nearby.

(e) Mr George, the gardener, and his colleague had access to the victim's home before investigating officers from the West Mercia Police Force arrived. What Mr George saw in the house revealed beyond any shadow of doubt that a systematic search of Hilda's home had been carried out. All the rooms, even the loft, appeared to have been searched. Mr George recalled later

171

that the telephone wires were not as described later in official statements. He even took the trouble to get his daughter to draw the condition of the telephone system: this sketch was then passed to a journalist from a national newspaper, only to vanish without trace. It might just be a coincidence, but the journalist involved has for some time been suspected of 'socialising' with the Security Services.

When he was interviewed by the police, Mr George gave a verbal statement which he says was tape recorded but it was not until nine months later that he was presented with a formal typed statement to sign. His attitude to the 'chance burglar' conclusion reached by the West Mercia Police was blunt. 'Casual burglar my eye', he said.

One final incident that tends to extinguish one's confidence in the police concerned involved both male and female officers said to be on duty at Hilda's house before the discovery of her body. According to a local witness who is reluctant to be identified, police guarding the house appeared not to be treating the whole matter of Hilda's disappearance seriously. One female plain clothes officer is alleged to have responded to neighbours' requests for information with the remark 'She may be dead'.

The investigation into Hilda's death was headed by Detective Chief Superintendent Cole, the chief of West Mercia Criminal Investigation Department. This was the same officer responsible for the 1983 enquiry into the Geoffrey Prime spy scandal and leakages of information from GCHQ, an officer with an impressive record of successful cases.

In addition to the ordinary CID murder enquiry, another more clandestine unit began research into Hilda's pre-death activities, with special attention being paid to her friends and contacts, some of whom had been helping with the preparation of her paper. The West Mercia Special Branch, it transpired, were also involved, seemingly independently of the murder investigation.

The introduction of Special Branch into what was from the

outset thought to be a straightforward murder by a chance burglar introduced a strange cloak and dagger ambience to the whole affair, especially since Special Branch operatives more than once posed as CID investigators. These acts of deception were not only committed by middle and low ranking officers: the actual Commanding Officer of the Branch visited witnesses, insisting that he was a CID officer. I am able to speak with authority on this point as I was one of the witnesses.

At the time, I was operating my own detective agency from offices in Egham, Surrey where I was visited by two well-dressed police officers who identified themselves as being from West Mercia CID. I had been forewarned by a journalist, Duncan Campbell, of the name of the Special Branch Chief so I was able to detect the deception immediately.

In a conversation which I managed to tape record this senior officer can clearly be heard insisting that both he and his colleague were CID detectives. At one stage they even denied being Special Branch. Eventually, after some cross examination by me, they admitted their true identity and brushed their attempted deception aside with a vague reference to helping out on the murder investigation. I was unable get the junior officer to comment on a very interesting tie he was wearing which had a dark background and sported an unusual pattern which looked remarkably like a radio mast transmitting some kind of signal. 'Could this have been a GCHQ tie?' I asked myself afterwards.

The investigation into the death of Hilda Murrell commenced officially on Saturday 24th March 1984. I say 'officially' because, quite frankly, I and many others believe that her death was known to the authorities some time before. The initial stages of the enquiry provided months of controversial copy for espionage-hungry journalists who highlighted so many contradictions and inconsistencies in the 'evidence' that one began to wonder just how efficient – or inefficient – were the officers taking part in the investigation. Shock-horror stories emerged, accusing detectives of failing to record accurate statements and of not having any real interest in solving the case.

At one point it emerged that a number of detectives had been suspended from duty for 'skiving off' to play golf when they should have been interviewing witnesses. There were Press allegations that the officers were aware the investigation was nothing more than a cosmetic exercise, and that they were not actually supposed to find the killer(s).

Regardless of police assurances that they were examining every source of potential information, a number of witnesses felt they were being treated with contempt, or at any rate not being taken seriously. Some, like Hilda, were opposed to the nuclear industry, others had been helping her with her research, yet murder investigators, or Special Branch agents posing as CID men, showed no real interest in what they had to offer. There was, however, a great deal of interest in Hilda's contacts. Constance Purcer (see previous chapter) experienced at first hand the lack of police interest in the evidence she had to offer.

Immediately following the murder, and still disorientated, Constance made a statement to police officers. However, because of her grief-stricken state, she forgot to mention the events of 19th March and Hilda's visit. Attempts to persuade police investigators to re-interview Constance were a waste of time: even personal approaches by Hilda's nephew Rob Green failed to provoke any interest.

Constance became so determined to persuade police to record her further statement that she bombarded Shrewsbury police station with call after call, demanding that an Inspector visit her.

Eventually, the police agreed to send someone, and on Wednesday, 16th April two junior detectives visited her. After voicing her complaint that she had specifically requested that an Inspector should call, she agreed to talk to them. The interview was something of an ordeal. Rather than simply asking Constance what she wished to say, the officers aggressively demanded to know whether Rob Green or anyone from Harlech Television had been to see her. They also accused Green of putting her up to making a further statement. At eighty-five years of age, Constance was already frail, and by now easily frightened. She became so confused and exhausted that she signed the further statement that they handed her, even though she felt it did not fully reflect what she wished to say.

If the attitude that the police adopted with Constance Purcer is typical of the Hilda Murrell investigation as a whole, it is not surprising that the killers are still running free. Negligence? Poor detective work? Unprofessional conduct? Or was it all a carefully constructed plan to discredit and neutralise valuable witnesses who could help uncover the truth about the murder of Hilda Murrell?

Two other potentially valuable witnesses who have already been mentioned, Trina and Malcolm, were overlooked despite their close friendship with Hilda. Trina, as we now know, was given a draft copy of the paper being prepared by Hilda: the police failed to discover this document. There was also the question of the identity of Malcolm's father who was, and still is, a serving Signals Intelligence Officer working for the Ministry of Defence.

John, whose name I feel obliged to obscure for security reasons, is a senior officer working at a Shrewsbury MOD unit. His work is classified, and necessitates regular positive vetting. I have been led to believe that during the Falklands campaign John would have handled numerous secret signals routed to and from the Falklands via GCHQ. From my limited experience of Signals Intelligence, I would suggest that such signals would have almost certainly not been in a raw form. My understanding is that classified signals in transit are always encoded before dispatch and it is therefore highly unlikely that any operator would know the contents. This theory would, of course, not apply in cases where an operator was expected to either encode (before transmission) or decode (after receiving). I am unable to comment on the intimate details of John's duties.

The first few months of the investigation into Hilda's murder must have been a very embarrassing time for the officers in charge of it. Apparent acts of negligence, discrepancies and controversy were highlighted every step of the way by the media. The 'chance burglar' theory was shot down in flames on television programmes and in every national and many local papers one way or another. This did not deter the West Mercia Constabulary: they steadily trawled the length and breadth of the country, giving the impression that an authentic murder investigation was taking place. There was no official mention of Special Branch involvement: they were almost certainly operating independently of the regular murder team.

To elaborate on the supposed progress of the police investigation as revealed through their briefings to the media would only introduce considerable contradiction and confusion, clouding any meaningful analysis of the whole affair. I will therefore concentrate only on those aspects of the case considered to be of genuinely major relevance, starting with the Medical Examiner's report.

Dr Peter Ackland from Edgbaston, Birmingham, was the Home Office pathologist responsible for the post mortem that was carried out on Saturday, 24th March at 6.15pm. The report presented at the subsequent inquest was scientifically objective, describing in detail the many injuries inflicted on the deceased.

Setting aside the inevitable technical jargon, Dr Ackland's report still reveals very little that would assist the layman in understanding or deciding what could have happened to Hilda. Having said that, there were a couple of points which made interesting reading. 'Two articles of footwear apparently belonging to the deceased were noted placed at intervals between the copse and the road', Dr Ackland reported. What a strange choice of words. Why not just report that Hilda's shoes had been found in such and such a location rather than categorically state that her footwear had been *placed* at intervals between the copse and road? There is no way a chance burglar would undertake an elaborate placing of his victim's personal items. His first and primary concern would have been to dump his victim and then get the hell out of the area to establish his alibi.

I and others find this mention of Hilda's shoes most peculiar and wonder how Dr Ackland can be so sure that the shoes were deliberately placed. This is not a medical or scientific conclusion reached as a result of a physical examination of the body but an investigatory conclusion that is normally provided by police investigators. If this is so, then my question to the West Mercia CID is simple: 'what evidence do you have that Hilda's shoes were deliberately *placed* at the spots found, and why would the murderer have done such a thing if he was only a *chance burglar*?'

Dr Ackland's report contains other interesting pieces of information that, if correct, should have been of assistance to the murder investigators. For instance, many of Hilda's injuries were inflicted with a knife, some of the wounds being to the hands and arms as though she had tried to fight off her assailant. There was also bruising that, according to Dr Ackland, could have been the result of punching, falling or kicking.

In his final analysis, Dr Ackland speculated on how Hilda may have come to be stabbed. He also intimated that had she received medical treatment immediately after the attack she would not have died.

'I think that an elderly lady with some moderately serious injuries, in very cold weather, would die of hypothermia within five to ten hours. Had she received medical treatment within that period she may have survived. I am cautious about drawing too many conclusions from the evidence we have had, but I think that from the evidence I saw, Miss Murrell may have been trying to escape from the car and was pursued, and possibly frog-marched with an arm across her neck, and the knife held towards her.

'A blood-stained handkerchief was found in the right pocket of her coat, which was adjacent to the stab wounds, but I am not sure whether the handkerchief was stained because of this, or whether she used the handkerchief to mop up some earlier injury. The evidence suggests she had been stabbed through her clothing.

'I'm firmly of the opinion that the body was not moved after death, although in a hypothetical case, if two people were involved in lifting her, it is possible. But I don't think that this is what happened. I certainly don't support the police in every case, but in this one I think they are right. It is my professional judgment that the cause of death was hypothermia because I do not think Miss Murrell died from her wounds.'

On hearing the evidence of Dr Ackland and that of Detective Chief Superintendent Cole, coroner Colonel David Crawford Clarke declared:

'It is clear that having driven her to Hunkington, at some point removing her from the car, or her getting out of the car, at the place in which she was subsequently found, he attacked her and caused the injuries which brought about her subsequent death. The only verdict that I can record in such a case is that the deceased was killed unlawfully.'

There is no doubt that Hilda was unlawfully killed. It is just unfortunate that *how* she died is not at all clear. One of the reasons for this is that the coroner has consistently refused to supply a full copy of the post mortem report. Rob Green, Hilda's next of kin, has not been able to obtain a copy of this report despite representation to the coroner's office so speculation about what it contains has led to all kinds of theories about how Hilda died. It is not my intention to discuss these, except to mention briefly the matter of hypothermia.

According to reputable medical sources, it is difficult to confirm the cause of death in a victim who has been dead for three days. Apparently, over such a period the core temperature of the corpse reduces to that of the ambient temperature, resulting in a more difficult task for the examiner who then has to rely on certain internal conditions to reach his final diagnosis. Referring to Dr Ackland's statement, other experts insist that the presence of punctuate erosions in the mucosa would not *in itself* be sufficient grounds for concluding hypothermia was the only cause of death.

On the contrary, there are said to be a number of possible conclusions about the cause of death one can reach from the presence of small dotted traces of mucus, multiple injuries and natural causes being two of them.

In due course a second post mortem examination was carried out. Once again controversy raged over why another examination should be necessary. The answer is simple: it is standard practice in such cases since any defendant is entitled to have available whatever evidence can be gleaned from a post mortem so that they or their lawyers can cross examine witnesses and present their case in possession of all the relevant facts.

While there does not appear to have been any ulterior motive in carrying out a second examination, the sudden request to remove Hilda's body from the morgue for burial as soon as possible does raise yet another puzzling question. After all, most modern hospitals and morgues have facilities suitable for storing corpses for years if necessary. For example, in the case of Helen Smith who died under mysterious circumstances her father insisted that her body be kept for some considerable time whilst he carried out enquiries into her death. Helen's body was subjected to no less than *four* post mortems, and it was not until the final one that it was proved that she was raped before she died, supposedly by jumping off a hotel balcony.

This kind of last-minute evidence can make or break a criminal investigation. Why, then, was there a sudden demand to remove Hilda's body from the morgue, knowing full well it would have to be disposed of?

Hilda was finally cremated on 25th August 1984, five months after her murder. At this time the police were no further towards an arrest. The suicide of Barrie Peachman had gone unnoticed, and the fact that private detectives, some with criminal records, had been spying on Sizewell anti-nuclear campaigners (some of whom were in contact with and helping Hilda) was totally unknown to the West Mercia authorities.

The months leading up to December 1984 must have been very stressful for the West Mercia police. The continuing serious allegations of a State-sponsored murder made the 'chance burglar' hypothesis something of a joke. It's not really surprising that a solution to the mystery proved so elusive, even after the services of a hypnotist and the American FBI (Federal Bureau of Investigation) were enlisted.

For Hilda's nephew, Rob Green, the murder caused tremendous personal grief. Having lost his mother at an early age, he had forged a particularly strong bond with his aunt. Regrettably, the uncaring attitude of the various authorities dealing with the case did nothing to help his state of mind.

The police took over Hilda's home during their investigation so Rob was unable to gain access to the property to use his own powers of observation in an attempt to find out what might have occurred in the house on 21st March. One would have thought that ordinary CID detectives would have been only too pleased to make use of the expertise of a highly experienced Intelligence officer whose investigative powers must have been equal to those of any of the officers employed on the case.

Rob was faced with an interesting situation when he eventually got into the house at the end of the police examination. Hanging from the walls were a number of microphones. His queries about why they were present were brushed aside with vague and unconvincing statements that they had been used for security purposes.

I find this explanation most strange. According to numerous police contacts I have spoken with, any form of security alarm system is an extraordinary method for safeguarding premises under investigation of this kind. Normally in such cases, the physical presence of a police guard is deemed sufficient. If this is true, then one can only surmise that the microphones found by Rob Green were in fact electronic eavesdropping devices originally installed to intercept Hilda's conversations, or perhaps even Rob's conversations with his wife Liz during their presence in the house.

The mention of such devices leads on to the contentious topic of Hilda's telephone. Initially, the official version was that the 'phone lines had been simply ripped out by the intruder to prevent outgoing calls. But expert testimony from a telephone engineer reveals that the wires had in fact been adapted by someone who obviously knew their stuff to ensure that the continuous ringing tone would be heard by any caller at their end while the bell tone on the phone in Hilda's house would not be heard.

In other words, to outside callers the line would appear in order, but Hilda would not know when to answer the telephone – an excellent and professional way of sabotaging incoming calls. Electronics experts inform me that this method could also be used to turn the telephone installation into a listening device for bugging conversations in the room and on the 'phone.

Despite extensive police activity throughout 1984, the killer(s) remained free. Confidence in the ability of the authorities to bring the case to a successful conclusion was waning, and there was still no official mention of private detectives keeping watch on the Sizewell protesters. Despite media and private investigations revealing that Hilda was frightened for her life, the police could not or would not even acknowledge that this was so, and any witness who mentioned anything out of the ordinary was discredited in one way or another. According to the press, there was a cover-up.

Hilda had mentioned to several people that she was worried about a house on the other side of the road. My own research into this aspect of the affair reveals that there had indeed been an empty house overlooking Hilda's address and that outside it, a few days before her death, a suspicious-looking van had been seen parked.

I was able to identify the owners (at the time of the murder) of this address as being the West Mercia police. According to local sources, the property was sold some time after Hilda's death. A former Special Branch detective feels that if Hilda's worries about being under surveillance were justified, then it is feasible that the police house was being used as an observation post.

By Christmas 1984 there was still no sign of progress. Contradictory descriptions of suspects had been issued, without any result. The 'chance burglar' line was still being pursued, with thousands of man-hours being expended by police detectives, some of whom were Special Branch men. Six days before Christmas, just when impetus was decreasing, Tam Dalyell, the Member of Parliament for Linlithgow, spoke before the House of Commons on the subject of Hilda Murrell. What was presented to the rather exhausted House at 3.51am injected a new urgency into the case plus another possible clue as to why her home had been burgled. Mr Dalyell, known for his impressive connections with Security and Intelligence, and a staunch critic of the *Belgrano* affair, had received a tip off from one of his inside contacts which led to his controversial speech on the 19th December 1984.

After the usual introductory preamble, Mr Dalyell launched a most impressive attack on the police investigation. He criticised the official line that Hilda had died at the hands of some wandering chance burglar, and insisted that the police interpretation of the case did not tally in any way with what was obviously a sophisticated break-in.

He then went on to describe how he had approached one of his official Security sources, whom he described as having been scrupulously accurate in the past. It was from this contact that Mr Dalyell learned that Hilda's nephew Rob Green had in fact occupied a key position in Naval Intelligence during the Falklands campaign. 'I was informed that Commander

Green was in a position to know about the receipt and dispatch of signals to and from HMS *Conqueror*, and intercepted signals from the *Belgrano* to the Argentine mainland and back, from both British and American sources', Mr Dalyell said. Following his introduction of the *Belgrano* and Hilda's nephew, Mr Dalyell went on to dissect all aspects of the police investigation, either by giving his own analysis or by posing searching questions:

'Miss Murrell's house had been carefully searched and her papers gone through, but in an orderly manner. Her telephone had been cut off in such a way that although it was dead from inside the house anyone calling would seem to hear it ringing out.

'The police agree that that is a sophisticated way of doing things – not exactly the actions of a common burglar looking for loose money and taking a chance. Moreover, not only had the telephone to Miss Murrell's home at Ravenscroft, Shrewsbury, been tampered with – the 'phone at her cottage over the border in Wales had been disconnected.

'Later the police said that the 78-year-old lady had been sexually assaulted. Why did they say that when it turned out, on their own evidence, to be untrue? What is the purpose of that kind of inaccuracy other than to sweep uncomfortable suspicions under the carpet?

'Does the police force which, I am told, has a good reputation for efficiency normally act like that or was it told on high authority to act in such an uncharacteristically incompetent and slapdash way? Why did the police behave out of character? Ministers should tell us. I am told by more than one of the people interviewed by the police that they instinctively felt that the police officers knew jolly well that their time was being wasted and that they were having to go through the motions of a large scale investigation for cosmetic reasons.'

On the point of Special Branch involvement in a simple chance burglar murder case, Mr Dalyell was very critical. He also asked why Hilda's next of kin had not been given a copy of the post mortem report. It was during this part of his speech that Rob Green's impressive Intelligence status was revealed for the first time. According to Mr Dalyell, Commander Green earned a special citation from the Commander-in-Chief of the fleet for his contribution to the organising of crucial aspects of the British fleet's activities in the South Atlantic. Mr Dalyell's continuing exposure of embarrassing aspects of the police investigation, and his incessant questions, all served to pave the way for the bombshell he was eventually to deliver to the House.

Navigating his way skilfully through the various reasons and theories about the reason for Hilda's death, Mr Dalyell searchingly examined every important facet of the case. His analysis of the nuclear angle was particularly illuminating, and in effect convincingly diverted the spotlight from this industry as a possible agent in Hilda's death:

'I have had dealings with many in the top echelons of the CEGB and the Scottish generating boards. I cannot believe for one mini-second that Sir Walter Marshall, any of his colleagues, my friend Con Allday and others from the nuclear industry would dream of authorising minions to search the house of a 78-year-old rose grower who had elegantly expressed, but unoriginal, views on reactor choice and nuclear waste disposal.

'Besides, I have been to the great Peter Pears/Benjamin Britten Hall where the Sizewell inquiry is being held. I listened to evidence on day 178 and talked afterwards to Sir Frank Layfield. Those people will not fuss about Hilda Murrell and her evidence, for heaven's sake', he said.

While much of Mr Dalyell's comment on the nuclear industry is simply an expression of opinion, a lot of what he says is common sense. Nuclear authorities would not have fussed over what Hilda was to present at the Sizewell hearing, for two very simple reasons. Firstly, although what she had written in her thesis was, and still is, embarrassing, there was nothing (as we already know) original in her submissions: it had all been said many times before. The second reason, a vitally important one at that, also corroborates Mr Dalyell's opinion, according to the evidence gleaned from letters between Hilda and Bunyard a few weeks before the murder. Hilda had, on the advice of Mr Bunyard, submitted a copy of the evidence that she wished to present to the Secretariat of the hearing with her application to appear!

So the nuclear industry had no possible reason to break into Hilda's home looking for something they already had in their possession. And they certainly had no need to abduct and kill her to stop her appearing: all they had to do was refuse her permission to speak.

This led Tam Dalyell to give credence to another version of events which was passed to him by his reliable security and Intelligence contact.

'The story that I am told is as follows. In the early spring, the Prime Minister and Ministers close to her were getting very nervy about incessant questioning on the *Belgrano* in general and about signals, intercepted signals, and GCHQ at Cheltenham, which would call into question their truthfulness to the House, in particular. This was pre-Ponting. There were a number of suspicions about people dating from 19 and 20 December 1983, when I tabled questions to the Prime Minister about GCHQ Cheltenham, which are recorded in the Order Paper and *Hansard*.

'Because Commander Robert Green was known to be unhappy about certain aspects of the Falklands War and was known to have wanted to leave the Navy, he came under a cloud of suspicion, wrongly, to the best of my knowledge, but certainly under a cloud of suspicion.

'It was thought that he might have copies of documents and raw signals that incriminated the Prime Minister, some of the originals of which had been destroyed on instructions from a very high level by the intelligence services. Just as those of us who have had certain documents have taken the precaution of keeping them in friends' or relatives' houses whilst we have them, so it was thought that some of Rob Green's supposed records might be in the home of the aunt to whom he was close.

'I am also given to understand – and I am happy to accept it – that there was no premeditated intention of doing away with Miss Murrell – only a search of her house when she was out. Alas, on Wednesday 21 March she returned unexpectedly to change. The intruders either arrived while she was dressing or were disturbed by her. Being a lady of courage and spunk, often found in that generation of women, Miss Murrell fought them. They too had to fight. They injured her and panicked.

'I am informed that the intruders were not after money or nuclear information but were checking the house to see if there were any *Belgrano*-related documents of Commander Green in the home of his aunt. Things went disastrously wrong. They had no intention of injuring, let alone killing, a 78-year-old ex-rose grower. Yet, being the lady she was and in her home, Hilda Murrell fought and was severely injured.

'She was then killed or left to die from hypothermia, and the cover-up had to begin, because I am informed that the searchers were men of the British Intelligence.

'If Ministers cannot solemnly deny my belief about the participation of Intelligence, on whose ministerial authority, if any, did the search of Miss Murrell's home take place? Was there clearance, or was this the Intelligence services doing their own thing? Did they do it on political orders, and if so, on whose orders?'

Having dropped his bombshell, Dalyell continued to offer suggestions as to how the Intelligence services could be monitored, none of this being very relevant to the Murrell murder. Just before 4.15am, Mr Dalyell concluded his speech, allowing Mr Paddy Ashdown, MP for Yeovil, to respond. In closing, Mr Dalyell said:

'It is from the head of our security services that Parliament should be demanding an explanation, because of one thing I am certain – that there are persons in Westminster and Whitehall who know a great deal more about the violent death of Miss Hilda Murrell than they have so far been prepared to divulge.'

Mr Ashdown did not contribute in any evidential way to the case, except to say that from conversations between himself and Commander Green, all Mr Dalyell's references to Rob Green were correct. Mr Ashdown also tendered an interesting and worthwhile constructive suggestion:

'In the absence of detailed answers to the detailed questions which the Hon. Member for Linlithgow has put, I believe that there is only one way forward: a full inquiry in front of a High Court judge. I hope that other Hon. Members will support that kind of inquiry. We merely say that if the Minister is unable or unwilling to answer questions of fact in detail, that is the only proper way forward.'

With regard to the accountability of the Security Services, Mr Ashdown was equally critical.

'The Hon. Member for Linlithgow touched on the broader issue of the Intelligence services. My party and I have always pressed the need for a Select Committee of Privy Councillors to deal with Intelligence matters. The Intelligence services are not sufficiently accountable to the House. The mechanism for such accountability needs to be chosen carefully. For reasons that the Hon. Gentleman mentioned, my party has always believed that there should be a Select Committee of Privy Councillors. It would have been much better if the Hon. Member for Linlithgow had been able to take his case to such a Committee in private, rather than being forced to raise the matter on the Floor of the House.

'At the very heart of this issue lies the system that we now refer to as "clearance". The Intelligence services have to receive clearances at various appropriate levels, including at the very highest level – that of the Prime Minister – before taking any action. I have no doubt that action such as that mentioned by the Hon. Member for Linlithgow would, under normal circumstances, have had to be approved at the very highest level.

'If what the Hon. Member says is true, it is inconceivable that it could have occurred in normal circumstances other than with agreement at the very highest level. But if that did not happen, there must have been a significant breakdown in the way that our Intelligence services are controlled. One must reach one or other of those conclusions if the Hon. Gentleman's thesis is supportable. Either a politician at a very high level was involved in taking the decision to allow such action to go ahead, or there must have been a very serious breakdown in the democratic and political accountability and control of our intelligence services,' Ashdown said.

Paddy Ashdown is no ordinary MP: as a former member of the Foreign and Commonwealth Office, he worked for MI6, so his comments should be seriously noted.

At 4.27am, Clive Soley, MP for Hammersmith, responded. 'My Hon. Friend has given us the sort of story that would tax the ingenuity of a novelist. However, it is precisely at such times that we should remember that truth can be stranger than fiction. I hope that the Minister will not attempt to dismiss it as some form of creative literature or to put it down to a colourful imagination. My hon. Friend has put very real questions to the Minister and they deserve answers.

'It is important to remember that my hon. Friend has pursued this matter and the related matter of the *Belgrano* in a way that has not only respected the integrity of those involved in the military operation, but revealed the extraordinary accuracy of his research. He has, literally on a one-man operation, been able to demonstrate that the Government's arguments have not held together over a period of time. They have had to change their story from time to time, and it must be to my hon. Friend's credit that his research has brought that to light.

'Not only is my hon. Friend's research accurate, but so are the sources of his information. I know those to be extremely good sources of information. The Minister and many others must be deeply disturbed by the quality of the information that is always available to my hon. Friend. He uses that information to deploy his case well.

'I hope that if the Minister cannot give us answers today, he will be able to reassure the House that he will ensure that those answers are provided at some stage and in some context', Mr Soley said.

Finally, at 4.33am the most important respondent of all, the Minister of State for the Home Office, Mr Giles Shaw, responded to Mr Dalyell's speech. His lengthy response failed to move the case on, and he declined to elaborate on certain aspects of the case, on the grounds that the investigation was on-going. Not an unreasonable attitude to adopt in a *genuine* murder enquiry.

A few interesting facts and figures about the number of witnesses interviewed were forthcoming, but other than that nothing of any real substance was offered.

'From the considerable information that has been made available to me by the police it has become quite clear that the West Mercia police have devoted substantial resources to the investigation of what they see as a very grave offence. We all share their concern – that undoubtedly goes for the Hon. Member for Linlithgow – that the offender is still at large.

'I shall give some of the figures about the extent of the police inquiry. Some 3,500 people have been suggested as the potential offender by the public, police officers or by research on local and national intelligence indexes.

'Out of this number, 962 people have been identified for interview, and over half of them have already been interviewed. Over 1,300 telephone messages had been received by 30 November, over 2,000 statements taken and over 55,000 items of information recorded, both manually and on computer in the incident room.

'As at 30 November again, nearly 12,000 people had been interviewed, over 4,500 houses visited and over 1,500 vehicles checked. I make these points not just because I think that this is an example of the tenacity and thoroughness with which the

West Mercia Constabulary are investigating this matter, but because even if some believe the inferences drawn by the Hon Member for Linlithgow, there has still been a massive orthodox investigation into the tragic events surrounding Miss Murrell's death.

'In the initial stages of their investigation, the police made full inquiries into suggestions that Miss Murrell had been murdered because of her connections with various anti-nuclear organisations, in particular that she was at the time of her death preparing a paper to oppose the Sizewell B project. I am grateful to the Hon Member for Linlithgow for dismissing that suggestion out of hand, with the probity that we know him to possess.

'The Hon Gentleman is entirely right. A senior investigating officer assigned a small team specifically to inquire into those aspects, but I am sure that the Hon Gentleman will be glad to note that no evidence has been found to link those activities with her death', Mr Shaw said.

The proceedings closed, with brief reassurance from Mr Shaw that Mr Dalyell's questions would receive full consideration and a proper and comprehensive reply.

The introduction of the *Belgrano* angle was just what the media needed to resurrect the Hilda Murrell affair. It also manoeuvred the spotlight onto Clive Ponting, a senior civil servant arrested in the summer of that year for leaking top secret papers about the *Belgrano*. Whilst some people disagreed with Mr Dalyell, he did make a lot of sense. After all, the State had been monitoring and harassing anti-nuclear campaigners for years without actually killing them. 'What harm could a little old woman do to the nuclear industry?' was now becoming the general consensus of opinion.

The day after Tam Dalyell's Commons speech, an incident occurred in St Albans that added credibility to his *Belgrano* claims. The home of a former Naval officer, Peter Hurst, was broken into.

At first it appeared to be an ordinary breaking and entering job for the purposes of theft. But a number of easily disposable consumer goods and other valuables were left untouched. What, then, could have been the reason for the search? Peter Hurst, like Rob Green, was a former Naval Intelligence officer, and had served with Rob at Northwood during the Falklands war. He too was disillusioned by the *Belgrano* affair, and had also resigned his commission. His knowledge of secret signals to and from the South Atlantic was such that, had he decided to speak out, the British Government could well have experienced major embarrassment. Although nothing was stolen from his flat, it was obvious to Mr Hurst that his personal papers had been searched, that he was under surveillance and that his telephone was being tapped.

Much has been said about the Falklands war, especially the decision to sink the *General Belgrano*, an antique ex-US cruiser and survivor of Pearl Harbor, which was due to become a floating museum in 1983. Perhaps it was the circumstances surrounding the torpedoing of this inferior vessel, while it was 59 miles *outside* the total exclusion zone, sailing away from the Task Force, that frightened the powers-that-be into dispatching secret agents to search people's homes. After all, what politician would like the world to know that orders had been given to kill 368 sailors whilst their backs were turned?

If it was not the circumstances surrounding the sinking of the *Belgrano* that caused Whitehall to panic, then could it have been the fact that nuclear weapons had been taken to the South Atlantic – and that serious consideration was given to using them? Some of these very weapons are now lying at the bottom of the ocean.

The questions posed by the Falklands war are many, and it is impossible to do them justice in this book. Nonetheless, Hilda's nephew, Rob Green, is said to have had access to secret intelligence about that conflict, some of which was in the form of raw signals. The information contained in such signals would undoubtedly have been highly embarrassing to those responsible for the several questionable aspects of the campaign. One only has to recall the trial of Clive Ponting to appreciate just how paranoid those in Whitehall had become, and how far they would go to try and keep the skeletons in the cupboard. The thought of Hilda having such sensitive information must have been too horrifying to contemplate.

To understand something of the complicated issues arising from the Falklands war, and hence why British Intelligence would search the home of an anti-nuclear protester related to a senior Naval Intelligence officer, it is essential to read the ECOROPA leaflet distributed by Hilda.* The twenty-four questions in this document were posed by ECOROPA and answered by Tam Dalyell MP, formerly Chairman of the Parliamentary Labour Party Foreign Affairs Group (1974–76) and Opposition Spokesman on science, until he was sacked by Michael Foot in 1982 for his courageous and outspoken views on the Falklands war.

My own work during this time with Nick Davies of the *Observer* involved acquiring the official company reports from Barrie Peachman's organisation, Sapphire Investigations. We also managed to trick Vic Norris into admitting his affiliations to the Home Office, doing their 'dirty work.' In a series of tape recorded conversations, Norris made it quite clear that the Sizewell investigations had continued throughout 1983. He said 'It went all the way to Whitehall'. If this then was the case, it is very feasible that the object of this assignment was in fact to detect any *Belgrano* information that might have been circulating among the anti-nuclear fraternity. This would certainly help to account for the specific request concerning 'contacts with the media and political leanings.' This hypothesis gains strength from David Coughlan's admission that as far as he was aware the Sizewell assignment was carried out on behalf of MI5.

The *Observer* story broke on 27th January 1985 and to add fuel to any speculation, Nick Davies and I had identified thirty

* See Appendix.

security and intelligence officers, including a Security Service vetting officer, who were members of the Institute of Professional Investigators (IPI), the private organisation controlling the activities of the majority of the country's private detectives. Peter Hamilton, the instigator of the Sizewell project, was also a member.

Immediately following the *Observer* report, Paul Foot of the *Daily Mirror* revealed that Victor Norris, alias Adrian Hampson, had been convicted in 1973 of sex offences and had served a six-year prison sentence and had a further conviction in 1976 for carrying an offensive weapon. Norris was also exposed as the leader of a satanist sect calling itself the 'Anglican Satanic Church.' In addition to his satanic activities, Norris was also the founder of two other organisations, the Nazi Phoenix Society and The 5000 Group. No one is saying that he was one of those who broke into Miss Murrell's house and abducted her. But as Paul Foot said, 'It is just a chilling thought that such a person is used by the Home Office, and to watch the Sizewell protesters.'

The rest of the year buzzed with spy-related activity. Television programmes reported on the various aspects of the Murrell case, and West Mercia police set out to investigate the detectives exposed for spying on the Sizewell protesters. There was also the famous Ponting trial which kept the *Belgrano* and Signals Intelligence in the spotlight.

I worked with Thames and other TV contractors interested in pursuing the Murrell case, and it was during such a project for TV-AM that I received a telephone call from a very sinister-sounding individual informing me in no uncertain terms that he intended to kill me. At this particular time, all of my telephone calls were being taped – by me – and I was able to identify the caller as a well known Private Investigator connected to the Security Services.

What with Tam Dalyell's speech and the Ponting trial, the *Belgrano* issue refused to die, even more so when Ponting was found 'Not Guilty' of leaking secrets. According to Mr Justice

McCowan's summing-up in the trial, democratic dissent from and legitimate activity against the Government policy of the day could actually be construed as being not just anti that government or that particular policy, but actually anti-State and against the interests of national security.

If this then is the general opinion held in Government circles, the reasoning behind any authorisation for a break-in to private premises such as Hilda Murrell's becomes very obvious.

Irrefutable evidence of the Government's feverish paranoia about individuals and groups actively dissenting from its nuclear policies was contained in the contentious Channel 4 television programme produced by 20-20 Vision, in which former MI5 officer Cathy Massiter revealed that much of the work of her department had involved 'phone tapping and mail interception against dissenters targeted by MI5. From the available evidence, even excluding Tam Dalyell's valuable contribution, there can be no doubt that people like Hilda Murrell were victims of a long-term spy operation.

One would have thought that with these new lines of potential enquiry the West Mercia Police could have uncovered some small clue as to who was responsible for Hilda's death. But it would appear not. Some of the private detectives concerned, but not all, were interviewed and as for the *Belgrano* slant, what possible chance of co-operation could the police expect from the Security Services? Intelligence officers are well known for their secrecy with each other, so it is hardly likely they would release details of MI5 operations even to a Chief Constable.

Not surprisingly, the West Mercia Police reacted strongly to the criticism of their failure to catch Hilda's killer. 'We've had every amateur detective in the country putting forward hare-brained schemes and theories about the killing. It's got to a stage now that it is seriously hindering our enquiries because officers are having to waste time following up leads which don't exist', a spokesman said.

I, and I'm sure others, find it frustrating that police officers attached sufficient importance to hare-brained ideas put forward by amateur detectives instead of concentrating on more important clues collected by competent investigators and journalists.

In addition to the above comment, in January 1985 the police also issued an eleven-page statement which was said to be intended to dispel confusion. This was followed by a further statement by Robert Cozens, the Chief Constable, who on 28th January referred to an interview with Tam Dalyell by his officers. In a nut shell, the statement simply said there was no evidence to lend substance to Mr Dalyell's claim that Miss Murrell's death was linked to British Intelligence.

Mr Dalyell was told that he had a public duty to reveal the identity of his informant within the Security Service, and he was assured that any evidence which might be forthcoming would be very thoroughly investigated. He refused to identify his source.

The detailed statement again referred to the possible involvement of British Intelligence officers, and confirmed that police enquiries to date had revealed no evidence to suggest such an involvement. But one report did not explain exactly what police enquiries had been carried out and it also omitted any mention of the possible use of civilian contractors working on a freelance basis, although this was a well known aspect of covert intelligence work. So, since it would seem that the official investigation had neglected to examine this crucial facet of the case, it was technically true for the statement to claim that police enquiries had failed to unearth any evidence of the involvement of Intelligence agents. If you don't dig, you don't uncover.

The lengthy report then went on to give the official explanations of why police officers working on the case were suspended, and of why specialist officers (Special Branch) are often called upon to perform non-specialist roles when manpower demands are great. It was claimed that in the Sizewell B situation they were used because it was thought their experience best fitted them to deal with the enquiry. There was no mention of Special Branch men posing as CID officers and on occasion denying their actual status.

The rest of the statement simply went over old ground, justifying the use of a hypnotist and the enlisting of the American FBI. Apart from clarifying several established problematic points of the case concerning the red Escort car, sexual assault and the sequence of events leading to the finding of the body, the statement did nothing to encourage confidence, and certainly failed miserably to move the case forward in any way. There was also mention of the moving of the body, and interestingly enough, confirmation that the house was thoroughly and systematically searched.

The comments about the telephone were also very interesting. Whilst the police opinion was that whoever had interfered with Hilda's phone had done so in an unsophisticated manner, the police agreed the end result was as previously described: the ringing bell actually inoperative but to the caller sounding as though it was emitting the usual ringing sound. I know from my operational experiences as a detective and private intelligence agent that this is a regularly adopted way of sabotaging a target's phone calls, so simple it could be considered unsophisticated. However, in terms of effectiveness such a simple method is indeed *very* sophisticated. The police statement could more accurately have described it as 'technically unsophisticated'.

In an attempt to clear up the mysteries about Hilda's Welsh cottage, the reason given for a similar fault on this telephone was that, because of a storm, a capacitator had failed, thus creating the problem. This sounds all well and good, except that there are no records of any storms around that time. Ironically, the Welsh cottage was seriously damaged in an arson attack shortly before publication of the *Observer* story. The statement concluded by reiterating the official opinion that Hilda had been the victim of a burglary that went tragically wrong.

During the police investigation, a number of experienced

burglars were visited by the police who (according to the burglars) seemed to be trying desperately to pin the murder on anyone they could lay their hands on. One such individual, Robert James Higgins, who was awaiting sentence for a number of offences, told the press (via his solicitor) on the 8th January 1985 that he was frightened the police were trying to pin the murder on him. He felt that the circumstantial evidence against him was formidable.

Higgins, who pleaded guilty to various offences, was taken to Miss Murrell's house. His own home was searched and an anti-nuclear leaflet was discovered.

Mr Delwyn Williams, solicitor acting for Higgins, released a statement to the *Evening Standard* when it became apparent his client was living in fear of being fitted up for the murder.

The unfortunate Higgins was not alone in this respect. Another suspect, a man with a history of petty crime, was arrested and, according to a friend, was denied access to a solicitor. He was interrogated at length about Hilda's death and was convinced the police were going to charge him. However, after three days of isolation, he was released.

The most dubious attempt to pin the murder on a 'nobody' with a bit of 'form' was the case of David McKenzie, an unemployed hotel worker convicted of two killings who confessed to ten more, including the murder of Hilda.

In 1990, McKenzie was convicted of the murder of Henrietta Osbourne, 86, and Barbara Pinder, 76. At his trial, the prosecution intimated that he would also be facing trial for the Murrell murder. However, because he was suffering from a mental disorder, it was decided that formal charges could not be brought against McKenzie, although a report was submitted to the Director of Public Prosecutions (DPP). In essence, this appeared to be the end of the Murrell case: a suspect who was unfit to plead, and had already been convicted of similar murders. However, subsequent appeals by McKenzie against these convictions were upheld.

In July 1992, a surprising turn of events took place in the Court of Appeal: McKenzie was dubbed, not a serial killer but a serial *confessor*, who had admitted to crimes that had not even been committed. It also transpired that he could not have killed Hilda Murrell because forensic evidence, held for years by the police, would have shown that the person who killed Miss Murrell and masturbated over her body had undergone a vasectomy. A simple medical examination of McKenzie would have eliminated him from enquiries.

The case of David McKenzie was yet another travesty of justice, involving as it did false confessions taken during a week of intense questioning – and in the absence of a solicitor.

There are many other complicated facets of the Hilda Murrell investigation. While some are legitimate spin-offs from central aspects of the case, others are nothing more than distortions caused through conflicting evidence and the pursuit of red herrings. So I do not intend to delve any further into these particular anomalies.

'Murrell watchers', journalists and relatives anxious for results waited patiently throughout 1985 for some indication of an arrest. They were disappointed. Once again the police failed to uncover any clues: both the *Belgrano* and Sizewell were quickly discounted and the chance-burglar theory increasingly became the accepted explanation for Hilda's death. Gradually, the public appetite for fresh revelations dwindled, and eventually only a few people, myself included, continued to search for the truth. It is only now, after eight years (at the time of writing), that further information has come to light.

On the 10th June 1992 Hilda's 'niece', Trina, visited the office of a Lincoln solicitor where, on my advice, she signed a sixteen-page affidavit and attested on oath that the contents of her statement were true.

In her statement, Trina outlines her current occupation and her past relationship with Hilda. She also reveals that, as a result of part-time work as an unofficial prison visitor, she made contact with serving inmates who alleged they had knowledge of the Hilda Murrell murder, and in particular knew who was responsible. If the information in Trina's statement is to be believed, then it would appear there has been a conspiracy to pervert the course of justice from inside the very heart of the Government, the police and the Security Services.

Since the dramatic revelations contained in this affidavit could well become relevant to a future public enquiry, or even a hearing in a criminal court, the names of the persons concerned have been replaced by initials:

AFFIDAVIT:

'1. I am over twenty-one years of age and currently employed as a Publications Manager for the Royal Society for Nature Conservation based in Lincoln. In my spare time I act as an unofficial voluntary visitor to Her Majesty's Prisons where I offer general assistance to convicted prisoners.

'2. I am making this statement at the request of Writer-Investigator Gary Murray who is of the opinion that I am in possession of important evidence relating to the outstanding murder of anti-nuclear protester HILDA MURRELL, who died in March 1984 shortly before she was due to appear at a public hearing convened in the County of Suffolk. It was Miss Murrell's intention to present her own researched thesis complaining of various aspects of nuclear waste and safety associated with the Pressurised Water Reactor (PWR) that was at that time being planned for Sizewell B Power Station. I was a close friend of the deceased and had an intimate knowledge of her anti-nuclear views, I was also aware of the fact that she was preparing her own paper for presentation at the Sizewell B public hearing where she would have highlighted various aspects of waste disposal and security.

'3. My relationship with Hilda developed when I was a young woman, after getting to know her via my mother. We became very friendly and occasionally went on holiday together. It would be accurate to describe our relationship as being very similar to that of an aunt and niece. I was aware of Hilda's passion for the countryside and her worries about the nuclear industry and pollution. This concern was such that she would write regularly to newspapers and members of Parliament. On one occasion she even wrote to the Prime Minister to voice her complaints. We would often discuss her views on nuclear issues and from time to time she would talk with me about her paper. During November 1983 Hilda passed to me for checking a draft copy of her lengthy paper, approximately 19 pages in all. I have passed this on to Gary Murray for safe keeping.

'4. Throughout 1983 I was associating with a male friend who I shall now refer to as "LM". We were very close, and in fact lived together a short distance from Hilda's home in Sutton Road, Shrewsbury. LM, Hilda and myself would often spend time together at Hilda's house. We even went on holiday together to Anglesey a few months before the murder. On these occasions we would often discuss Hilda's paper. All three of us even attended meetings of The Shrewsbury Peace Group, a local organisation concerned about the threat of nuclear war.

'5. Under normal circumstances such a three-way relationship between a high-profile campaigner and like-minded colleagues could well be considered nothing out of the ordinary. However, in this case there were a number of anomalies that appear to have been overlooked or perhaps conveniently ignored by police investigating the murder:

'(a) I was a close friend and confidant in possession of documents passed to me shortly before the murder. The contents of these papers related to embarrassing deficiencies within the nuclear industry.

'(b) My boyfriend, LM, was the son of a Signals Intelligence Officer who was, and as far as I am aware still is, employed by the Ministry of Defence in Shrewsbury. His work is said to be top secret and he requires regular positive vetting by the Security authorities.

'6. Immediately following the announcement of Hilda's murder, my boyfriend and I were initially in a state of deep shock, so much so it did not occur to us that we might be valuable witnesses. Consequently we did not bother to contact the police.

'In any event friends, known to both myself and Hilda,

and who had been interviewed, informed me that they had told police officers of my identity and the fact that I was a close friend of the deceased, and that it might assist their enquiry if they contacted me. I find it most strange that after eight years my boyfriend and I have been totally overlooked, despite assurances from the authorities that investigators have exhausted their efforts in a nationwide search for Hilda's killer/killers. I am unable to accept the official line, that she was murdered by a chance burglar.

'7. After the hue and cry surrounding Hilda's death had subsided, I found that my own personal circumstances had changed, resulting in a move from Shrewsbury to my current address in Lincoln. I managed to resume a fairly normal life, until January 1988 when a series of unpleasant events led me to believe that my home had been searched and my telephone calls intercepted. However, after contacting a local solicitor my circumstances stabilised.

'8. Despite my heavy work schedule I have never forgotten my close friend Hilda Murrell, and at every opportunity have sought advice and/or questioned numerous sources in the hope of uncovering some small clue that might lead to the truth.

'It was on such an occasion in November 1991, when I was speaking to an ex-prisoner, that I was told a current serving prisoner had considerable knowledge of the Hilda Murrell affair. I obtained his identity and made arrangements to visit him.

'9. I was astounded when he revealed that he had shared a prison wing with another long term prisoner who had stated that he had been in charge of a small group responsible for the surveillance of Hilda. I immediately contacted Gary Murray and after lengthy discussion it was agreed that I would visit this prisoner over a period, for the purpose of collating as much information as possible. I was specifically briefed by Mr Murray in methods of cross-examination, and also provided with a number of key questions that were designed to test my informant's reliability. Over a number of weeks throughout 1991 I carefully questioned my source, whose full name and location have been made known to Mr Murray. The following story emerged.

'10. Having been moved to a prison close to York, my

informant shared a wing with a long term prisoner serving 15 years for armed robbery. They became close friends and it was as a result of this friendship that the following data came into the possession of my informant.

'11. The armed robber, whose identity and location have also been made known to Gary Murray, stated that he had been in charge of what was described to me as a "cell", a group of four men and one woman who had been engaged in regular freelance work for same kind of secret intelligence department. One of their assignments had been to search Hilda Murrell's house for papers or information relating to signals intelligence, specific mention was made of the *Belgrano* and the Falklands. The most frightening aspect of the informant's story is that the leader of the group was said to be reporting to the Cabinet Office via an MI5 Liaison Officer and that the team, in addition to their government work, were also engaged in all manner of other illegal activity, including armed robbery for which they were arrested some time after Hilda's death.

'12. On the occasion of the search of Hilda's house in March 1984 there were allegedly three male and one female operatives searching the property when she unexpectedly returned home. Confusion and panic ensued and one of the perpetrators became very unstable and subjected Hilda to violence and threatened her with a knife, accompanied by obscene sexual acts involving masturbation.

'At this point in the proceedings one of the team, plus the woman member who dressed up in Hilda's coat and hat, left the house and drove off, returning some time later, at which time Hilda was removed from the house and taken to a local area which has been described to me as some kind of military base or former American airfield known as "Little America", or simply "America". I understand that Gary Murray has located such an area just outside of Shrewsbury. Two days later Hilda was taken to the copse where her body was eventually found.

'13. According to my informant, the other criminal activities of the team resulted in one of them dying of gunshot wounds during a police chase. A second male member of the team was, and still is, incarcerated in a secure psychiatric hospital. The team leader is currently serving 15 years for armed robbery and is insisting he was "fitted up". The female operative received a two-year sentence on other criminal charges and has now been released. Nothing is known about the whereabouts of the remaining member of the group, who has been described as a Nazi enthusiast in the habit of adopting names of German military colleagues of the late Adolph Hitler.

'14. I have applied considerable thought to the testimony and credibility of my informant and do of course understand the value of hearsay evidence.

'However, given all the unusual and controversial circumstances surrounding the death of Hilda Murrell, I verily believe that it is in the public interests to activate either a public or judicial investigation into her death, and that in view of past, unrelated, events involving the use by Security Services of criminals on freelance assignments, serious consideration should be tendered to my informant's statement.

'15. I would like to conclude by saying that I am fully aware of the offence of perjury and that I swear this affidavit with the sincere belief that the claims of my informant may well be relevant to the murder of Hilda Murrell. I am of sound mind and body and am not making this statement for any pecuniary advantage. The identities of the team said to have been responsible for Hilda's murder, along with the personal details of my informant have been supplied to Gary Murray.

'16. Finally, I respectfully point out that as a prisoner isolated from society, my informant has no protection and should it ever become known that he has supplied me with this information and assistance, it is more than likely his life will be in danger.'

It took me several weeks to analyse the contents of Trina's statement, after which my initial reaction was simply to dismiss the informant as a time waster, bent on alleviating his boredom. However, further pieces of information gleaned by Trina suggested that her source was producing information that could have been known only to someone inside Hilda's house at the time of the abduction. Then there was the question of the former American air base, allegedly used by the murderers to hide Hilda's body, and the mention of a woman being involved. This corroborated the evidence of a previous witness, Mr George, who informed me that he had seen, on the morning of the abduction, a suspicious off-duty policeman type of person, together with a woman wearing a cloak.

I finally became more inclined to believe Trina's informant when I located the site of a former American air base, very close to where Hilda's body had been found. The area, now known as Atcham Industrial Estate, was at one time the home of the 31st US Pursuit Group. There are still a few military buildings, now used by various civilian companies, and in 1984, at the time of the murder, there were even more secluded spots that could have been used to hide a body, the most suitable being bunkers built on the perimeter of the base and having easy access from the main road. The distance from the copse where Hilda was found is 4.5 miles, a journey that could have been completed very quickly.

To complicate matters slightly, I also discovered another site, some twelve miles from the copse, that also matched the 'American' description supplied by Trina's informant. Just off the A5(T) road leading to Wales, there lies a Ministry of Defence training area surrounded by an area called . . . America: this name actually appears on Ordnance Survey maps. The whole area has great potential as a temporary dumping ground for a body, and there are many old farm and ministry buildings that could have been used by Hilda's kidnappers. The only reservation I have about this site is that it is too far away from the scene of the crime to risk a midday drive through heavy traffic with an unwilling kidnap victim in the vehicle. All the evidence and my instincts point to an area much closer to the murder scene: the former Atcham Air Base, only 4.5 miles from Hunkinton Moat, would have made an excellent temporary 'safe house' for Hilda's abductors.

By the time I had completed research into this aspect of the allegations contained in Trina's statement, her informant was supplying further information. Incidentally, as far as we are aware, he has never been to Shrewsbury, so there is no question of him having local knowledge about the Atcham Industrial Estate.

According to the source, whom for convenience I shall call George, two statues of dogs were removed from Hilda's house at the time of the burglary. This is doubly important, firstly because one of the abductors was a part-time antique dealer and secondly because, according to reliable information, Hilda actually did have two such items.

Other bits and pieces of information obtained by Trina concerned the identities of members of the gang, along with suggestions that they had been responsible for dirty tricks – undercover work – during the national miners' strike. It is my understanding that their brief was to create scenes of such violence that the Home Secretary would be forced to authorise the arming of police officers. There was also mention of John Stalker, the former Deputy Chief Constable of Greater Manchester, and a reported plan to kill him during his controversial Northern Ireland enquiry.

After weeks of debriefing Trina, who in turn had carefully questioned and cross-examined 'George', the following composition of the team said to have been responsible for Hilda's death emerged:

Team member 1 – Currently in prison serving fifteen years for armed robbery. Said to have done a deal in exchange for his silence. Has been transferred to a prison convenient to his family, and as at the time of writing refuses to talk, or even to respond to my letters requesting an interview.

Team member 2 – Now serving sixteen years for armed robbery. Has been committed to a secure psychiatric hospital where he has been receiving treatment for severe depression after an incident that occurred while in the same prison as team member 1.

Team member 3 – A violent professional criminal, who is said to have terrified all those who came into contact with him. Now deceased after being accidentally shot by his own gun during a police chase.

Team member 4 – 'Helga' received a two-year sentence, and after release vanished without trace.

Team member 5 – A former policeman, operating under the interesting code name 'Demeter' (the Greek goddess of agricultural fertility). Is alleged to have been the direct link with the MI5 liaison officer attached to the Cabinet Office at the time of Hilda's murder.

Casual associate – A 'low life' known to use German nicknames, his favourite being Spengler.

The overall code name said to have been adopted by this five-handed team was 'Ceres' (the Roman goddess of agriculture).

The hardest part of checking out the allegations made by 'George' was gaining access to the only two remaining available suspects. Team member 1, who I thought would at least agree to a visit, if only to test my knowledge and/or reasons for wishing to speak with him, totally ignored my request for a chat, despite a carefully worded discreet letter of introduction. This I find most strange. In all the years I have worked as an investigator, he is the first resident of Her Majesty's Prisons who has declined a visit. Normally, prisoners are only too pleased to receive mail and visits from anyone who will help pass the time. The only other avenue of research open to me was the secure psychiatric hospital holding team member 2. Fully expecting an outright refusal to a request to speak with doctors and the patient, I contacted the authorities, never dreaming I would end up face to face with this particular suspect.

I must say that as a result of this visit my opinion of psychiatric staff has changed dramatically. Never before have I witnessed such concern for a patient and his welfare. Even though they were dealing with a convicted criminal, the staff at this particular hospital, without breaching patient or official confidentiality, gave invaluable assistance, allowing me not only to talk to the prisoner but to question him about Hilda's death, albeit in a very roundabout way.

Surprisingly, this patient was not as I expected. Although very apprehensive and frightened, he remembered the events leading to his conviction for armed robbery. He also was able to describe briefly events that he insisted were untruthfully presented or exaggerated by the prosecution, and he claimed that he was persuaded to admit to offences he and his associates had not committed. When questioned about the accidental shooting of team member 3 by his own gun, he replied 'That's not true, the police shot him to keep him quiet'.

The object of speaking with this suspect was not just to obtain his comments about his own circumstances, but also to show him pictures of Hilda and photofits of the suspects, as prepared by the police at the time of the murder. At an appropriate moment during the interview, in the presence of a qualified senior psychiatric nurse, I produced a 10 × 8 picture of Hilda, together with the police photofits superimposed alongside another picture of Hilda in her famous hat, worn at the time of the murder. Immediately on seeing these pictures, the suspect reacted by refusing to look at them. He became very agitated and said 'I'm not saying anything, I've said too much already, that's why I am in here'. He then got to his feet and started pacing the small room, as though seeking an escape.

Proceeding with my plan, I then mentioned several names of people said to have been involved in the Murrell murder, one of these names being that of a private detective associated with a London security firm. According to the expert opinion of the senior psychiatric nurse present, his patient reacted positively to the names, and in his opinion they meant something to him. This was obvious in the case of the private detective, whose nickname I used to great effect: the patient actually admitted knowing him, but then changed his mind, saying he did not wish to discuss it further. Eventually, we reached a stage where it was obvious the patient was getting very distressed. He kept repeating he was to blame and that he had said too much. It is impossible to say if he was referring to Hilda Murrell with this statement. When questioned about visits to Shrewsbury, he vehemently denied ever being in that area.

The interview ended with the patient saying that it was just a matter of time before he was dead. When reassured that he would be OK and that he should not talk like that, he simply said there was nothing that could be done for him, repeating that it was just a matter of time. After this interview, the psychiatric nurse accompanying me examined the police photofit pictures of the suspects. Pointing to one of them, he said 'That looks like your man when he was first admitted.'

Inevitably, 'George''s allegations are one-sided, and because of the circumstances cannot be checked out without some sort of genuine investigation, by way of either a public or a judicial inquiry. To reveal any more at this stage would jeopardise such an investigation, especially one in which a jury might have to deliberate.

If it were not for the dreadful track record of the Security Services with all sorts of past wrongdoing, I would dismiss 'George''s statement as utter nonsense. Alas, the sad truth is that both MI5 and MI6 do *not* have unimpeachable reputations, and both organisations are known to use experienced criminals on 'intelligence' operations, with burglary, other theft, blackmail and telephone tapping regular features of such work. It is therefore easy to understand how someone like Hilda Murrell can die in mysterious, unexplained circumstances. A former Security Service officer, who asked not to be identified, said 'In certain cases, criminals are the best type of people to use.'

CHAPTER 10

Other Victims

Had the case of Hilda Murrell been a one-off, then it is highly likely the 'chance burglar' explanation would have been accepted. But numerous other incidents involving protesters speaking out against nuclear weapons and power point the way to the obvious conclusion. Hilda, along with others (about to be named), was the victim of the Security Services, aided and abetted by Special Branch.

On the morning of Saturday, 6th April 1985, yet another nuclear mystery began when Australian Air Force pilot Alan Crowe stopped his car at a lay-by on the A87, north of Fort William in the Highlands of Scotland, to investigate what he initially believed to be some kind of motor accident. Lying across a stream was a maroon Volvo car. Inside, the driver, William McRae, a radical Glasgow lawyer, was slumped in his seat with what appeared to be dried bloodstains on the side of his head. He was barely alive. The car was perched precariously across the stream and was leaning to the right.

The driver's window was wound down and the door jammed in such a manner it could not open more than a foot. The scene had all the appearance of a simple road accident: it seemed that the car had simply run off the road, injuring the driver.

After stopping other motorists on the main road, Mr Crowe

called for an ambulance, which arrived about an hour later. McRae was taken to Aberdeen Royal Infirmary – where doctors found a bullet in his brain. The overall damage was such that medical staff were unable to save him, and he died the following day.

Police investigations at the scene of the shooting recovered a revolver (owned by McRae) some distance from the car. Press reports at the time described the weapon as having been fired twice, and found several yards from the car. Also found about twenty feet away from the vehicle were a neat pile of ripped-up documents and McRae's watch with its face smashed.

After the investigation, which lasted only two days, the authorities for Inverness announced that the death had been fully investigated and that McRae had committed suicide.

Little or no explanation was given how, after shooting himself, the victim had managed to throw his gun some distance from the car. There was also the question of how McRae, sitting in his Volvo with the driver's door wedged shut, had succeeded in piling up his torn documents in a neat pile quite a distance from the car. Then there was the matter of his two briefcases which he always carried with him. These were eventually returned to his brother by the police, who were unable or unwilling to reveal where they were found. According to witnesses who discovered McRae, there were no briefcases at the scene, or in the vehicle.

The mystery deepened when McRae's legal work was highlighted by the media. It transpired that, like Hilda Murrell, he too was passionately opposed to the dumping of nuclear and other toxic waste. He was probably the nuclear industry's most formidable opponent in Scotland, and many believe that it was his speeches in the Mullwharchar Enquiry in 1980 which overturned plans for nuclear dumping in the Ayrshire Hills. 'Nuclear waste', he said, 'should be stored where Guy Fawkes put his gunpowder'.

At the time of his 'suicide', McRae was planning to take

part in a public enquiry into the processing of nuclear waste at Dounreay, and his law firm was on the list of official protesters.

His work was very similar to that of Hilda Murrell: collecting evidence for presentation at a public enquiry. He was also writing a book on the same subject, and the two briefcases he was known to carry everywhere contained most of his material for both the campaign and his book.

In the weeks before his death, several of McRae's friends recall him referring to some secret information he had obtained, and how one occasion he said 'I've got them'. Although he refused to be drawn on this secret information, it was understood that it concerned his 'nuclear' work. Once again, the similarity with Hilda Murrell is overwhelming, if we recall Hilda's words shortly before she died: 'If they don't get me first, I want the whole world to know that one old woman has seen through their lies'. Perhaps the secret information uncovered by Willie McRae attracted the attention of the same covert investigation unit that was dealing with Hilda Murrell, and indicates that their insatiable desire to track down Falklands secrets had expanded to Scotland.

Born in 1923 in Wester Ross, Northern Scotland, McRae was a precocious student, and from an early age politically active in the Scottish National Party (SNP). After Army service during the Second World War, he joined the Royal Indian Navy, where he served in Naval Intelligence.

He learned to speak Urdu and began addressing public meetings in India, his pet topic being freedom for the people. Once again, he became politically active when he joined the Indian Congress Party, at that time an illegal organisation involved in an underground war against the British occupation of India. This work brought him into contact with Indira Gandhi. His political work in India finally brought him to the attention of the British Security Services who, for various reasons, found it necessary to keep him under continued surveillance up to the time of his death. Like Hilda Murrell, Willie

McRae was a focus of attention for MI5, Special Branch and the Nuclear Police.

McRae's work was not only devoted to anti-nuclear campaigning. He also directed his workaholic energies against the drug trade operating in the West Highlands, an area which, because of its secluded sea lochs and sparse population, made an excellent entry point for drug smugglers. So it would be true to say that he was unpopular with the nuclear industry, elements of the criminal fraternity and some members of the police whom he had accused of conniving with drug pedlars.

One of the strangest aspects of the McRae case is the disparity between accounts of his state of mind just before his death. As a workaholic bachelor, his lifestyle can only be described as hectic. He was prone to heavy drinking and bouts of depression that necessitated treatment by a psychiatrist. However, despite these various personal problems, Willie always exercised a great sense of responsibility towards his clients and his anti-nuclear campaign. Sadie Patterson, a client and friend, saw McRae shortly before his death and described him as being 'radiant'. Mary Johnston, a former SNP activist and close friend of Willie, said 'He couldn't have done it, everything was going well for him. He had a great many responsibilities to do with clients. He was not the sort of man who would push that aside and kill himself'.

Other friends also point out that McRae was combative by nature, a fighter who would not give in to pressure, official or personal. He always courted trouble and adventure and had many enemies, especially ones in official positions. There are a number of possible answers to the mystery of the death of Willie McRae, but the suicide theory has been firmly ruled out by the Willie McRae Society, set up by friends to keep the case alive. Despite their continued lobbying for an official enquiry, the Scottish authorities have declined to reopen the case and stand by the final verdict reached after the two-day investigation, namely that McRae shot himself.

Similar to the Murrell murder in so many ways, the Willie

McRae case is saturated with mystery and unanswered puzzles. It is clear that he had been under surveillance for many years because he even knew the Special Branch men by their christian names and would speak to them when they attended his political meetings in Scotland. His telephone was tapped, and his mail was regularly examined by the Security Services. The Special Branch surveillance was so blatant that he was able to obtain details of their car registration numbers. One vehicle, a brown Chrysler, registration number XSJ 432T, occupied by two operatives, followed him to his home a few days before his death. According to local friends and media investigators, this vehicle was on official records as belonging to the Strathclyde Special Branch.

Shortly before his death, McRae's cottage in Dornie was burgled and his friend Mary Johnstone maintains Willie said 'They didn't get what they were looking for'. Could this have been the nuclear documents in his two briefcases?

McRae's was not the only property visited by unidentified burglars; in Edinburgh, the office of the Scottish Campaign to Resist Atomic Menace (SCRAM) was also burgled and set alight. It is interesting to note that SCRAM was listed on the Sapphire Detective Agency's Sizewell report as being targeted for investigation.

In addition to these unexplained break-ins, there is also the evidence of John Conway, ex-policeman turned legal rights campaigner and member of JUSTICE. After investigating the McRae case, he submitted a report to the Lord Advocate in which he stated 'There can be no doubt that some time after the crash and the first people arriving on the scene, someone searched through McRae's pockets and also ransacked the car'. Conway is also critical of the police two-day investigation, that he believes was stopped short by the Home Office because of MI5 involvement. He claims: 'It's just like when Henry II says, "Who will rid me of this turbulent priest?" and then the word is passed on'. Two years ago, Mr Conway was run over by a motor bike, receiving horrendous injuries. He is covinced that this was a 'frightener' that went wrong.

The bizarre twist in this linking of McRae's death to that of Hilda Murrell involves a red Ford Escort seen several times outside Miss Murrell's house and at the scene where her body was discovered.

On Saturday 6th April 1985, the day McRae was found by Australian Alan Crowe, a party of walkers a few miles from where McRae's car crashed reported that during the afternoon a man drove up the road, parked, got out and fired a number of shots in their direction. His car was . . . a red Escort.

Not only are there many similarities between the respective circumstances of the Murrell case and the death of McRae, there is also the attitude of the investigating officials to be considered. In both cases, investigators failed to interview important witnesses who could well have contributed valuable evidence. A former Strathclyde police officer, who does not wish to be named, said 'The ability to overlook possible sources of information in a murder enquiry is not always down to negligence. If an investigator knows he is wasting his time, or has been instructed by superiors to adopt a specific course of action, then what's he to do, waste his time or disobey his orders?'

Two years after McRae's death, Hamish Watt, a former SNP MP and Councillor in Grampian, told the *Aberdeen Press & Journal* that a nurse working at Aberdeen Royal Infirmary, where McRae was admitted, had told him that *two* bullet wounds were found in his brain – a fact that would clearly rule out suicide.

The nurse said that she was assisting at the time, in the theatre where doctors tried to save McRae. This statement conflicts with the Crown Office claim that after the x-rays showed the extent of the damage to McRae's brain no attempt was made to prolong his life.

Here is a summary of the similarities in the Murrell and McRae cases:

MURRELL	McRAE
Red Escort observed at scene	Red Escort observed at scene
Activities of interest to MI5, Special Branch, Atomic Energy Police	Activities of interest to MI5, Special Branch, Atomic Energy Police
About to appear at public hearing dealing with nuclear issues	About to appear at public hearing dealing with nuclear issues
Passionate anti-nuclear campaigner	Passionate anti-nuclear campaigner
Under surveillance by Security Services	Under surveillance by Security Services
Witnesses overlooked by police investigators	Witnesses overlooked by police investigators
Drove/driven to death scene in own vehicle	Drove/driven to death scene in own vehicle
Death scene: quiet country spot outside of town	Death scene: quiet country spot outside of town
Victim was said to have discovered something specific about nuclear industry	Victim was said to have discovered something specific about nuclear industry
Authorities refused enquiry into death and murder investigation wound up	Authorities refused enquiry into death and murder investigation wound up
Conflict in official statements about evidence	Conflict in official statements about evidence
Victim's property broken into and burned down	Victim's property broken into and an associate's also burgled and set on fire
Anomalies concerning nuclear papers	Anomalies concerning nuclear papers
Associates and friends attempting to pursue the case become victims of burglary and/or acts of violence or damage to property	Associates and friends attempting to pursue the case become victims of burglary and/or acts of violence or damage to property

215

A former senior police officer now living in retirement abroad, when presented with the fourteen similarities between the Murrell case and that of Willie McRae, said 'I'm astounded, *genuine* investigations into mysterious deaths have been ordered on a lot less evidence than that shown here to me. It's obvious something has gone on that is not at all proper'.

Was Hilda Murrell a victim of the State? And what about Willie McRae: did he die at the hands of nuclear spies or, perhaps, agents working for Special Branch? I will discuss these possibilities in due course. Meanwhile let us look at some more cases where anti-nuclear campaigners have been subjected to violence, surveillance and harassment.

In 1985, writer Dora Russell, staunch CND member and widow of philosopher Bertrand Russell, claimed that she was the victim of Secret Service violence. The 91-year old campaigner (since deceased) complained that she was dragged from her bed at 3am by a political burglar seeking documents to do with a book she was writing. Mrs Russell suffered internal bruising and injuries to the right foot.

In discussion with the author, Mrs Russell revealed that she was under surveillance and had received a number of threatening telephone calls, some of them mentioning Hilda Murrell and claiming that the same thing would happen to her if she did not abandon her book. She also received notes from unidentified persons claiming to have knowledge of the Hilda Murrell killing. At the time of these incidents in 1985, Mrs Russell was simply dismissed as an eccentric old lady who was prone to imagining things. Nothing could have been further from the truth: like Hilda Murrell this lady, as might be expected of Bertrand Russell's widow, was an articulate and alert woman who, despite her advanced years, was perfectly capable of describing her experiences accurately.

Another Security Service victim, Madeline Haigh, an anti-nuclear campaigner and chairperson of West Midlands CND, was able actually to identify the perpetrators of a covert investigation mounted against her in the early 1980s. Her story shows just how Special Branch officers use their skills against British citizens who are simply exercising their democratic rights. It also shows how Hilda Murrell's early letters to the Press would have been intercepted.

In 1981, Madeline wrote to a local newspaper voicing her anti-nuclear sentiments, while clearly condemning any sort of violent demonstration or public disorder. Immediately following publication of this letter, she received three visits from police officers identifying themselves as CID, wishing to question her about a mail order fraud perpetrated in her name from her home address. She was woken on several mornings at 5.40am by the telephone ringing and as she stumbled out of bed along the hall to answer the calls, the 'phone stopped ringing. Not only did she observe a number of men in parked cars outside her isolated house, where she spent most days alone, but telephone conversations with friends were often interrupted by the line going dead.

Because letters and documents in her possession were important to her work, Madeline became very security conscious, so much so that she began to photocopy all such materials, carrying the originals with her everywhere she travelled, not unlike Willie McRae and Hilda Murrell.

After seeking legal advice, Miss Haigh decided to make a complaint to the European Commission of Human Rights against the United Kingdom for breaching her right to hold opinions and to receive and impart information and ideas without interference by public authorities. She embarked on a complex and lengthy process, with little expectation of getting very far. Her efforts have proved successful in collecting considerable evidence about the way the State operates against those who dissent.

After an eight-month struggle, the West Midlands Chief Constable, much to everyone's surprise, finally admitted that the Special Branch had investigated Miss Haigh. She is still frightened by her experiences and is also angry at the arrogance of those who she says have thrown away our real freedom and security and seek to silence us by corruption and intimidation.

In a personal message to fellow anti-nuclear campaigners in *Sanity* magazine in August 1986, Miss Haigh said 'My request to each anti-nuclear campaigner reading this is, please don't let them get away with anything in your life. If we try to protect freedom on the little space we occupy individually, maybe we can collectively keep a big space free enough for long enough for better days to come. The alternative is too terrible to contemplate.'

During the seven years it took to research this book I met so many anti-nuclear campaigners complaining of beatings, telephone threats, and surveillance that I eventually came to believe that somewhere nesting deep within the Security and Intelligence fraternity was a secret organisation dedicated to dealing with anyone considered any sort of threat or embarrassment to the Government or the Security Services. Because of the covert nature of this 'firm', I decided to nickname it 'Q Squad', the quiet men (and presumably some women) who engage in clandestine dirty tricks directed against anyone upsetting the status quo.

The nickname 'Q Squad' applies to an organisation I now know to exist which operates along the lines described in a statement by former Military Intelligence Officer Captain Fred Holroyd. This organisation has been responsible for many covert operations against peace protesters at the Greenham Common Air Base in Berkshire.

In a nine-page statement, Miss Jane Powell and 60-year old Hazel Rennie describe a horrific attack by two men dressed in SAS-style clothing. On the 10th April 1985, these two ladies, who had spent almost twelve months protesting outside Greenham Common Air Base, were sitting around their fire chatting before getting into their sleeping bags for the night. They were very close to the perimeter of the Air Base which, for security reasons, was normally well lit around the fence. At approximately 10.45pm the lights were unexpectedly

ENEMIES OF THE STATE

extinguished. A short while later, rustling was heard in the trees and gorse below the campsite and a minute or so later a man was seen approaching the camp fire in a crouching run. Suddenly, the women found themselves confronted by two men dressed in similar dark combat-style uniforms and wearing ribbed woollen hats with the bottom edges turned up. The two men set about the women and systematically beat them, severely injuring both of them. The men used sticks and boots and not a word was spoken.

Miss Powell said 'My overwhelming impression at the time was that the man attacking me got nothing from it. There was no sign of anger or hatred, no indication he was getting something out of his system. At the time of the attack one of my preoccupations was that the man was not enjoying himself, he was just doing his job. Thinking about the events afterwards, I cannot work out their brief. If they wanted to kill us they failed and botched the job, although they had plenty of time. On the other hand, if they simply wanted to scare us, they only narrowly escaped murdering us. I was told that I would lose the feeling and use of my arms and legs, persistently kicking our heads was also dangerous and it was touch and go as to whether or not they had damaged my friend's kidneys.'

The initial diligence of the Ministry of Defence and Thames Valley Police concerning the incident wore off very quickly. Apart from a trip to Newbury to help make a photofit picture of the attackers, the victims were not contacted again by the police.

Approximately six months later, Miss Powell met one of the RAF top brass with whom she was quite friendly, an officer who was normally very co-operative and sympathetic to the campaigners protesting at Greenham. Powell had in fact come to know this man fairly well, and decided to tell him of the attack and to ask if he could investigate on her behalf. He agreed, and returned a short while later but would say nothing. Normally he was very forthcoming on pretty well anything going on inside the Base, particularly Base politics. On this occasion it would appear he was upset, uneasy and monosyllabic. He refused to comment on the attack or offer any opinions, which she found most strange. A short while later, she received an anonymous letter informing her that MI5 were investigating her activities and had been watching her at Greenham. The letter indicated that undercover agents were searching through campaigners' rubbish, and that she (Jane Powell) and her friend were of particular interest to the Security Service.

The injuries sustained by these women at Greenham Common were extremely serious, and even at the time of writing both are still suffering from their severe beating. Having had time to review the events of that night, they are now more certain than ever that they were the victims of an SAS-style 'hit team' acting on behalf of the British Security Services (MI5). If this is the case, then is it not likely that such teams were also responsible for the deaths of Hilda Murrell and Willie McRae?

Dominy Hamilton, another anti-nuclear campaigner who described herself as being 'on the periphery of Cruise Watch', became concerned about her telephone in the spring of 1983 when she found herself being frequently cut off in the middle of conversations. This experience was shared by many other anti-nuclear activists, including Carol Lewton who, during telephone conversations, would suddenly be interrupted by a man's voice shouting 'Oi, you' before the line went dead.

On other occasions, Miss Hamilton found herself connected to Dial-a-Disc when she tried to contact other members of her Cruise Watch cell. Despite complaining to British Telecom, she was told there was no question that her 'phone was tapped and it was simply a case of crossed lines. She also had the fairly common, and unnerving, experience of dialling a number and hearing not a ringing tone but people moving about in a room. Dominy admits to having been shocked and frightened: as a result she made a conscious decision to become high profile, her theory being that the more well known she was the safer she would be.

Campaigner Dr Di McDonald was protesting against Cruise missiles in June 1984 when she encountered physical intimidation, as a Cruise convoy was on its way back to Greenham Common. She went into a 'phone box to call a Newbury fellow campaigner and was followed in by a policeman who physically prevented her from dialling the number. Eventually, in a sarcastic tone of voice, he said 'It's engaged isn't it?' The number was indeed engaged. So this police officer for one was aware that telephone calls between the protesters were being blocked. Di also had difficulty with her 'phone at home, particularly with cut-offs in the middle of conversations. She noticed as well that her house was under surveillance for long periods by men sitting in cars.

Having satisfied myself beyond any reasonable doubt that an organised system for intimidating peace campaigners existed, I decided it was imperative that I obtain expert evidence from impeccable independent sources. One such source is Captain Fred Holroyd, a former Military Intelligence operative with regular service experience in covert operations, particularly with Special Branch.

Holroyd, like Commander Rob Green, trained at the Joint Services School of Intelligence in Kent, where he acquired the many clandestine skills needed for Intelligence operations. He agrees that this espionage school is the headquarters for spy training in England, where all the practical training for MI5, MI6, Special Branch and certain police forces takes place. Even the Central Intelligence Agency (CIA) are said to send agents to this unit for training. 'In that camp is a deep interrogation pod, where they actually carry out interrogation for real as well as for training. We learned burglary, actually busting open a safe, and how to make explosives in a wine bottle', he said.

This former Intelligence agent described his training in covert entry and surveillance as well as many other secret intelligence tricks, including lock picking and assassination. His testimony describes how MI5 would go about a covert operation directed against a nuclear protester, and reveals how a campaigner would be targeted. 'Well, first of all you put the house under surveillance and work out the modus operandi of the resident, and when she/he is going to be out. When you know you are not going to be disturbed, and you have decided the best time to break in, you put the person under surveillance. You have radio contact so that you know where that person is the whole time you are in the house: this way you get some kind of warning to give you a chance to tidy up and get out.

'Normally, you have a fixed point outside the premises controlling the operation, and once you've established that the person is shopping or whatever, your team goes in. The lock is picked in such a way it will not be detected: that is easy. The team then either searches, photographs or bugs the place before the resident returns.'

'The whole area is screened by the Special Air Service (SAS) in civilian clothes, who keep watch and intercept anyone who might visit the house. The SAS in this country have become an adjunct of the Security Services. They are no longer regarded purely as military troops. They now have a political rôle which is very much in the forefront with 22 SAS, and that is covert operations for the Security Services'.

The introduction of Britain's élite SAS killer troops into domestic intelligence work could well account for the military-style precision as well as the brutality of the attacks on the Greenham Common campaigners. Additional expert testimony from former senior police officers, Royal Air Force and Army Special Branch investigators, and of course my own experience, reveals that other forms of covert operations are conducted by other official agencies, independent of the MI5/SAS duties described by Captain Holroyd.

Fred Holroyd is a unique witness, who is able to give first-hand evidence of dirty tricks and illegal acts carried out by servants of the Crown. He is also a victim in his own right in that he was persecuted, threatened – and on one occasion nearly shot – not by terrorists or criminals but by serving members of the Security Services who were unhappy that he not only refused to get involved in criminal acts but took it upon himself to complain about the illegal behaviour of some members of the Intelligence Services working in Northern Ireland.

Fred's introduction to the secretive and dangerous world of military intelligence began on a bright summer afternoon in 1973. As a Captain in the British Army, he had been selected for special training at the Joint Services Intelligence Centre just outside Ashford in Kent. Knowing full well that he was destined for service in Northern Ireland, Fred found that much of the intensive training he received at Ashford actually had very little to do with what he ended up doing in Ireland. However, some of the instruction was much more satisfactory. He was trained in such clandestine skills as surveillance, lock picking, firearms and photography.

On a course where there is only a 50% pass rate, Holroyd performed just well enough to qualify eventually as a Military Intelligence Officer (MIO). What he lacked in academic ability, he made up for in loyalty, enthusiasm and enough common-sense to function effectively as an Intelligence operative working with MI6, MI5, Special Branch and the Special Air Service. Immediately following his graduation, Fred was posted to Lisburn, where he expected more experienced colleagues to show him the ropes. However, while a certain amount of on-the-job instruction was provided, he found himself floundering and left to his own devices a lot of the time. During one week he spent with a Major, Fred began to realise just how inadequate his Ashford training had been. His superior seemed to have no idea what he was doing or why he was doing it, and spent most of his time visiting a married woman in Dungannon. As the weeks progressed, Fred familiarised himself with MI5, Special

Branch and SAS, gradually managing to work out his own *modus operandi*.

After a few months of routine intelligence work, something happened that led to Holroyd being recruited into the Secret Intelligence Service (MI6). Early one evening, a colleague, junior in rank, entered Fred's office and suggested that he (Fred) might like to help out by doing him a driving favour.

There was something rather unusual in the junior colleague's attitude. He declined to elaborate on the reasons for this 'chauffeuring' job, simply stating that if Fred was prepared to do it he was not to ask any questions. For some inexplicable reason, Holroyd agreed. That night, he drove two non-commissioned officers through pouring rain to the outskirts of a Republican area of Lurgan. He parked the car and waited while the two, a Warrant Officer and a Sergeant, walked across a deserted field, returning after about twenty minutes. Over the following weeks there were further similar journeys, some of which were made into highly dangerous enclaves of Belfast.

Distinctly puzzled about what was going on, Fred finally pulled rank and demanded to know what was happening. The response surprised him more than he could have imagined. He was simply told that there was no reason why he shouldn't know, and that if he was agreeable he could undertake the work himself. Holroyd was still completely flummoxed and asked his colleague what on earth he was talking about. 'We want you to work for MI6. I'll take you to see my boss as soon as possible', he was told.

His work with the higher echelons of Secret Intelligence was not to Fred's liking. From the offset he made it clear he would not hide his MI6 involvement from his own Commanding Officer who, as it turned out, was delighted and fully expected Fred to provide him with copies of everything obtained for MI6. In effect, he was expected to spy not only on the terrorists but also on MI6. This kind of conduct was completely foreign to Holroyd's personality and he made his displeasure known both to his own boss and to MI6. In addition to working for MI6, he was still expected to carry out his own work as a MIO, the job he trained for at Ashford. He found this very difficult, and to make matters worse he became very disillusioned about what was expected of him in the dirty tricks department.

Now working as a civilian security consultant and investigator, Fred looks back on his experiences with anger rather than bitterness and is grimly determined to bring the Ministry of Defence to book over what happened to him. 'The dirty tricks I am aware of involved all branches of the Security Forces with whom I worked in 1974-75 – the Army, MI5, MI6 and the RUC. They were carried out on both sides of the border and ranged from the merely professionally disreputable to murder', he said.

MI5, according to Fred, brought in agent handlers from the Intelligence Corps and the SAS, and their general policy was not just basic but downright shortsighted: use whatever means, legal or illegal, to blackmail an involuntary 'recruit' into acting out of fear for his or her safety, then force them to carry out operations which cannot be traced back to the handler unless they are prepared to risk their life by confessing what they have done. This kind of conduct fragmented intelligence operations so that no one could afford to turn their back even on a colleague. There was no long-term future in this kind of manipulation, and the danger to those the Service needed to keep in place was so increased that any short-term gains were effectively nullified.

These general operational frustrations, along with the ongoing bitterness between MI5 and MI6, were as nothing compared to other more serious acts committed by serving Intelligence Officers of the Crown. Some were designed by MI5 to sabotage the credibility of MI6 operators who were struggling to inject some kind of professionalism into their spying duties, others were nothing more than outright illegal acts.

Despite displaying a certain amount of apparent reluc-
tance to commit itself wholeheartedly to 'dirty tricks', MI6
were certainly capable of running some dubious operations.
Bank robbery seemed to be their forte, as Fred discovered
in 1974. He says 'It was MI6 who organised the Littlejohn
brothers in their campaign of bank robberies in 1972, when I
was asked by my MI6 Controller if I would consider robbing a
bank. I declined, explaining that it was not part of the duties of
one of Her Majesty's Officers. It was never mentioned again'.

Robbing banks was not the only sort of criminal activity carried out by the Security Services during Fred's service in
Northern Ireland. Murder, blackmail and sabotage all played
their part in covert intelligence operations.

It is inevitable that, if a person is regularly involved against
their will in activity of which they disapprove, they will eventually adopt one of two courses of action: either they will
decide to fall in cynically with the activity concerned or
they will speak out in the hope of correcting what they consider to be wrong. Captain Fred Holroyd, being a loyal officer
with an admittedly 'inconvenient' code of ethics, decided to
speak out.

Holroyd's reward for his loyal service to the Crown was to
be removed from his post as an intelligence agent and ordered
to attend as a patient at the Royal Victoria Hospital
(Psychiatric Department), Netley, near Southampton. He was
admitted in May 1975. The alleged reason for this was that he
was suffering from stress following his father's death. This
official move was allegedly carried out in accordance with
military regulations in force at that time. In layman's terms,
Holroyd's bosses were saying he was mad.

During his stay at Netley, Fred was medically down-graded
on the grounds that he was emotionally unstable. What followed was nothing short of a nightmare, allegation upon allegation discrediting him almost on a weekly basis. He was even
ordered not to discuss his Intelligence work with anyone,
including medical staff.

Despite undergoing a number of tests that proved him to be normal, Holroyd was held incommunicado until his release on 30th June 1975, when he was supplied with a certificate that contradicted his 'normal' record report. In August the following year, after numerous discussions, arguments, and correspondence with medical and other defence authorities (all to no avail) Captain Holroyd submitted his written resignation from the army. Since then he has lobbied Members of Parliament, the Prime Minister and the Ministry of Defence in vain attempts to set the record straight. On behalf of Captain Holroyd, I would now like to provide extracts from his Ministry of Defence statement of service, and other sources that show him to be a sane, competent officer throughout his army career.

His official statement of service, as provided by the Ministry of Defence to Holroyd, reads as follows;

'Mr Holroyd joined the army in 1960 and was commissioned in 1964. He was promoted to Captain in 1969 and held this rank until his resignation in September 1976. Mr Holroyd's personal record shows him to have been a thoroughly competent officer who performed well in a wide variety of posts. His reports remark upon his enthusiasm and drive, and refer to his enjoyment of challenging physically demanding tasks. There is no reason why, had Mr Holroyd chosen to remain in the army, he should not have been able to pursue a worthwhile and fulfilling career.

'Mr Holroyd has expressed concern that an incident during his career in the army could affect his job prospects in civilian life. During 1974/75 Mr Holroyd was employed in a very demanding post, from which it was felt necessary to remove him as he was displaying signs of stress. However, after a relatively short period Mr Holroyd was considered to have recovered completely and his temporary problem did not in any way reflect adversely on either his character or his competence as an officer.'

In a letter dated 22nd February 1977, the Assistant Chief Constable of the Royal Ulster Constabulary, C H Rodgers, wrote 'to whom it concerned':

'Captain Fred Holroyd is well known to me. During his service with the British Army in Northern Ireland I met him almost daily. He was at that time a member of the Brigade Staff but attached to the Royal Ulster Constabulary. I found him to be a man of unquestionable loyalty, outstanding courage, with devotion to duty that one looks for but rarely finds today.

'During the two years he was attached to the Royal Ulster Constabulary, the force enjoyed a success record against terrorists in my area which has not been equalled before or since. It is my considered opinion that the part Captain Holroyd played made a very significant contribution to our success.

'His leadership qualities and dedication inspired the men around him, he always put the Service first.

'I understand that Captain Fred Holroyd intends to apply for a position in the Rhodesian Armed Forces, from my long years of experience dealing with terrorists I can say that he is exceptionally well equipped for any command position that requires loyalty, courage, dedication and anti-terrorist know-how.

'I recommend him unreservedly for the position he is seeking.

'I will be pleased to give answers at any time concerning Mr Holroyd's suitability.

(signed) C H RODGERS
Assistant Chief Constable, Royal Ulster Constabulary'

We need people like Fred, people for whom the principles of justice and truth to which most of us just pay lip service really do matter. In 1987 he was offered £15,000 compensation by the Ministry of Defence for his lost career. Despite being completely broke at the time, without even the price of a rail ticket from his home in Westcliff-on-Sea to London, he turned the offer down because at the last minute a string was attached: he would have had to keep his mouth shut.

It is now nearly twenty years since Fred engaged in professional fisticuffs with his Intelligence bosses, and from the offset his most difficult task was actually proving that there was an official conspiracy to silence him by having him committed to Netley Psychiatric Hospital. There were many colleagues who were aware of what was occurring, but unfortunately none was able to go on record to assist him, and the Mafia-like code of silence adopted by all concerned effectively sabotaged his fight for truth and justice.

Fortunately, this long-term silence was eventually broken on 23rd March 1990 by a former Army Doctor who had knowledge of the case. W H Thomas MD FRCS(C) FRCS(ED), a Consultant Surgeon for the Mid Glamorgan Health Authority, provided a detailed statement which alleged that attempts had been made to discredit Captain Holroyd by having him incarcerated in the Army hospital.

All in all, this is a disgraceful case involving MI5, MI6, and Army Intelligence, who in a desperate attempt to conceal illegal acts (including murder) committed by servants of the Crown, went to extreme lengths to have a loyal, dedicated Intelligence agent declared insane. With this kind of attitude permeating the Security Services, it's not surprising the cases of Hilda Murrell, Willie McRae and others are now dormant.

As a final tribute to Captain Holroyd, I now produce in its entirety the statement of Consultant Surgeon Thomas, who in the opinion of many, including lawyers and other professionals, produces a good case for a public hearing:

> Prince Charles Hospital
> Mid Glamorgan Health Authority
> Merthyr & Cynon Valley Health Unit
> Merthyr Tydfil C47 9DT

Mr Fred Holroyd
15 Sandleigh Road
Leigh-on-Sea   Our ref: WHT/EW
Essex SS9 1JT   23rd March 1990

<u>To Whom It May Concern</u>

<u>Re: Fred Holroyd</u>

I was senior Consultant Surgeon at Musgrave Park Hospital from 1974 to 1978 during which time I came to know about the case of Capt. Holroyd who had been admitted to Netley Psychiatric Hospital through referral at Musgrave Park Hospital. I was not involved in the assessment of this officer, but was made aware of the concern of my fellow officers about the case at the time. I would comment on his initial referral . . . not by any doctor, as being totally irregular. The Commanding Officer's obligation in such matters is to involve the Unit doctor for advice and referral. This was not the case in this instance.

I would also comment on the fact that the Unit doctor, had he been involved, would have had to assess Capt. Holroyd himself and assess the alleged circumstances relating to his family life.

I can only surmise that his assessment would have been unwelcome and I can only surmise that this was the reason for this highly irregular and precipitate action.

Had his Unit doctor been involved and had he found cause for further referral in Psychiatric terms, such referral would have been made either to civilian Psychiatric Consultants present at Musgrave Park Hospital, or to Army Psychiatric Consultants.

As it was, he was brought to the hospital and presented to a medical officer. This medical officer was hardly a person to adequately assess a supposed acute case, having had no Psychiatric experience himself and not knowing, as the Unit doctor automatically would, the background of the family concerned.

At the time of this incident, there was grave concern expressed by a Physician at the hospital who sought sanctuary in the operating theatre, in order that he would not become involved in this affair. For a Physician to enter the portals of a surgical theatre was unusual enough let alone to request to remain there for any length of time!

Subsequent transfer of an unwilling Capt. Holroyd was, I understand, made under threat of Court Martial and threat of physical removal to Netley. There was no Sectioning procedure and his transfer was thus deemed voluntary. Such 'voluntary transfer' under threat of Court Martial stand out as an obvious irregular act.

Not only was Military Law clearly broken in this instance, according to my own understanding of the case then and now, but all aspects of medical practice were transgressed.

His records at Netley ought themselves to carry due reference to the mode of his admission to Netley and I find it highly significant that no treatment of any kind seemed to have been given Capt. Holroyd which could equate with a diagnosis requiring Section.

The whole episode of his medical referral in this aberrant fashion, in my opinion, requires full investigation and may be a slur not only on his Unit, but on the medical profession engaged in his transfer.

Yours sincerely
[signed] W Hugh Thomas
W H THOMAS MD FRCS(C) FRCS(ED)
CONSULTANT SURGEON

If the 1984 experiences of Mrs Pat Davis are anything to go by, then it is not surprising that Hilda Murrell was living in fear of her life.

As the wife of a Naval nuclear submariner, Mrs Davis dared to speak out, complaining to the Ministry of Defence that radiation leakages in her husband's submarine HMS *Resolution* had been responsible for her son Stephen's hare lip and cleft palate. Mrs Davis gave birth to Stephen on the 16th September 1973 and now, almost 20 years later, she is still battling to obtain compensation from the MOD. No longer married to Petty Officer Danny Davis (now retired), Pat suffered surveillance and beatings when she was bravely contributing to a Yorkshire Television programme about nuclear contamination.

In a sworn statement to solicitors Boyes Turner & Burrows of Staines, Middlesex, Mrs Davis revealed the nature of her experiences:

'I am a divorced woman living alone with my son, Mark. I have one other son, Stephen, who attends a boarding school and is only home on odd occasions.

'My ex-husband is Chief Petty Officer Danny Davis who is employed on the nuclear submarine HMS *Resolution*. His

231

duties are top secret and he is positively vetted for his post as a Sonar Operator.

'During 1971, while married to Danny Davis, we were based in Scotland and we attended a Naval social function. During the course of this party a Naval Rating serving on nuclear submarines broke down and started crying. He mumbled something about *rad. counts* and stated that something had gone wrong with the reactor and there had been a serious leak. Between 1971 until 1973 I heard other mention of similar leaks and spoke to my husband about it, but he simply stated there was no problem.

'In 1973 my second son, Stephen, was born: he had a hare lip and cleft palate. Up until approximately 1975 numerous other children were born to Navy wives and again there were deformities. I eventually began to realise that something was terribly wrong and decided to enquire as to the possibility of nuclear leaks being responsible for these deformed births. I had no idea at the time that I would be embarking on a fight that would last ten years and result in a divorce and threats to my life.

'I commenced my campaign by talking with my then husband. He refused to get involved in discussions and simply stated that it was a coincidence. I then approached a Dr Morris who was responsible for the health of naval wives in the area; he was not helpful and I have reason to believe that he might have had contact with, or even been employed by, the Navy on an official basis. The situation became so hopeless that I then decided to approach a local MP, who in fact approached the MOD.

'They informed him that there was no leak and that my submissions were totally inaccurate. At this point in time I came up against a brick wall and began to realise that attempts were being made to frustrate my efforts for the truth.

'I had further discussions with my then husband but he stated that it was pointless pursuing the matter, he acknowledged that there was a high level of radiation in nuclear submarines but denied that there had ever been any leak. It is significant to note that since this time he has had growths removed from his body, which he stated were caused by bee stings.

'The years went by and eventually I divorced my husband during August 1983 and subsequently arrived at my current council home in Northfield Road during May 1985.

'During 1984 I had contact with Yorkshire Television and certain newspapers and decided to co-operate with a programme on nuclear leaks, my item to be part of an overall picture of the serious nuclear problem in this country. A number of small stories, some of them quite inaccurate and lacking in content, have been presented in certain newspapers – all in all, no national newspaper or television programme as yet has presented the whole truth of my problems.

'During the latter part of 1984 up until the present time I have received numerous death threats by telephone and by anonymous people speaking to me from cars displaying what appear to have been false number plates. The circumstances of these threats are as follows:

'I received my first threat on the 22nd or 23rd October 1985 at midnight. This was by telephone and the male voice, with a Scottish accent, stated that if I went ahead with my television programme I would be killed. On the 25th or 26th October 1985 at 1am I received another telephone call from the same Scottish voice and he asked me if I was still planning to go ahead. I answered in the affirmative and he became very abusive and stated that if I went ahead "we will kill you".

'Approximately a week later between 11 and 12 midnight, again the same Scottish accented male telephoned me and asked for Pat Davis. He became abusive and repeated the following words – "we've said before, we will make you a very dead woman".

'The following night I received another telephone call and the caller stated that "we're now nearer home tonight, you'll be dead". This call sounded very local and by this point in time I was terrified out of my mind.

'Three nights later, at 2.25am I received a telephone call, and the caller on this occasion sounded intoxicated and he again threatened to kill me and then rang off. I would point out that this was not a Scottish voice, there have been two different voices and the last two/three calls were in fact English speaking.

'Finally, two nights later, at 4am I received another telephone call from a gentleman who appeared to have technical knowledge of radiation and leakages. We had a long discussion about my proposed statements on television.

'During October 1985, I cannot remember the actual date unfortunately, I left my home at approximately 7.15am in the company of a local female by the name of Jenny who walked to the bus stop with me. A black car I believe to be a Scirocco was parked in the road. Sitting behind the steering wheel was a gentleman dressed in a suit, reading a newspaper. He had fair short curly hair and was about twenty-five or thirty years of age. The following day, the same car was parked in the same position, the time again being 7.15am. As Jenny and I walked around the corner to the bus stop the car started and drew up alongside me and the window wound down as though electrically operated. The male driver asked me if I was still planning to go ahead with the television programme. He stated "You must know by now you won't be allowed to go ahead". He laughed and drove off. He was English and reasonably well spoken.

'I must correct part of my statement – Jenny was with me actually the following day, a Wednesday. The car was not parked in the same position on this occasion but it pulled up alongside me suddenly by the bus stop. Jenny was walking a few feet ahead of me, and the driver said to me "Mrs Davis, you are a very dead woman".

'I said to one of the girls in the office that "that was the bloke who has been following me".

'I also received a threatening telephone call at my place of work, again threatening my life. I literally broke down after the

234

telephone call, after shouting obscenities at the caller, and had to be taken off the switchboard. Members of staff at work witnessed my condition and Mr Murray, a private investigator who has been retained by Yorkshire Television for a short period of time to assist me, has spoken to one of these witnesses. This witness is of course very frightened about the situation and does not want to be mentioned by name.

'Shortly before Christmas 1985, the Saturday before to be exact, I received my final threatening telephone call which terrified the life out of me.

'It was from an English speaking individual who described the personal activities of my son, Mark, and the fact that his friend had a criminal record. He also mentioned the name and address of Mark's girlfriend and described my recent visits to dry cleaners. It was obvious to me that I had been watched. I immediately called Mr Murray who then attended my premises and it was agreed that the police would be informed, although I must say my previous complaints to the police appear to have been totally ignored. However, on Mr Murray's advice, I did report the matter to the police. As I suspected, this was a total waste of time, I received little or no assistance from them since my complaints.

'On the occasion of the last telephone call, Mr Murray installed on my telephone tape-recording equipment to enable me to record all incoming calls. Also on this date Mr Murray telephoned my ex-husband Chief Petty Officer Davis in Scotland to enquire as to whether or not my youngest son Stephen, who was staying with my ex-husband, was safe and well. Unfortunately on this occasion, whilst in a frightened state, I let it slip to my ex-husband that my telephone calls were now being monitored and since this date I have received no further calls of a threatening nature at my home or work. The police in Staines are also aware that my telephone calls are being monitored and they showed more concern about Mr Murray's involvement than my complaints.

'They have not taken any statements from the witnesses, have not carried out any enquiries in the neighbouring houses that would have confirmed the existence of the black Scirocco vehicle. However, Mr Murray has contacted the DVLC in Swansea and from a conversation with them it would appear that the motor vehicle licence numbers that I recorded are not registered, although the registration numbers are in fact appertaining to a Birmingham registration but the car itself appears not to be registered.

'On Friday 3rd January 1985 I made arrangements, over my home telephone number, with Mr Murray to attend my home for the purpose of taking a detailed recorded interview with me. During our telephone conversation it was arranged that a certain witness who actually intercepted one of the threatening telephone calls would be present, for the purpose of giving a statement of corroboration.

'On Saturday 4th January 1985 at 10.15am, by arrangement, Mr Murray attended my house and while we were waiting for the witness, Stephen Chubb, to arrive, uniformed police officers arrived at the house stating they wished to interview Mr Chubb in connection with what they described as a trivial offence. They were anxious to discuss with him a certain traffic matter that would only take, according to them, half an hour of his time.

'Mr Chubb, a young man of 18, was eventually arrested and incarcerated in Staines Police Station until after 2pm that day. The result was that Mr Murray was unable to interview him on this occasion. Since this time Mr Chubb appears to have been lodged in a probation hostel in Richmond, what the circumstances are surrounding this man's whereabouts and activities I am unable to elicit from the Staines police, but it is my opinion that he was deliberately arrested and kept incommunicado to avoid a statement of corroboration being made to Mr Murray.

'Since the 4th January 1985 there have been two occasions when I believe my house has been broken into. On the first

236

occasion I returned home from work to find all the lights on, the front and back doors open, but nothing apparently stolen. I did not bother on this occasion to report the matter to the police, for obvious reasons.

'On the 5th February 1986 I received a telephone call at approximately 9.15/9.30pm from [name deleted for security reasons], the Public Relations Officer for the Ministry of Defence, Navy, in Faslane Submarine Base. I recorded the conversation and at the end of the same I switched off my tape recorder and went upstairs to have a bath.

'While upstairs in the bath I heard a noise downstairs. I came downstairs, the time being approximately 10pm, to find the front and back doors open and the tape-recorder having been tampered with and in fact the whole of the conversation with [name deleted] had been recorded over. Mr Murray, the private investigator, has this tape and fortunately the identifying voice of [name deleted] is still identifiable. On this occasion Mr Murray suggested that the police be informed. Mr Murray attended my premises along with one local police officer who appeared not to be too interested in my complaint. Mr Murray discovered in the back garden footprints that in my opinion came from the intruder, they led to the fence, across the garden, and then vanished. The police officer examined the garden and during the course of his examination destroyed all of the footprints, these were seen by Mark, my son, Mr Murray, the private investigator, and his assistant. The policeman eventually left my premises at approximately 11.30/ 11.45pm, after stating he would make a report.

'Mr Murray has attended Staines CID where he has spoken with a Detective Constable Marwick and a Detective Sergeant Jones and on my behalf Mr Murray attempted to encourage them to take my complaints seriously.

'However, Mr Murray has reported to me that they were totally uninterested in my complaint and in fact seemed more concerned about his involvement in the affair and that he should be retained by Yorkshire Television or have contact with any other journalists interested in my problem.

'Mr Murray, I am confident, will give a statement of corroboration to this effect.

'All in all, I am extremely terrified; I have read carefully the stories of Hilda Murrell and other people who have received similar threats and it is obvious that people in official circles will do nothing to help such people. In the case of Hilda Murrell, this lady was also remonstrating or voicing her opinion about the inadequacies of the nuclear reactor at the Sizewell Plant in Suffolk. She also had contacts, via her nephew Lt. Commander Green, with the Royal Navy and reading the reports leading up to the death of this lady, it would appear that she experienced almost identical happenings as myself. I do not know where to turn, no one takes me seriously and there is the continuing problem of nuclear leaks from submarines. The Navy have knowledge of not just leaks from HMS *Resolution*, but other leaks, and the rate of deformed births is far too high to be a coincidence.

'Finally, I would like to conclude by stating that Mr Murray, the private investigator, has a tape-recording of a conversation between himself and my ex-husband Chief Petty Officer Davis. From the contents of this tape-recording and statements made by the current wife of Chief Petty Officer Davis, it is obvious that Royal Naval authorities have given instructions for abortions to be carried out on naval wives. This horrifies me and I am desperate that the truth be revealed to enable the nuclear leaks to be stopped and naval wives' interests to be protected. It is too much to ask that compensation be paid to these individuals, but if I can at least successfully call for an enquiry into the truth of the incidents on the nuclear submarines then at least I will have achieved something. From conversations I overheard between naval personnel, it would appear that the core of the nuclear reactor had been fractured during refit in 1971.

'I have read over carefully the above Statement and it is true. I am willing to give evidence at any hearing, board of enquiry, and/or make a sworn Affidavit if required.'

For weeks prior to the transmission of the Yorkshire Television programme, Pat Davis received threatening telephone calls from sinister-sounding unidentified men, telling her she would be killed if she continued with her campaign. Although she had learned that she was under surveillance by mysterious vehicles following her to work and watching her house, and despite the threats and harassment, she doggedly continued her fight for compensation. Then, in May 1986, instead of just threats and surveillance, she received an actual visit from two 'military types' who ransacked her home – and physically beat her.

In spite of this terrifying experience, Mrs Davis was not deterred, and to-day she is still pursuing her legal claim against the Ministry of Defence. She continues to be the victim of harassment: very recently, during May 1991, she received another painful beating from two unidentified assailants. This terrifying incident occurred in southern Ireland where Mrs Davis had moved from Middlesex. It would appear that sometimes there's no escape.

The examples of intimidation, harassment and worse in this chapter are all supported by solid evidence which has been supplied by responsible and intelligent individuals who, to the best of my knowledge, have never acted in any way that could be considered a threat to the defence of the realm.

As for the organisations and individuals who physically carried out the various burglaries, beatings and harassments, and the murders of Hilda Murrell and Willie McRae, it is a sad fact that these faceless agents, with their twisted ingenuity and unparalleled powers of deception, will more than likely never be brought to book.

The best we can hope for is that, with the newly introduced Security Services legislation, accompanied by, one hopes, new regulations to control the private investigation business, perhaps the shadowy operators of British Intelligence and Special Branch will decide at long last to play by the rules.

A public enquiry into Hilda Murrell's death would certainly be an encouraging step in the right direction.

CHAPTER 11

The Libyan Connection

Some time during the early part of 1988, the Honourable Dale Campbell-Savours, MP, received a letter addressed to him at the House of Commons. This 'date as post marked' communication was from an inmate of Her Majesty's Prison, Maidstone – B73886 Hassan Assali.

The letter was mostly about the (then) recently published book by former MI5 officer Peter Wright – *Spycatcher* – which exposed thirty or so MI5 agents said to have been involved in illegal dirty tricks operations. Assali mentioned one of these officers by name and said that at that time he was running a security company out of Great Queen Street, London EC4. Assali claimed that although to all intents and purposes this agent was trading as a private detective and security operative, he was still employed as an MI5 officer under a 'civilian wrapper'. Assali also explained to Campbell-Savours that he (Assali) was in prison as a result of false charges.

On the 16th April 1984, Squadron Leader Moralee, the officer commanding 27 Squadron of the RAF Regiment, prepared a report on the trial of passive infra-red equipment for RAF Fire Unit Defence. The designer of this sophisticated security system was an MOD contractor (who had security clearance from MI5) called Hassan Assali.

On various dates during 1983 and 1984, a private security

electronics firm, Radiofort Sentek Ltd, trading from Shenley Road, Boreham Wood, Hertfordshire, made a number of business deals with the Royal Ordnance Factory, Blackburn. This firm also conducted business with several defence companies linked to the Ministry of Defence. Radiofort Sentek and its directors had also been security-cleared by MI5. The name of the Managing Director of Radiofort? Hassan Assali.

On the 30th May 1984, armed police officers, accompanied by members of Special Branch and Customs agents, raided the premises of a private security firm in North London. Officers entered the premises with firearms at the ready and, according to witnesses, sharpshooters were stationed outside with an impressive array of firepower. Directors and staff of the firm were ordered to place their hands on their heads while police carried out body searches of all detained.

When asked by the primary 'target' what was going on, a police inspector explained they were looking for 'firearms and bombs'. There then followed a systematic search of the premises, which culminated in the removal of what were said to be a number of bomb timers and unlicensed firearms. Running in parallel to this raid, Customs officers at Heathrow apprehended what they described as a laser weapon allegedly for export to the Middle East. Searches at the Shenley Road, Boreham Wood address resulted in the removal of other items, including numerous documents.

The suspect – arrested at the Boreham Wood premises – was eventually transferred to St Albans Police Station, where he was questioned about his possession of the alleged bomb timers and the unlicensed firearms. Customs officials also interrogated him about the export of other items.

The following months turned into a nightmare for the suspect, with lengthy periods of questioning, and accusation heaped upon accusation. Eventually, criminal charges were preferred against him and in May of 1985 at the St Albans Crown Court, before His Honour Judge Blofeld QC, he was convicted of offences relating to the manufacturing of timing devices contrary to the Explosives Substances Act 1883 Section 4(1). The name of the defendant was Hassan Assali and his sentence was 9 years.

I first came into contact with Assali quite by accident, shortly after he wrote to Dale Campbell-Savours MP. My interest in the case was aroused by the mention of the private security operative alleged by Assali to be a former MI5 staff officer, supposedly working undercover through his own firm in London. I recognised this man's name: he was associated with a number of London-based security firms, including the Zeus Security group of companies run by Peter Hamilton, the organiser of the Sizewell surveillance project. I was able to track Assali down to Maidstone Prison, where after satisfying himself about my credentials he obtained the necessary permission for a visit.

I met him several times, even travelling to the Isle of Wight shortly after his transfer to Albany Prison. Bearing in mind what we were discussing and writing about, I cannot help feeling that his move to Albany was an attempt by the authorities to limit his contact with me. It did not take me very long to identify Assali as a highly intelligent individual with an outstanding knowledge of electronics who was very bitter about his predicament. From the outset of his trial, he had insisted that the timing devices responsible for his conviction were definitely not designed for use with explosives, as claimed by the expert witness for the Crown, Alan Feraday.

I can say that, from my own experience of basic electronics, I was able to make sense of Assali's technical explanation describing how the timers were not designed for use with explosives but for domestic use. And when he disclosed details of other work which he said he had done for Zeus Security, my every instinct drove me to investigate further.

Despite being Libyan, Assali is in fact a British citizen. His father (now retired) is a former barrister and there is no evidence to suggest that any member of the family has ever been involved in terrorist-type acts. On the contrary, Assali's work appears, beyond any reasonable shadow of doubt, to have been done for British Security and Intelligence, various civilian contractors, the Ministry of Defence and other British defence companies, including British Aerospace and Marconi. From his company records, plus the evidence gleaned from copy tape recordings of the interrogation by Customs agents, there can be no doubt that Assali told the truth about his work within the defence industry.

Concerning his work for the Security Services, Assali says 'My company had over 1,500 accounts, including Peter Hamilton of Zeus Security. I first met Hamilton after he responded to one of my trade adverts in August 1978'.

In a lengthy statement, written under very restrictive conditions in Maidstone Prison, Assali described how he supplied via a former MI5 officer, Jeremy Wetherall, general alarm equipment and other more clandestine devices suitable for bugging and surveillance to Zeus. 'I have on several occasions supplied to Zeus, to Wetherall, remote control equipment modified for other use. At the same time Wetherall enquired what bugs I could supply him. Some I did and some others I informed him where he could get them from, essentially all to do with bugging and surveillance', he said.

Throughout his relationship with Zeus, Assali believed that both Hamilton and Wetherall were connected to British Intelligence. He said 'Wetherall and Hamilton always seemed to wish to impress me with their high level contacts in British Intelligence. Hamilton even told me, boasting to make an impression, that he was in the past of some rank in MI6 or MI5. All that concerned me was that I was not breaking the law. Hamilton stressed that neither was he breaking the law.'

The most interesting part of Assali's statement concerns Hamilton's activities in the period 1983–84, the time of the Sizewell surveillance and the death of Hilda Murrell. 'At the time – 1978 briefly, the years 1983–84, also in 1982 – I knew that Wetherall and Hamilton were concerned with surveillance on behalf of British Intelligence, which seemed perfectly legal and in the public interest' said Assali.

It goes without saying that evidence obtained from criminal sources has to be corroborated, checked and re-checked. After all, a person convicted of such serious criminal offences as manufacturing bomb timers has much to gain by impressing journalists with exciting stories of secret intelligence operations linked to private detective and security agencies. Having satisfied myself that there was nonetheless *some* substance in Assali's allegations, I set out to check his claims about Mr Wetherall's connections with the Security Services. To start with I got hold of a copy of Mr Wetherall's company brochure. The short biography of Mr Wetherall in this brochure makes very informative reading:

JEREMY WETHERALL – MANAGING DIRECTOR

A Cambridge honours degree in law, followed by service in the Metropolitan Police and in British Intelligence. This exposed him to a wide variety of sensitive areas in the UK and overseas.

Initial employment in commercial security was as a senior kidnap negotiations adviser, operating overseas in both political and criminal cases.

A co-director of Lynx Security Services Ltd was named as David Godfrey who, according to the company profile, had spent thirty years in security and intelligence mostly for the governments of New Zealand, Canada and the West Indies. Mr Godfrey was also said to have attended courses organised by the police and Security Services in the United Kingdom.

Hamilton and Wetherall were not the only contacts Assali had with Zeus. He also met very briefly with Lord Chalfont and Antonio Von Marx once when he was commissioned to service an alarm installed in Chalfont's Knightsbridge flat. According to Assali, both Lord Chalfont and Von Marx played a vital part in Zeus company operations. This of course does not necessarily mean that Chalfont, Von Marx, Wetherall,

Hamilton – or for that matter anyone connected with Zeus – were involved in any illegal acts. However, one can question whether security services should ally themselves to private security firms to conduct intelligence operations – something which is certaintly not illegal.

Assali's relationship with Zeus was such that other government work emanating from South Africa and Rhodesia was put his way. He said 'Wetherall seemed better connected than Hamilton in that area.'

Having satisfied myself that Assali had a credible case and was not attempting to manipulate me for his own ends, I set about the difficult task of learning whether or not he was the victim of an irregular conviction. It did not take me very long to discover that this strange case had not received the amount of media attention one would have expected. After all, journalists are renowned for their insatiable appetite for anything to do with terrorism, the Ministry of Defence or spying. I'm not for one moment suggesting that there was some kind of conspiracy to maintain a low level of publicity for the trial so that some kind of improper conviction could be obtained, but it does seem to me that for such a media-worthy case to slip the newshounds' net is most strange.

Having said that, it is true to say that any case tried at the Old Bailey will almost certainly receive more publicity than one dealt with, for example, by the St Albans Crown Court. To further restrict publicity, the prosecution could simply persuade a Judge to hold much of the trial in camera (closed court) and a lot of what is presented in defence or mitigation can have little, or even the wrong, effect on the jury. In the case of Regina v Hassan Assali, the trial location was, in fact, St Albans Crown Court, and some of the case was indeed closed to the press.

This, of course, is not by any means evidence that there was an orchestrated legal operation by the authorities to 'fit up' Assali quietly. But it would be interesting to know just how many 'secret' angles there were to this trial and, indeed, why there should have been any at all.

A major factor in Assali's conviction was the damaging technical evidence of the prosecution expert, Feraday. It is not my intention to go into the complicated details of this evidence and the defence's cross examination of this witness, except to say that his final conclusion was that the timers in question could *only* have been manufactured for the detonation of explosives. In addition to Mr Feraday, the Crown produced additional verbal evidence from Mr Wetherall, who was described in court as a former member of the Security Services connected to Zeus Security. What Wetherall told the court about his relationship with Assali had a very damaging effect on the defence and without doubt strengthened what would have been a much weaker prosecution case relying primarily on technical evidence which is still in doubt to-day. It must be said, however, that documents were also said to have been recovered from Assali's company records, documents which the Crown claimed proved that the timers were being supplied to a Middle Eastern client. Of course, as Assali is a Libyan and closely associated with Arabs the effect this had on the jury was significant.

Another witness, a former employee sacked by Assali some time before his arrest, one Philip Bidwell, also gave verbal evidence to the effect that he (Bidwell) had been instructed to work on bomb timers for export abroad. This really closed the lid on Assali. Bidwell corroborated Wetherall's evidence and vice versa: all that was left was for the technical expert to nail down the coffin lid – which is just what happened.

My own investigation into the technical evidence led me to a qualified independent expert based at the National Institute for Higher Education, Dublin, where he is Head of the School of Computer Applications. Michael Scott PhD, MSc, is a scientist well qualified to assess the Crown's claims stemming from the technical evidence. Fortunately I was able to provide Scott with a transcript of Mr Feraday's statement, along with photographs of the timing devices. After a lengthy analysis, Dr Scott supplied a comprehensive report on all aspects of the timers. His opening paragraph in the covering letter made encouraging reading: 'Please find enclosed my report on Mr Feraday's evidence, which is clearly seriously flawed in this case', he wrote.

The report itself would, in my opinion, convince any Appeal Court seriously to consider quashing the original convictions against Assali, and had an independent expert like Scott been produced for the defence an entirely different verdict might have been reached.

Dr Scott's opinion of the cross-examination of Mr Feraday is that it was, relatively, effectively conducted, but he said 'I would defy the most brilliant barrister to pin him down unless they also happen to be themself an expert in the field of electronics'. He highlights various aspects of the technical evidence, reviewing and criticising much of Feraday's testimony, especially the closing submission when Feraday said 'I am of the opinion that they [the timers] have been specifically designed and constructed for terrorist use.'

According to the defendant, the police refused to allow him access to a solicitor during initial and subsequent questioning, and all official guidelines concerning the interrogation of suspects were ignored. That, insists Assali, was why he refused to make any formal statement during the early stages of the enquiry. He is adamant that from the very start he was considered a terrorist, working for some kind of anti-Gaddafi organisation.

If this was so, why didn't the appropriate police or intelligence department set up some kind of long-term surveillance to locate his contacts and learn the full extent of the Assali network in the United Kingdom? And why impose reporting restrictions? After all, to be seen capturing a terrorist could enhance the police's and Security Services' reputations.

After reviewing this case carefully, it occurred to me that all the defendant had to do was produce suitable witnesses to give evidence on his behalf and the prosecution would have collapsed. I was not surprised to hear that every time an attempt was made to produce such a witness, something occurred that resulted either in a weak, unimpressive defence statement being produced in court, or in witnesses failing even to appear. One such witness was an Italian businessman, a Mr Zotti, a resident of Padova. Being in a similar line of electronics to that of Mr Assali, and familiar with the design of timing devices, he could have clarified a number of technical points. Regrettably, Mr Zotti changed his mind at the last moment, causing irreparable damage to the line of defence that Assali had planned.

I spoke with Mr Zotti by telephone on Wednesday, 22nd July 1992. He explained to me that just before his intended journey to England he was contacted by the local police and told they had information that Assali was connected to the Red Brigade terrorist group, and that he (Mr Zotti) would get himself into trouble giving evidence. It is therefore not surprising that he changed his mind.

On the surface, the case of Assali appears to be yet another travesty of British justice. A deliberate conspiracy? Who knows? One thing is for sure, there are enough dubious elements in the prosecution's evidence to lead any sensible jury to reach a 'not guilty' verdict. Sadly, this did not happen for Assali, who is now a free man after serving just over six years of his sentence.

An obvious question that springs to mind in considering this peculiar case is, why didn't Assali appeal? His answer to that is simple. 'I was never allowed to appeal. Every time I made an attempt to get an appeal accepted, some reason or another not to proceed was always given by the authorities. I stood no chance.'

Overall, Assali seems to have had a very raw deal and perhaps with hindsight he regrets dabbling in technical timing devices that maybe could have been adapted to detonate time bombs, as described in a *Times* story on the 25th May 1986. This brief story described how the defendant was engaged in the designing and building of devices specially for use by terrorists to explode time bombs. It also mentioned how the former MI5 officer, Jeremy Wetherall, gave evidence to the St Albans Crown Court, but there is no mention of his affiliations with Zeus Security and that Assali had been supplying Zeus, via Wetherall, with devices specifically for use in British Intelligence operations. Had the jury known of this, and had they also known that in 1984 the firm (Zeus) with which Wether-all was associated had been involved in a massive unortho-dox spying mission against harmless anti-nuclear protesters, then my guess is that Assali would have been found not guilty.

The extent of Assali's relationship with Hamilton and Zeus was made clear on the 24th May 1983, when Assali was given a book entitled *Espionage, Terrorism and Subversion in an Industrial Society*. The author – Peter Hamilton – wrote a personal message on the inside pages:

> 'Hassan Assali, with the author's compliments and thanks for your friendship,
>
> Peter Hamilton 24th May 1983'

There are many questionable facets to the *Crown v. Assali* case that even to-day should be investigated by an independent enquiry. Many will be unable to fathom why a Ministry of Defence electronics expert, responsible for the design of a Rapier missile site protection system, presumably vetted to a reasonable standard by the Security Services, suddenly found himself accused of being a terrorist. Then there is the question of his association with Zeus Security, who he insists were engaged in work for British Intelligence.

CHAPTER 12

Media Espionage

After two decades of clandestine investigations for private and Government clients, I found it a welcome change of pace and style to work with the media. Apart from the frantic competitive spirit that exists in every Press office and, of course, the political pressure that sometimes leads to an occasional hiccup or accidental falsehood in a story, I found the work extremely rewarding. There is nothing more worthwhile than seeing the results of a difficult investigation in print, or on screen. It is a double bonus when one's efforts lead to the exposure of conspiracies or criminal activities.

Despite the occasionally 'showbusiness' aspect of media assignments, the majority of serious journalists, contrary to popular belief, make every effort to get it right. The average person would be amazed at just how much attention is paid to detail, and what legal ramifactions there are to a story finally hitting the screen or appearing in their daily newspaper. Unfortunately, from time to time different interpretations of events and circumstances are deemed by the courts to be untruthful, resulting in massive libel payouts.

Within the media, there are a number of capable investigative journalists who have created for themselves reputations as guardians of the public interest. Most of these Press detectives would make highly competent intelligence agents: in fact, it is true to say that some of them do indeed liaise with government agencies and have been known to operate as freelance spies for many years.

Although the basic method of uncovering newsworthy material is similar to detective work and intelligence gathering, the disciplines of investigative journalism mean that the media spy has to adopt a slightly different approach. Not only has he (or she) got to collect accurate evidence, it has to be presented in an entertaining, eye-catching manner that will attract the maximum number of readers or viewers. This makes compiling a final report in the form of a story a more difficult task than when it only has to be seen by one client. To make the job even tougher, there is often an element of personal risk to the operative. The attempted murder of ex-London Weekend Television (LWT) journalist Gerry Gable serves as a good example of what the more adventurous type of media investigator can expect when reporting on controversial subjects.

Gable, a reputable veteran journalist formerly with LWT, was going about his business of publishing the well-known anti-fascist magazine, *Searchlight*, when in 1986 he received an astonishing telephone call from a reporter working on the *Daily Mirror*. He was shocked to learn that the *Mirror* had received information from a security detective working for a private company that his employers were planning to abduct, question, and then eventually actually kill Gable. Being very capable and streetwise, Gerry set out to investigate the plot. His findings confirmed that his informant was speaking the truth. Mysterious individuals were seen watching his office, and a number of attempts were made to obtain his home address on various pretexts. Gable's next step was to speak with a friend in Special Branch who decided to arrange armed bodyguards to watch over him.

The circumstances eventually became public, and a very upmarket security investigation agency was identified. However, no action was taken against the suspects and Gable, legally prevented from publishing all of the available facts in the case, had to be content with his life and a general write-up of the plot in *Searchlight*.

With Mr Gable's kind permission, I have been able to review his story.

The police investigated astonishing allegations that a Tory MP had been implicated in the conspiracy to kidnap and murder Gable, in an attempt to block *Searchlight* investigations into extremism in the Conservative Party. They concluded that such a conspiracy had indeed been hatched. At this point, *Searchlight* was unable to name all of those involved, even though their identities were known to their reporter – and to the Prime Minister who had been officially briefed on the affair previously. As there had been no official action against the plotters, *Searchlight* decided to make public the basic facts of the case.

Gable wrote 'The MP involved linked up with an up-market private security firm reputed to carry out contract work on behalf of the intelligence services. Its board of directors includes two former senior military officers, one of whom was implicated more than 10 years ago in discussions in military circles about a possible coup d'etat against the then Labour Government of Harold Wilson.'

Between them, the MP and the company's major shareholder hatched the conspiracy to deal with Gerry Gable whom they called 'this evil man' and whom they believed to be largely responsible for *Searchlight*'s series of revelations of links between the Conservative Party and the extreme right. They were particularly anxious to establish how far other investigations had gone, especially any concerning the MP himself, who is known for his hardline right-wing views.

It was decided to contract out the work to a small, recently established security firm based in south of England but, in order to conceal the relationship between the two, no money for the deal was to change hands. Instead, the smaller firm was to be rewarded with lucrative security work in Africa and the

Middle East which the larger company would be able to arrange.

On 26th June 1984, a meeting was held at the larger firm's head office in London. Present were this company's main shareholder, a director of the smaller company, and one of his partners. At this and subsequent meetings, surveillance of Gerry Gable's movements was organised and arrangements for dealing with him were discussed.

Because of his initials, Gable was codenamed 'Horse' on company case papers. Another *Searchlight* company director was codenamed 'Rider'. The plan of campaign decided upon was to monitor Gable's movements at the *Searchlight* offices, and then to determine the best course of action.

He was to be abducted, first to a farm in Berkshire and then to a safe house in Dorset where he would be interrogated to discover what other investigations concerning the MP were in progress. Once the public interest in his disappearance had died down, he was to be killed and his body disposed of.

In the weeks that followed these meetings, certain arrangements were set in hand to carry out the plot. Gable said 'A female associate of his partner twice called personally at *Searchlight*'s office, enquiring about the availability of back numbers. She was keen to be allowed onto the premises, but in accordance with our normal security procedures was made to wait at the front entrance. A few days later, the director of the firm and his colleague were positively identified walking around outside our office premises, studying them closely. Then they carried out Companies House checks on Searchlight Publishing Ltd and tried, unsuccessfully, to find my home address by a trace on my car registration. Not long afterwards, they obtained my ex-directory home telephone number and, pretending to be a firm of builders, called me asking to be allowed to visit and quote for any building and decorating work I might want done. By this time, however, we were well aware of what was going on and I declined to give them my home address.'

Instead, Gable reported the matter to the police and it was investigated by Special Branch officers who concluded that the evidence was firm enough to offer him special police protection. From there the matter was referred upwards, and when the police enquiries were concluded a report was given to Mrs Thatcher at a meeting in Downing Street and to Lord Bridge, then Chairman of the Security Commission. What happened from that point on is unknown but what is certain is that the conspiracy against Gerry Gable was brought to an abrupt halt.

What is surprising is that charges were never brought against any of those involved. The police view appeared to be that, even it if was not a full-blooded conspiracy to murder, it was at the very least an attempt to intimidate Gerry Gable. However, the evidence, much of which *Searchlight* is still unable to publish, points to the more alarming conclusion that a plot was genuinely in progress to silence Mr Gable once and for all and to put a stop to *Searchlight*'s embarrassing disclosures about the Tory far right.

Among other things, Gerry Gable's *Searchlight* reports described in detail the activities of an English private detective using the name Lutz, a nickname adopted from Adolf Hitler's most trusted officer, Viktor Lutz.

Currently based in Wiltshire, 'Lutz' is now running his own detective agency, working for government departments and local business organisations. He is a firearms enthusiast and owns a number of weapons. As a member of a military gun club, he acts as a key holder to the army shooting range at Tidworth Barracks, and has a background in clandestine activity, including work in Whitehall. According to reports, he has convictions for firearms offences.

In the 1950s Lutz, the son of a British army officer, was a junior bandsman in the Royal Marines, but after a short period of service he was dropped as 'unsuitable'. During the 1950s he was a member of the Young Conservatives, and there have been suggestions that his family may also have had a connection with the Diplomatic Service. By 1961, Lutz became a member of the original British National Party, and eventually became a full member of their paramilitary wing, Spearhead. He went on to become the official security officer for the notorious Column 88, and as their intelligence officer was responsible for the planning of their clandestine operations.

He was later investigated for carrying a gun and was exposed by the *Sunday Telegraph* for his private spy missions. During this time, he was employed in Whitehall as a civil servant.

Gable's expert research shows that this country has seen several paramilitary bodies of a right wing nature created with the official or unofficial blessing of the Security Services since the Second World War. But a number of actual Nazi paramilitary groups have also been brought into existence, and although they received no formal blessing from Whitehall, there is no doubt that officials conveniently turned a blind eye.

The most notorious of these is Column 88. This group has existed, in one form or another, since the end of the war. It took its name from the Nazi Fifth Column operating in Vienna before Hitler took over Austria. 'One of its two key members is a former army officer living in the south. He was the organisation's military commander, and for many years ran training courses for would-be right wing guerrilla fighters. Among those who graduated from his training school were the British Movement's Leader Guard', Gable said.

In the early 1980s, the Major 'safe housed' three key West German Nazi terrorists. One escaped the police raid that netted his two comrades, and was later arrested in the Paris apartment of a Lebanese terrorist. While still a school master in the 1960s, the Major used his old Marine Commando contacts to gain access to their facilities on the south coast to train his Viking Youth Commandos. Despite several exposures in the Press, Parliament and on television, he has remained untouched by the law.

When other members of the original British National Party and Spearhead split away to form the National Socialist Movement, Lutz went with them as a security officer. When some months later Spearhead was exposed by an ex-paratrooper who had infiltrated the NSM and the leaders were jailed, Lutz disappeared from view. According to Gable 'Some time later he turned up working for the then Labour Government in the Ministry of Economic Affairs.'

Despite his far right connections, Lutz had no problem in getting a job in Whitehall. When anti-fascists and the *Sunday Telegraph* set up an investigation into his activities after hearing he was carrying a gun, it was the anti-fascists rather than Lutz who were raided, the purpose of the Special Branch visit being to deprive the investigators of any paperwork to do with their Lutz investigation. However, they failed to secure all the photocopies that had been made of Lutz's Spearhead membership card and other documents concerning his role as a courier between the British and illegal Austrian Nazi movements. 'After pressure was brought to bear on the authorities, Lutz was charged and convicted of possession of an illegal firearm and ammunition. In court he denied Nazi connections, but days later he was asked to leave the Civil Service without a fuss as his Nazi membership record had surfaced in both Whitehall and Fleet Street,' said Gable.

By the late 1960s, Lutz had taken on another rôle, this time as a regional director for a detective agency specialising in tracing and debt recovery. According to the firm's owners, when Lutz applied for the job he said he had worked for British Intelligence carrying out special operations on the Soviet-Finnish border, in the course of which he had been wounded. Lutz's mistress said that he once brought a very distinguished elderly man to their home and introduced him as his controller.

Intelligence experts in Europe viewed Lutz as a runner and odd job man for British Intelligence, and very much a hardline Nazi whom his masters appeared not only to tolerate, but to go to great lengths to protect. The same sources suggested that if Lutz had a bullet wound it could well have been obtained in a skirmish in the shooting war in the South Tyrol between the Italian police and Austrian Nazis.

A startling fact revealed by Lutz's employers at the detective agency was that his connections in the various branches of the Defence Ministry were so good that he could get traces carried out on serving military personnel within hours.

In 1970, Lutz played a key role in the formation of the National Democratic Party. Similar in its policies to the National Front, its job was to establish 'Forums' that would act as a bridge between the far right of the Conservative Party, the Monday Club, and the Anglo-Rhodesia Society. Others involved in the NDP included a Tory MP.

In Sussex, the Forum was used to bring certain people into the Monday Club, and in East Anglia it arranged secret meetings between Tory Party officials and leading Nazis, one of whom had been a member of Column 88 since the age of 19. When in the mid 1970s this man grew too big for his jackboots, with 17,500 members in the NF, a source of funding from contacts in the City and secret negotiations with a man closely linked at the time to intelligence circles and involved with others in the setting-up of Unison, Column 88 pulled the rug from under him and helped to create the National Party and the League of St George. The latter's role was to give the Column a semi-public face for the first time. Lutz and others turned up to guard League camps with shot guns, issuing security passes in Column 88's own name.

In 1975, questions about Column 88 were asked in the House of Commons. Labour Government spokesmen, misinformed by Special Branch, appeared to have no real knowledge of the organisation, and denied claims that it had infiltrated the Territorial Army.

A week later, the Press splashed an exposé revealing that Lutz, the convicted gunman, was a commissioned officer in the junior army and had set up joint training exercises for the

TA and Column 88. He was then living in Savernake Forest, Wiltshire, in a Crown property. This Press, parliamentary and television exposure led once again to his disappearance.

Gable's intensive investigation in 1980 revealed that Lutz resurfaced in Bedfordshire, running a detective agency with a partner. The London address of this business was the home of a leading light in the League of St George, who was honoured by SS veterans at an annual reunion in Belgium around that time. She is also believed to have had a Whitehall connection, working as a part-time translator for the Ministry of Defence.

In 1981, with Gerry Gable hot on his heels, Lutz attracted public attention when television's 'World in Action' revealed his involvement in a conspiracy with others to supply weapons to the far right. After the programme had been transmitted, the solicitor fled to the Irish Republic and Lutz, not surprisingly, dropped out of sight yet again. At this time he was using a former Young Conservative as his Column 88 courier. Mysteriously, the Leicester police did not seem at all keen to prosecute any of the Column 88 personnel.

Lutz resurfaced in Wiltshire during the summer of 1985, again working as a private detective. Much of his work was for the local farm owners' establishment and local authorities, his main job being to keep a peace convoy out of the area. He tried an unorthodox way of doing this – by offering guns and ammunition to members of the convoy, who refused after realising that Lutz was trying to set them up. The police eventually carried out one of the most violent attacks on women and children in this country seen this century, when they cornered the peace convoy in a field. As a result of TV and press coverage showing the police in a poor light, most of the charges against those arrested that day were dropped. No action was taken against Lutz.

Locals who knew Lutz said his home was full of weapons, and that he regularly attended military shooting competitions – not bad for a man with a firearms conviction and a long record of links with the Nazi terror network. As far as is known, he continues to run his Wiltshire detective agency and as for his other activities – that's anyone's guess.

Gerry Gable is not the only journalist to live in fear of his life. My own work for the BBC, London Weekend Television and Central TV also attracted the attention of hit men.

As a researcher working for LWT, I was commissioned to investigate British mercenaries alleged to be fighting for drug barons in Colombia. After successfully making contact with a number of notorious Hampshire and London 'mercs', we had reached a stage where we were going to film a meeting in North London secretly. However, due to an accidental leakage of information out of the production office, my true identity became known and the targets of investigation managed to obtain my home telephone number and the name and address of the presenter of the programme.

Late one afternoon, a few hours before the intended interview, I received a telephone call from a quietly spoken Scot who calmly informed me that should *anything* ever be transmitted about the mercenaries in Colombia and the drug barons, both the presenter and myself, plus our families, would be killed. He described what he knew about us both, where we lived and even our movements. When I informed him cleverly that I was tape recording the conversation, he just laughed it off and said 'Then you will be able to listen carefully to what I'm telling you.' There was no ranting or raving, just a simple calm statement telling me what we could expect if the programme was ever transmitted.

Journalists get threats frequently but not all are genuine, many are just nuisance calls intended to intimidate. Duncan Campbell and I received such calls for several years after exposing the criminal activities of a Windsor private eye who, we discovered, was paying serving police officers to steal official information from the Police National Computer. Even today we still receive the occasional call, which we suspect is from this man.

In my early days of media work, much of what I did was in association with or for the doyen of investigative journalists, Duncan Campbell, who is currently Chairman of *The New Statesman & Society*. Campbell, a Scot, went to school in Dundee, after which he graduated from Oxford University in 1974 with a degree in physics. He then went to work for a number of years in community Press, including the *Aberdeen People's Press*. In 1978 he was appointed to the editorial staff of the *New Statesman* and in 1980 received the Cobden Trust award for writing on civil liberties. He won this award for three years' investigative journalism writing articles that revealed widespread illegal 'phone tapping, secret bunkers prepared for Government Ministers in the event of a nuclear war, and foreign surveillance of West European Governments. Duncan has also written several books and has appeared regularly on television and radio.

In 1977 he was catapulted into the headlines because of the infamous ABC case, in which he was prosecuted for contravening the Official Secrets Act by interviewing a former junior intelligence soldier, also for being in possession of a number of items, including a photograph of the Post Office Tower. The ABC case arose out of investigations he and others had carried out into threats to civil liberties posed by Britain's intelligence bureaucracy. The case was unsuccessful for the Government, and only served to bring to light the many unacceptable activities of the Security and Intelligence Services.

Following the unsuccessful ABC trial, Campbell and his associates were targeted for special long term surveillance by the Security Services and Special Branch. For nearly a decade his telephone calls were monitored and his mail was intercepted, with particular attention being paid to an alleged network of sympathetic 'moles' thought by the authorities to be in numerous government departments, and who, it was assumed, rendered occasional assistance to him. For some inexplicable reason, spy masters had developed a paranoid suspicion that Campbell was engaged in espionage and subversion.

Duncan would often jokingly refer to himself as 'public enemy number one', meaning of course that he was a priority Intelligence target; little did he realise just how true that was. The official situation, as far as Duncan Campbell was concerned, was far more serious than he realised. The lengths to which government agents and Special Branch were prepared to go to get him exceeded most if not all of the rules of criminal legislation. And as for the ageing Maxwell-Fyfe directives about Security Service operations, I doubt very much if these guidelines were even considered when dealing with Duncan Campbell.

Indicative of the Government's attitude towards Security and Intelligence exposés by the media, the recently revised Official Secrets Act now prohibits writers and broadcasters from exposing most forms of official information, including that considered to be of public interest. Although it does not directly say so, this now means that criminal acts or conduct considered contrary to the public interest must remain a State secret. What better way to keep the skeletons locked in the cupboard while you go about the job of manipulating democracy to suit political requirements?

The types of assignment handled by media investigators vary from consumer fiddling to complicated criminal conspiracies, not forgetting, of course, antisocial activities of high profile individuals such as MPs and entertainers. Whatever the type of investigation, the journalist is more often than not involved in some kind of covert intelligence-style operation.

My own work, most of which has involved surveillance and undercover work, has included monitoring the activities of suspected Nazis and probing into the sleazy world of paedophiles. To be able to expose such people gave me more satisfaction than any of the work I carried out for the Security and Intelligence Services. One rewarding undercover operation, carried out for the BBC's 'Secret Society' programme, resulted in the arrest and conviction of several police officers and private detectives who were discovered poaching official information from the Police National Computer (PNC).

The PNC is based in Hendon, North London, and holds details of criminal records on nearly five million people. It was set up in 1969 and became operational in 1974. Linked via hundreds of terminals to police stations throughout Britain, it is described as the largest police intelligence system in Europe.

Despite being cloaked in secrecy, there is considerable evidence that PNC data is being leaked to private detectives and security officers. This was certainly the case when a BBC television programme decided to launch their own top secret investigation into the activities of Britain's private spies.

In early 1986, BBC Producer Brian Barr and Director Dennis Cosgrove felt that it would be in the public interest to investigate the activities of a Basingstoke gumshoe, Stephen Bartlett, who was suspected of attempting to sell his services as a provider of official information protected under the Official Secrets Act. Barr and Cosgrove decided that the BBC investigation would be conducted as part of the controversial 'Secret Society' series. They had no idea at the time that the series would culminate in Special Branch raids on BBC offices and the private homes of journalists working on the project.

Because of my intimate knowledge of the detective and security profession, the BBC decided to employ me as a researcher on the programme. I was teamed up with Duncan Campbell of the *New Statesman* and together we set out to infiltrate a group of private detectives and police officers suspected of dealing in the sale of official information.

By now, Campbell and I were quite an adept double act when working covertly on assignments of this nature. Carefully worked-out cover stories were prepared and Campbell, with the co-operation of the BBC, adopted the *nom de plume* 'Duncan Sinclair,' working for the firm McNair

Matthew Sinclair operating from 21 Havelock Street, Glasgow. Our plan of action included the installation of a special telephone by the BBC to present a convincing front to the suspect, Bartlett. Suitable business cards and letterheads provided the final touch to a foolproof plan.

With the scene set, Bartlett was led to believe that I was a private eye in the market for official information. And on 8th April 1986 I responded to his offer illegally to acquire and sell government data protected under the Official Secrets Act. In a secretly tape recorded discussion, Bartlett gave me his sales pitch. He described how he was able to provide most kinds of official information. The taped conversation revealed the quality of service:

> Murray: 'What kind of information are you specialising in?'
>
> Bartlett: 'Well, I don't specialise, you know, if you wanted somebody traced, then they can be traced, CROs, car registration numbers.'
>
> Murray: 'That's fantastic, so if I give you a car index number, you could trace it for me.'
>
> Bartlett: 'Yes, no problem.'
>
> Murray: 'And what about someone's criminal record?'
>
> Bartlett: 'That's no problem at all.'

He then continued by describing his background and discussing his previous employers, Nationwide Investigations.

At one stage, I introduced into the conversation the subject of the assassination of the Seychelles dissident Gerard Hoareau and, much to my surprise, Bartlett confirmed to me that at one time he had actually been employed by the firm involved in surveillance of the Seychelles exiles in London.

When asked if there was any truth in the rumour that a private detective had been involved in the assassination, Bartlett named an individual he alleged had been responsible for setting up the 'hit'.

Questioned about the availability of other kinds of official information, Bartlett indicated that this was easy for him:

> Murray: 'OK, you mentioned CROs and car checks. What about DHSS information?'
>
> Bartlett: 'Yes, yes, that's no problem at all.'

I then asked about the possibility of penetrating Ministry of Defence records. Bartlett explained difficulties involved, but confirmed that he could acquire such information, despite the fact it would be 'a bit dodgy.'

He went on to describe his methods of operation, and said that he had a contact in the police force who was carrying out about twenty CROs a week. When asked how long it would take to produce MOD information, Barlett said 'At the moment, about two days.' He went on to brag that he had half the Basingstoke police force working for him.

In accordance with the 'Secret Society' plan of action, I responded in such a way that Bartlett thought that he would indeed eventually be asked to acquire information supposedly protected by the Official Secrets Act.

In a series of further conversations conducted between April and June 1986, Bartlett's trust was won and eventually a meeting was arranged between him, myself and Duncan Campbell who played the rôle of company director Duncan Sinclair from the Scottish firm McNair Matthew Sinclair. It was to take place at the Ladbroke Motel, Aldermaston, near Basingstoke. The object of this rendezvous was to test Bartlett's method of operation, and in particular to set a chain of events in motion that would lead to the identification of serving government officials who might be conspiring with him to break the law.

At the meeting, Campbell and I were fitted with radio microphones, and a motor vehicle was strategically placed in the hotel car park. BBC television cameras installed in an upstairs bedroom were trained on this vehicle. From noon, Campbell played the part of the Scottish company director urgently seeking criminal record checks on a number of people.

Names were passed to Bartlett, and he was filmed accepting money on account of services to be rendered. Film and sound recordings were made of all the events.

My part in all this was to pose as a corrupt private investigator, anxious to acquire a source of official information on behalf of my client – Campbell alias 'Sinclair.' During the early stages of the operation, Campbell and I had no idea the evidence we were about to collect would result in a major Official Secrets trial at the Winchester Crown Court.

Further meetings and telephone conversations were held with Bartlett over a period of weeks. Eventually the evidence, which was all collected by clandestine tape recording and filming, was so strong the BBC decided to hand over details of the investigation formally to the Hampshire Constabulary. In the final stages of the investigation, when he was actually providing information from the police computer, Bartlett began identifying the whereabouts and identities of his police contacts. It also became apparent that he was using the services of other private detectives who had access to official records.

On receipt of the BBC dossier, a special police unit was set up to investigate the affair. Headed by Detective Chief Superintendent Mandry, ably assisted by Detective Sergeant (now Inspector) Rushton, the unit carried out a most impressive investigation that took them the length and breadth of the United Kingdom, interviewing serving police officers and numerous private detectives.

At one stage, a firm of London detectives was raided by undercover police officers who had the patience to stick together shredded documents which turned out to be valuable evidence. All in all, the private detective and security industry was now in turmoil. Detectives all over the country were in fear of a visit from the police, so much so, I heard on the grapevine, that a number of worried suspects were desperately trying to discredit me in the hope they could neutralise the evidence I would be presenting for the prosecution. At one stage during 1987, a message was passed to me indicating that should I decide to give evidence I would be 'sorted out'.

Eventually the police enquiry concluded, with Official Secrets and conspiracy charges being preferred against serving police officers and a number of private detectives.

The defendants, two police officers and five private detectives, including Stephen Bartlett, all pleaded not guilty to charges of conspiring to obtain information contrary to the Official Secrets Act. Two defendants were also charged under the Prevention of Corruption Act.

The trial began in January 1989, and lasted for one month at the Winchester Crown Court. The jury heard how this case was the 'tip of an iceberg', and how private detectives from London, Essex, and Wolverhampton had milked official data from the Police National Computer for years prior to 1986, long before the BBC had enlisted the services of myself and Duncan Campbell to investigate. Two of the defendants turned out to be employed by Nationwide Investigations of Balham, London, and another detective had established such longstanding and close contact with a serving police officer that their relationship was described in Court as 'blatant corruption.'

As expected, I attended Court for the prosecution and, despite severe cross examination by five barristers, I was able to satisfy the jury of the authenticity of the evidence collected by myself and Duncan Campbell. The trial ended in guilty convictions, but surprisingly the only prison sentences were suspended ones.

The Judge obviously considered that breaches of the Official Secrets Act and corruption by serving government officials were not serious enough offences to warrant incarceration.

The Winchester trial highlighted the activities of Britain's private espionage agents, and just how easily they are able to penetrate the official files of this country. It also showed how private detectives with foreign intelligence or terrorist connections could potentially wreak untold damage on the security of this nation. The case also illuminated serious operational flaws in the Police National Computer.

In researching this book, I collected much evidence that, when examined overall, reveals a massive abuse of the Police National Computer and other official information sources. According to Detective Chief Superintendent Mandry of Hampshire Constabulary, it is impossible to audit all computer interrogations. The alternative would be to make access so tight that it would become almost valueless because it would not be possible to provide instant response. This is obviously true: however, it goes without saying that if existing legislation was altered to control the activities of private spies, this would inhibit those at present tempted into corruption and breaches of the Official Secrets Act. Such deterrence would be especially effective if stiff penalties of imprisonment and disbarment from practice became part of a regulatory system.

On 23rd October 1981, Duncan Campbell submitted a sworn statement to the Thames Valley police. This document described a *New Statesman* investigation into the activities of a former Thames Valley police officer-turned-private-detective, working from a small sleazy office in Windsor. The events leading to Campbell's statement involved another protracted undercover operation carried out by the Murray-Campbell duo. This investigation illustrated the ease with which private eyes were able to corrupt serving police officers who were willing to impart official data.

The sequence of events started in June 1981, when it came to my notice that a Windsor private detective was using serving police officers to acquire illegally Police National Computer information. I also discovered that he was posing variously as a Post Office and Inland Revenue official, also as a police officer.

I considered this man's conduct quite illegal, as well as unethical and contrary to the public interests: I therefore set out to expose him.

After deciding against informing the Thames Valley Police

(because there was a strong possibility that officers from that force were involved) I decided to start a media investigation with my colleague Duncan Campbell. Following an initial briefing, it was agreed that a dummy company would be set up, and that I would pose as a private detective with a client in the market for official information. Campbell assumed a false identity and London address, and we set out to expose the culprit. Over a number of weeks, we cultivated a relationship with the suspect, and the identities of his police contacts were gradually established. These officers were based at a number of stations in the Thames Valley area, and they were all former colleagues of the Windsor detective.

Eventually, we reached a point where a test had to be carried out to confirm beyond any shadow of doubt that access to official records was possible. From the many tape recordings that had been made by myself and Campbell, it appeared that Special Branch records were also being penetrated.

A grand finale was arranged at the Skyline Hotel, Heathrow, where it was planned that transactions between Campbell and the culprit would be taped, and photographed by hidden cameramen.

All went according to plan and, in the presence of an official from the Thames Valley Police Authority, reports containing confidential information from government and criminal records departments were handed over in exchange for money. At the conclusion of the transaction, the Windsor private eye was informed of the true identity of those present, and it was explained that his activities had been monitored for a number of weeks. When asked if he had anything to say, he was too shocked to respond.

Extracts from a tape recorded conversation of 20th October 1982 showed what easy access this man had to the PNC:

> Private eye: 'Well, a red Ford Cortina turned up. We did a check on it right away and it came out in another guy's name.'
>
> Murray: 'Say that again.'

Private eye: 'It came out in another guy's name.'

Murray: 'I'm sorry, I'm not quite with it, came out of what?'

Private eye: 'The registration number for that vehicle came out as being owned by a man who lives at that address.'

Murray: 'How the hell can you tell that at that time of night?'

Private eye: 'Well, the Police Computer.'

Murray: 'Ah, you did one of those.'

Private eye: 'Yes.'

The conversation also revealed how the suspect was able to acquire copies of actual police files from a CID contact. Names of officers were also mentioned, and Special Branch was referred to, as well as many other private detectives.

Despite the arrest, followed by an intensive police investigation, no criminal charges were ever preferred against any of the culprits, even though it transpired serving police officers were actually working for the detective agency and had received substantial payments by cheque in exchange for official information.

These transactions were even documented in the agency's books, and there was plenty of evidence of corruption, conspiracy, and breaches of the Official Secrets Act.

On 25th February 1982, a letter from the Director of Public Prosecutions to Campbell at the *New Statesman* made it quite clear that the matter would not be pursued. The final paragraph of this communication reads: 'I have carefully considered the evidence and have reached the conclusion that the public interest does not require the institution of criminal proceedings under Section 2 of the Official Secrets Act 1911.'

Although frustrated, Campbell and I were pleased to hear that Thames Valley officers had resigned and/or been disciplined. It seemed this was to be the end of the matter. However, not so. Despite the fact that over ten years have elapsed since the conclusion of this case, we have received a stream of abusive and threatening telephone calls, some of which have been tape recorded, and the culprit is easily identifiable as the Windsor private detective. Complaints have been lodged with the appropriate authorities, but it would appear his police contacts must still be very strong as no action has been taken in spite of the overwhelming evidence confirming his identity.

CHAPTER 13

Stealing Official Data

Evidence collected during research for this book confirms beyond any shadow of doubt that *all* areas of government are at risk from pilfering private spies. Virtually every official department has been penetrated. Scarcely any have escaped the attentions of these greedy men and women who, on occasion, have passed illegally acquired confidential information to prestigious professional clients including High Street banks and finance houses, solicitors, public companies, industrial organisations, private individuals and foreign embassies. Even foreign intelligence agencies, during the Cold War period which has only recently ended, had access to this kind of information.

In a number of cases, private detective agencies have been found to be employing convicted criminals, with some detectives themselves having criminal records and enjoying long term relationships with organised crime. The jigsaw that has been pieced together by this book reveals an alarming picture of breaches of the law by clients and spies alike. Their conduct can only be described as illegal and completely contrary to the public interest.

I can do no better than give some examples of this data theft:

On 24th November 1983 I spoke with a well known brewery

using the services of a Surrey private detective. A representative of the brewery confirmed the identity of the detective, and also that he was providing a personal 'cloak and dagger' service to the managing director. This involved the illegal acquisition of information from the Police National Computer: the fees charged for the service were said to be expensive.

On 8th April 1982, in a taped conversation with another established private investigator, it was explained to me how a professional organisation was vetting its members by using the services of a Scotland Yard officer-turned-private detective. I have established that this detective is a former policeman from the Yard's Robbery Squad who has been using the services of his old police colleagues for years. During this unofficial liaison, vast amounts of money have changed hands, including payments made to Scotland Yard's own staff. Complaints to Scotland Yard and the Home Office have been ignored.

On 17th February 1985, in a taped conversation with a Warwickshire private investigator, I was informed that the agency was able to obtain criminal record information from the PNC, also Ministry of Defence information about former and currently serving members of the armed forces. The head of the agency is a convicted felon and has been jailed for industrial espionage offences.

On 27th February 1985, I approached covertly a major cellular telephone supplier in London. A Sales Director for the firm confirmed that his company had access to criminal records via a Midlands private detective who charged £60 per check.

On 9th April 1983, in another tape recorded conversation with Norfolk detective Barrie Peachman (now deceased), I was informed that a former Scotland Yard detective-turned-private-investigator was a Director of the IPI and that his sole job was checking out potential applicants to this organisation via . . . the Police National Computer. I have confirmed that this man, based in Surrey, has received substantial payments for this service.

On July 31st 1981, also on 22nd August 1985, I spoke with officers of a nationwide industrial vetting organisation, the Economic League. They admitted they were able to provide details of criminal records and other sensitive political information that could only be obtained from Special Branch or Intelligence databanks. The firm also admitted using the services of private detectives – I have already mentioned that Peter Hamilton of Zeus Security was used by the League.

On 17th December 1970, a Birmingham-based private detective agency submitted a report to clients, extracts from which read as follows:

'We are checking with our Birmingham CID contacts to see if they have any records. Our contact is on leave at the moment and will not be back on duty until next Tuesday. We will telephone you with the result of the enquiry.'

On 1st January 1971 the same agency communicated again with their client:

'We have now heard from our contact in the Birmingham CID, who informs us that the above-mentioned has a criminal record for fraud and larceny.'

On 29th January 1971 the same agency again wrote to a client:

'The only information we can obtain from our CID contact is that the case was heard in 1968.'

On 14th March 1984, a private detective agency on the Isle of Wight submitted a report to a nationally known plc finance organisation. Extracts from this report reveal access to DHSS records, as follows:

'I had hoped that unemployment records may have revealed something, but my source has been unable to locate a claim in his name.'

On 25th July 1983 a Portsmouth detective agency submitted a report referring to DHSS information to a firm of solicitors:

'Thereafter we made enquiries of a confidential source and were able to learn that the subject had been claiming Social Security until March 1983, when he gained employment with the Co-Operative butchery department in Havant', it read.

On 21st January 1987 I tape recorded a conversation with a private detective based in the Channel Islands. This investigator admitted to being able to provide criminal record information.

On 9th March 1984 another Channel Islands detective agency provided a report to a Surrey-based client (a firm of detectives). Contained in this report were confidential details of registered owners of motor vehicles that could only have been obtained from the PNC.

On 17th October 1984 a Surrey-based detective agency reported to a solicitor client in Kingston-upon-Thames. In this report were the identities of Derbyshire police officers said to be assisting the private spy agency on a specific case.

On 16th December 1983 a detective agency in Surrey reported to a firm of solicitors in Oxford. This report contained details of confidential ex-directory telephone numbers. The same agency communicated, on a later date, with another member of the detective profession and on this occasion reference was made to DHSS information.

On 25th July 1983 a Hampshire detective agency reported to a firm of solicitors, referring to DHSS information.

On 10th December 1970 a Surrey-based private investigator, now a well-known member of the profession, reported confidential car registration details to a client. Similar information was again passed on subsequent occasions.

In 1988 a former Royal Air Force Security and Intelligence officer, operating a private security firm in Southampton, attempted to persuade a Surrey private eye to acquire political and Special Branch information from New Scotland Yard.

This catalogue of examples is just (as mentioned at the Winchester Crown Court trial) 'the tip of the iceberg'. This unofficial access extends to the records of Special Branch, MI5, MI6, the DHSS, CRO, MOD, Inland Revenue, banks and Customs & Excise. Virtually every government department has been at risk for at least three decades. The truth, if ever revealed, would embarrass many very senior officials – politicians as well as civil servants – so I doubt very much if corrective action will ever be taken.

The situation is serious and not many members of the detective and security industry are willing to come forward and expose the secrets of their profession. Even the honest firms and individuals prefer to go quietly about their own business, and choose to ignore the stink of corruption that permeates the industry. However, a number of professional detectives of principle, who frown on the activities of the unscrupulous practitioners, have spoken out.

Dennis Byrne, a director in the detective agency Byrne Gaskill, previously of Kingston-upon-Thames, Surrey, has expert personal knowledge of what goes on in the industry. Most of his adult life has been spent in the police or private detective and security industry. As a result he has an intimate knowledge of methods used by Britain's spies. In a series of interviews, Byrne revealed how he had actually seen confidential Scotland Yard files in the possession of civilian private eyes. 'I was a member of the Board of Governors of the IPI responsible for the control of the day to day business of the Institute. What I witnessed concerned me, but I could do nothing about it', said Byrne. He continued 'I was present at one board meeting when I saw an actual Scotland Yard criminal intelligence file in the possession of unauthorised private investigators. The information in this file was being used by a number of directors involved in the running of this organisation. I became so concerned, I eventually resigned'.

Byrne described the availability of official data from official records. 'It's there for the taking. CRO, Inland Revenue – private eyes can easily get hold of anything through one of their contacts.'

Another witness, Leslie Prince, went on record for Mark Hollingsworth and Richard Norton-Taylor, authors of *Blacklist*, the inside story of political vetting. Prince served in the West Midlands police for thirty years, and on retirement had reached a senior rank. On discharge from the service he entered private practice, and held several prestigious investigatory and security posts. Prince was quite explicit when he said 'Employers taking on ex-police officers as their security staff have known that he or she will in all probability have some form of access to criminal records. Although such checks are rarely admitted, the practice has existed for years, and in many companies it has been an integral part of security procedure. These checks were usually made under the old pals act, and if any reward was received by the police officer it was nothing more than liquid refreshment. This, of course, is not so in every case, and there have been instances of police officers accepting quite lucrative rewards for providing information.'

Byrne also claims that information from Special Branch records has been on sale amongst private investigatory firms in the United Kingdom. 'If private investigators have the right contacts, it is there for them to take', he said.

Depending on what is required, there are a number of different ways to harvest sensitive official information. Whatever method is used, it must involve the services of a current serving government official such as a police officer, tax inspector, or whoever. By far the best method is to use a senior police officer of detective status. The ultimate contact is a Special Branch operative who can access almost any other government department, including the Ministry of Defence, Inland Revenue, and even the Security Services and armed forces. Some private detectives have close relationships with military or other armed forces security units, and this can also be used to advantage.

The contact procedure is quite straightforward. The client approaches the spy, who in turn contacts his own source which may involve a direct link with an official or alternatively a cut-out in the form of another private spook who actually has the personal contact. The information is then acquired normally by accessing a computer and/or signing out a file. It is then passed on to the external contact, who in turn passes it down the line to the client. Photocopies of official documents or printouts are frequently provided. Depending on whether or not money changes hands, there could well be a serious offence of corruption. In most cases, there is usually a breach of the Official Secrets Act; further offences of conspiracy are also usually committed in the process.

Perpetrators of these offences very rarely confess. Most of them plead not guilty and deny the offences, so it has been very difficult to persuade any member of the spy industry to acknowledge they have engaged in such skulduggery. However, one Cardiff-based private detective revealed 'a lot of private investigators are ex-coppers, so it's natural that we have got links with the Force. Look, if you're a copper you can get things done real quick, get information and so on. What would take me a week to get will take a bloke on the Force a couple of hours. You've got the computer, you've got records and contacts, it's all dead easy if you're a copper.'

This detective, now running his own vetting agency, is a former policeman with ten years' service. He admitted carrying out police computer checks and vetting enquiries involving political information.

During the final stages of research for this book, I discovered another firm of detectives breaking the law. This organisation readily agreed to obtain secret government information. I also uncovered a number of additional cases that complete a jigsaw, revealing corruption and pernicious breaches of security going back over three decades.

In 1988 a Police Constable, Robert Green, boosted his wages by supplying a private investigator, Ian McLaren, with the names and addresses of keepers of motor vehicles, extracted from the police computer. Constable Green of the Essex Police Headquarters, Chelmsford, also carried on business as a private enquiry agent while a serving police officer; Scantell Services was the trade name he used to make extra money during his off-duty hours. Both men were eventually convicted.

An extremely grave case surfaced in 1988, when a senior Scotland Yard detective and a private detective were arrested by Scotland Yard's Anti-Corruption Squad. The top Yard 'tec' was said to have been involved in payments of huge sums of money by a well known private company, in exchange for illegal use of the Police National Computer. The Anti-Fraud Squad were also looking into allegations that villains under police surveillance were being tipped off.

It was claimed that a multinational City conglomerate had been using the PNC to gather information about commercial rivals. Police believed that at one stage more than two hundred checks a month had been run through the computer on the company's behalf. The suspects were arrested after several weeks' surveillance by Special Branch officers.

The officer was described as a former member of the Flying Squad, with over twenty years' service in the Metropolitan Police, and one-time head of a secret unit responsible for collecting intelligence and keeping watch on major criminals. The private eye from South East London was described as working for prestigious City organisations with links to the Royal family. A senior detective said 'If the allegations are true, it means there has been a major breach of security.'

During the early 1980s, Duncan Campbell exposed a private security company in Berkshire (employed to protect a VIP) which had carried out over one hundred illegal criminal and political checks via a serving officer in the Thames Valley Police Force.

The personal opinion of a senior official from a major police force, who spoke off the record to me, is that 'The private detective industry is nothing more than a private espionage network, earning its members vast amounts of money. It's just very sad that serving policemen and other officials cannot act in an ethical and responsible manner when dealing with these people. Regulation and control must be considered by the Home Office.'

With the network of corruption linking civil servants and

private detectives still growing, many people, in and out of Government, are becoming very concerned. The National Council for Civil Liberties expressed concern at the wide use of the police computer by unauthorised individuals and private organisations on the grounds that it could unfairly jeopardise people seeking employment. 'We have a number of cases where convictions sent out by the PNC were totally wrong', Ms Madelaine Colvin, legal officer, said.

Labour Home Affairs spokesman Mr Barry Sheerman MP said 'I am amazed at the laxity which surrounds access to the PNC.' Mr Alex Carlisle QC, Secretary of the all-party Barristers Group, said 'This demonstrates a clear case for putting the PNC under the control of someone like the data protection Registrar, who could exercise quasi-judicial authority to determine whether an enquiry should be made of the computer.'

There are many ways to control this high-tech pilfering by unauthorised persons. The most effective would be to declare any breach of regulations a major offence, punishable by long terms of imprisonment. Also, strict control of the private detective profession with exclusion from practice as well as heavy fines and/or long terms of imprisonment as punishments for offenders would deter potential data thieves.

On 2nd January 1985, Dennis Byrne, former President of the Institute of Professional Investigators, became so concerned at the extent of unofficial access to government records that he wrote to Peter Heims, Public Relations Officer and Investigations Committee Chairman for the Institute. Byrne's concern was provoked by overwhelming evidence indicating that the IPI had access to criminal records information. He wrote:

'One point I am very concerned about, there is no record of your statement that you as Committee Chairman had instigated an official police enquiry concerning a member of IPI and a serving police officer in respect of misuse of the Police National Computer.'

Three weeks after Dennis Byrne's complaint (which appeared to be ignored) another former IPI Board member made a twenty-six-page statement to Detective Chief Inspector August and Detective Sergeant Inch of New Scotland Yard. On 28th January 1985 this complainant accused a number of British private detectives of serious criminal offences, including breaches of the Official Secrets Act – and murder. Pages thirteen and fourteen of this statement describe how secret intelligence operations had been conducted by private detectives for the Security Service. Particular reference was made to the nuclear industry and the death of anti-nuclear protester Hilda Murrell. To date no action has been taken, and the purchasing of secret information is still very much a feature of the private detective business.

On the 1st September 1992, an example of the most blatant abuse of a serving police officer's position of trust surfaced, quite by accident, when I enlisted the services of a former female CID officer now operating her own detective agency in Yorkshire.

Requiring some general background research for this book, I enlisted the services of Mrs J E, who, it turned out, was married to a serving CID detective. Her brief was simple, and certainly did not require official inside information. However, her final report referred to checks that had been carried out by her husband with the local Police Collator (Intelligence Officer), the result being that she had acquired specific information from this source which she included in her report. She also got another police officer to carry out some enquiries on her behalf, and even had the audacity to refer to him by description in her report, and on an invoice.

Throughout my brief relationship with this woman, I only ever spoke with her on one occasion. Her husband, the serving CID officer, seemed to have control of the business, and in a number of taped conversations gave me the impression (rightly or wrongly) that he was using his official position for private enterprise purposes. As I've shown, he's certainly not the only one.

Epilogue

Since 1973, there have been several attempts to introduce some form of official regulation of the private spy industry. However, despite the manifest need for such legislation, all such attempts have failed. One of the most difficult problems for those who might draft the laws concerned is just how to describe Britain's 'dogs of law', and in particular just what kind of professions should be considered subject to the intended legislation.

In August 1988, the *Police Review* considered the general conduct of the profession so questionable that it decided to run a series of articles. The report described dealing with Britain's private police as being very much like encountering the most dangerous jellyfish in the world – the Portuguese Man-of-War. It read in part:

> 'It's too nebulous to define its shape or tentacles exactly, but if you touch it . . . by gosh, you certainly know it's there! For a start, nobody knows the precise size, and there is considerable disagreement over what it includes. Most observers accept that detectives, general security and guarding firms, alarm-installing, and cash-in-transit carriers, are all part of the trade.
>
> 'Others insist that locksmiths, safe manufacturers, producers of electronic surveillance equipment, as well as in-house security staff, should also be included.'

If one is to accept all of these occupations as being part of the overall scene then, allowing for the numerous specialist firms supplying undercover agents and bodyguards, plus the vetting organisations, and of course the *corps élite*, mercenaries, the total number of people employed in this controversial business would exceed the number of official serving police officers. The Managerial Administrative Technical and Supervisory Association (MATSA) has 30,000 members working in the security field, and estimates that there are more than 10,000 working in the industry which has a turnover of around two billion pounds. Other estimates run as high as 250,000 employees, which is twice the size of the combined police forces of England and Wales.

The MATSA estimate does not take into account all the private investigators quietly going about their clandestine business all over the country and also excludes all military types involved in mercenary and intelligence operations.

There are a number of private 'federations' whose members are technically subject to codes of practice that are set down, and in the event that a member is in breach of the relevant code he can be expelled. However, this does not prevent an offender from continuing to practise their trade. In fact, many clients are totally unaware of the existence of these private trade associations, and are willing to employ detectives or security men simply on the strength of the quality of the service they provide.

The failed attempts on the rocky parliamentary road to legislation are as follows:

1973 Norman Fowler MP suggested a security industry licensing bill

1973 Michael Fidler MP also instigated a doomed attempt at statutory control

1976 Bruce George MP failed to make progress with recommendations to introduce statutory control of the industry

1981 Lord Willis attempted to introduce a security

officers' control bill, but after experiencing extreme pro-
crastination by the Government of the day, decided to
give up

1984–89 The Institute of Private Investigators (IPI)
launched an entirely new approach to the matter of controlling Britain's private spooks and security operators.
Their approach was to introduce a Private Member's Bill
into Parliament which, if accepted, would have ratified
self-regulation, supported by official legislation over the
whole of the industry.

Former IPI President Dennis Byrne said of this Bill 'It
would be like the inmates being in charge of the asylum. If
the profession is ever granted statutory powers to look
after its own affairs there will be an explosion of skulduggery and illegality on a most horrific scale.'

Whilst Mr Byrne's opinions may sound rather extreme, an
examination of recent announcements by the Government of
their intentions to privatise some official departments (including prisons) helps one to appreciate just how easy it is for an
honourable and knowledgeable member of the profession to
become so concerned.

The numerous approaches to Government have all been
blocked by the Home Office insisting on self-regulation which,
considering some of the characters involved and how they go
about their dirty business, could be quite disastrous. One
simple way to resolve the problem could be a licensing system
operated by either the Office of Fair Trading or a special unit
created to act as a watchdog over the industry. Firms and
individuals would have to satisfy basic requirements for the
issue of the licence and, in the event of any criminal offence
on breach of ethics, magistrates could be empowered to withdraw the practitioner's licence. This system is in operation
very successfully in the United States, and the private spook
industry there is tightly controlled.

Annual subscriptions from all practising members of the
security and detective industry would finance the running of
such a regulatory body. And if stiff penalties were applied

against offences such as bugging, telephone tapping and other criminal acts that have proliferated over the years, the unethical and criminally minded might at least try to change their ways.

The Institute of Professional Investigators (IPI), as already mentioned, is a very unusual organisation in that, despite being a private body, its membership is not limited to *private* investigators. In fact, according to a past register, police, armed forces and other government officials with links to the security and intelligence services share membership of the IPI with their private-sector brethren. According to former IPI President Dennis Byrne, who resigned after becoming dissatisfied with the conduct of IPI officials, this kind of joint membership is most unhealthy. When asked if it was correct and proper he said: 'Categorically NO! Undue familiarity among such people, particularly on a social scene, gives a scenario for relationships that undermine service regulations and possible status. One can foresee a possible situation of having to serve two masters, not only to the detriment of his or her employer but to the public at large.'

The Association of British Investigators (ABI) is perhaps the best established trade association of the private detective industry. This organisation contributes, albeit in a small way, to the self-regulation of the profession by monitoring its own five hundred or so members, scattered all over the world. The ABI has no legislative teeth, and sadly the Government will not respond to the many approaches made to it by them. Most members of the ABI – which is keen to see statutory legislation introduced – are considered reputable, and this appears to be the case. Only occasionally do members commit breaches of the Association's guidelines, and then they are dealt with accordingly.

Unfortunately, there are hundreds of non-ABI members operating in England free from even the token restraint that membership entails and left to adopt their own codes of ethics. This has resulted in certain individuals and firms conducting their business activities in a highly questionable and, at times, illegal manner. It must be said that not all non-Association members are of this calibre.

According to current legislation, *anyone* can set up in practice as a private detective or security operative, and no qualifications or *ab initio* training are required. Even a convicted felon can walk out of prison to-day and set himself up in the business of tapping phones, bugging offices and all manner of other 'secret intelligence' operations for any client who is willing to pay for his services. In 1986, TV personality Judith Chalmers and her family found themselves victims of a detective agency controlled by such a criminal who had previous convictions for a number of serious offences, including illegal possession of a firearm.

According to newspaper reports, the agency, headed by Trevor Witherley, a private eye operating out of an office housed above a doctor's surgery in Banstead Road, Purley, Surrey, had been approached by Susan Hughes, wife of Peter Hughes, editor of the Judith Chalmers travel programme 'Wish You Were Here', to keep watch on Miss Chalmers and Mr Hughes. In his report, Witherley alleged that the couple had a secret love nest in Regents Park, and that they had been observed exchanging a loving kiss outside the home of Miss Chalmers in Highgate, North London. On paper the evidence appeared convincing: however, an in-depth examination of the investigation carried out by this agency told a depressingly different story.

Apart from having no formal training or qualifications in the trade, middle-aged Trevor Witherley had enjoyed a life of crime stretching back to the early 1960s. At the age of fifteen he was given two years' probation for housebreaking and theft.

In 1972 he went to prison after appearing at Kingston Crown Court on a total of twenty-two charges, with a further thirty-one offences which he asked to be taken into consideration; there were thirteen charges to do with obtaining stolen property by deception, one of theft of cheques, and two of forging cheques. There was also one charge of illegal possession of a firearm. Witherley was sentenced to three years and seven months' imprisonment, and actually served two years and three months of the sentence.

In 1977 he again ended up in prison, sentenced to twenty-one months for criminal deception. This was reinforced with a further six months, to run concurrently, for theft of cash. As well as his lack of investigatory qualifications, Witherley had a remarkable knack of employing individuals even less well qualified than himself.

Nicholas Godden, a sixteen-year old school leaver, was employed by Witherley to tail Miss Chalmers to a rendez-vous with her boss. Godden, who later admitted to never having done this kind of work before, reported that he saw the couple kissing, but that as far as he was concerned the whole matter was a joke and that in his opinion the kiss did not indicate a love affair, seeming more like the kiss of close friends.

Godden admitted that, whilst he was tailing the couple, he lost them on four occasions. This inability to carry out a fairly straightforward mobile surveillance was not the only problem this schoolboy sleuth had.

In addition to his spying activities, Witherley engaged in a secondary occupation – that of junk dealer. From a pitch directly opposite his office in Purley he was found dealing in bric-a-brac and secondhand furniture! At weekends, he would swop his gumshoe raincoat for tee shirt and jeans to set up his business outside a boarded-up shop where he displayed a motley collection of antiques and furniture.

Not content with just compiling a fictitious report, Witherley then released what purported to be a confidential document to a national newspaper which ran the story at a time Miss Chalmers was out of the country on a television assignment.

*

Another private spy, hired to kill his client's wife, was unfortunately successful in carrying out his assignment. The 'hit', which took place in Bristol, was rather gruesome in that the sleazy operative hacked his victim to death with an axe. His fee for this assignment was £10,000. He is now serving life imprisonment.

The role was reversed in the case of private investigator Daniel Morgan. Instead of being the hunter, he became the victim when he was brutally murdered in the car park of a public house in London. Left to die with an axe embedded in his head, Morgan took many secrets to his grave. An alleged hit man is said to have carried out the killing. A Scotland Yard investigation resulted in serving police officers being questioned, and there was much speculation about Morgan's relationships with serving Yard officers. Arrests were eventually made, but to date no trial has been announced.

In 1986, top New Scotland Yard cops were accused of being homosexuals and sharing unofficial relationships with London- or Home Counties-based private detectives. A report was submitted to the Director of Public Prosecutions, but nothing has been heard on the progress of this case.

Another Metropolitan Police officer was suspended in 1987 for his involvement in a stolen car racket operated in Croydon, Surrey. Also implicated in this affair was a senior Yard official and a private detective. This is yet another strange case that has vanished into obscurity.

In 1987, private security men and detectives were said to be involved in a firearms fiddle. Scotland Yard investigators and the Military Special Investigation Branch announced that they had uncovered a series of illegal arms deals involving serving soldiers, private security operatives and a detective. Several large caches of ammunition were found, along with military equipment and firearms, all valued at thousands of pounds. Included in this find were a number of hand grenades and explosives.

There was an announcement in June 1985 that private detectives and police officers had framed a thirty-four-year-old Luton man. His house was raided without a warrant, and private detectives harassed witnesses in an attempt to gain support for a police prosecution. This was followed by a *News of the World* exclusive, exposing a rent boy scandal involving a top Scotland Yard policeman who was reported to be involved with a firm of London private detectives. Homosexual favours were said to have been accepted in return for secret data from the Police National Computer (PNC).

The activities of Britain's private police and intelligence services were so dubious that even Metropolitan Police officers were advised to exercise caution should they ever find themselves having to deal with any of the persons listed on a confidential Scotland Yard document compiled during 1980/81. This lengthy list contained the names of numerous private detectives and security operators known to the police. The ACC's *Consolidated Instructions,* as it was known, was leaked to *Time Out* magazine, who took it upon themselves to publish a story under the title Police Black List Revealed, along with the names and personal details of some of the people mentioned.

It is impossible to predict the future of the private spy fraternity. However, it is reasonable to assume that as long as unqualified or criminal types are allowed to come and go as they please within it, the continued absence of official regulation will only help the lawlessness that has dominated the industry for nearly four decades to grow. Many concerned observers have asked 'Why on earth doesn't the Government do something about these cowboys?' One answer to that question could be that police and government departments find it convenient to use the services of the private sector, regardless of their pedigree. One just has to read a letter dated 25th February 1986 from a Mr Gregg Montgomery of 10 Hyde Park, Dublin, seeking work with a London detective and security agency, to realise just how unqualified some agents are.

Accompanying his letter is a curriculum vitae which reveals that the applicant has no formal trade training in any aspect of police, security, or intelligence work, unless one accepts that his previous employment between 1984 and 1986 as a chef and chauffeur qualifies him for employment involving physical and electronic surveillance and working in close connection with the police and government departments.

In complete contrast to Mr Montgomery, in 1984 a David John Waters applied to the same firm for a change of employment. This man's pedigree is somewhat different in that he has what can only be described as an impeccable background in security and intelligence. At the time of his application, he was employed by Network Security Management Ltd, 63 Piccadilly, London W1. Prior to working for this firm, Mr Waters had served for 23 years in Army Intelligence where he reached the rank of Major. At one stage in his career he was a Senior Staff Intelligence Officer in Cyprus, and between 1982 and 1984 he was a Senior Instructor in the Security Wing of the School of Service Intelligence, Ashford. Part of his job was liaison with civilian firms and government agencies. An interesting point put forward by Mr Waters in his letter of the 23rd October 1984 mentions his 'recent high level government security clearance.' From the general tone of his correspondence, it seemed that this clearance still applied to him in his civilian life.

It goes without saying that Mr Waters is admirably qualified for employment within the private intelligence community, but should this remove the necessity for some kind of regulation of his activities? Definitely not. Even though, as far as I am aware, Major Waters is a responsible and ethical individual, his background, knowledge and, more importantly, his access to government agencies are good enough reasons to impose guidelines controlling his private security work.

In January 1987 I submitted a report and suggestions to the then Prime Minister, Margaret Thatcher, stressing the need for official control of the spy industry. Apart from receiving an impersonal 'thank you' letter from a Hazel Clark on the PM's behalf, informing me that the matter had been referred to one of the principal government departments, no useful course of action was taken by the Government, except to send a Home Office letter to me on the 8th April 1987 stating that it looks to the industry to regulate itself. In other words, let the inmates run the asylum.

From 1987 until the time of writing (1992), Britain's private secret services have continued to go their uncontrolled way. In June 1990, most national newspapers reported a plot that had many of the ingredients of a bestselling thriller.

Former Army Captain Jane Turpin was employed by a company formed by Colonel David Stirling (now deceased), founder of the Special Air Service. Her job was to infiltrate the firm Europarks, a London-based car park firm, for National Car Parks (NCP) who were locked in a bitter commercial war with Europarks. Two executives at NCP were charged. At an Old Bailey trial said to have cost £4 million it was stated by Judge Richard Hawkins that it was not a crime to commit industrial espionage; the defendants were acquitted.

On 10th May 1992, yet another exposé, this time by *The Mail on Sunday*, reported that acts of private electronic espionage were being conducted on a scale that no one had so far thought possible. With the assistance of a counter-surveillance expert and specialist equipment, they eavesdropped on the streets of London for days, picking up conversations from accountants' offices, the security offices of National Car Parks, a luxury apartment complex in Park Lane, and the Mayfair branch of an international finance firm.

While these firms were obviously being monitored for commercial reasons, a more serious and sinister situation was uncovered in Whitehall, when the presence of a bug was detected near Number 10 Downing Street.

Sophisticated receiving equipment also intercepted conversations within a hundred yards of the Conservative Party headquarters, and from the offices of a well known prominent foreign political figure.

During the course of their investigation, *The Mail on Sunday* interviewed David Benn of Lorraine Electronics, suppliers of bugs and telephone tapping equipment (mentioned in earlier chapters). He said 'We have plenty of dealings with government departments both here and abroad. We also deal with the corporate world and public limited companies.'

A further espionage-related story hit the headlines in July 1992, exposing a plot to assassinate a former South African security policeman, Dirk Coetzee, living in London. According to a Colonel John Horak, himself a former South African Secret Police agent, there are some 150 South African agents working in England, and many are private detectives contracted to collect information on organisations and individuals. Some of them engage in more sinister activities, such as arms dealing – and murder.

Over the years, this total absence of regulation has led to a devil-may-care attitude among many by members of the private spy fraternity. Some operators openly brag about their assignments in such a manner that it is obvious they consider themselves immune from prosecution. I came across an example of this cavalier attitude when I was interviewing a private security agent for television earlier this year.

Having concluded the interview, we were having a drink in a Richmond public house talking about security and detective work generally when, much to my surprise, he embarked on an amazing boast of how his firm had been commissioned to spy on Greenpeace and Friends of the Earth. I wasn't surprised that these organisations have been targeted for investigation: after all, both were infiltrated by Sapphire Investigations and Victor Norris on behalf of Peter Hamilton of Zeus Security, but it was the man's carefree, bragging attitude in a public place over such a sensitive issue that gave cause for concern. From what he told me, it sounded as though the headquarters of both organisations had been infiltrated by undercover agents. Telephones had been tapped and listening devices placed in their premises – and the homes of both organisations' directors had been penetrated.

Greenpeace are, of course, longstanding targets for infiltration by undercover agents. Not only were they targeted by private agents in 1983, they were also victims of a French Secret Service covert operation that culminated in the blowing-up of one of their ships, the *Rainbow Warrior*, in New Zealand. A spokesman for Greenpeace said 'We assume from day to day that our activities are being monitored, by either the Security Services or the nuclear industry.'

Now that the Cold War has gone into suspended animation, the only other official targets of investigation for the Security Services are terrorist groups, particularly the IRA. I hope the Intelligence Services will concentrate their efforts on these *bona fide* problems instead of wasting time, money, and manpower infiltrating and harassing, via the use of 'civilian' agents, environmental groups such as Greenpeace and Friends of the Earth. These groups may find some small consolation in the knowledge that they are simply the latest in a long line of innocent victims of a Secret State more interested in the soft option of terrorising its own peaceable citizens than in rooting out genuine subversive threats to our collective security.

With the enormous amount of 'civilian' spying in Britain today, one wonders if, had there been some form of official accountability and control in place ten years ago, Hilda Murrell and Willie McRae might still be alive today. 'Who will watch the watchers?' is a problem at least as old as the nation-state. Without an effective means of control over the 'domestic' activities of our self-appointed guardians and their freelancers, there is a genuine and frightening risk that it is they who will continue to be the real Enemies of the State.

References

DEATH OF A ROSEGROWER   Published by Cecil Woolf 1985
  by Graham Smith

WHO KILLED HILDA MURRELL   Published by New English
  by Judith Cook   Library 1985

WAR WITHOUT HONOUR   Published by The Medium
  by Fred Holroyd   Publishing Co. 1989

THE POLITICAL POLICE OF   Published by Quartet Books 1977
  GREAT BRITAIN
  by Tony Bunyan

MI5 & MI6   Published by Bison Group 1989
  by R G Grant

BLACKLIST   Published by Hogarth Press 1985
  by Mark Hollingsworth
  and Richard Norton-Taylor

SPY CATCHER   Published by Viking 1987
  by Peter Wright

ON THE RECORD   Published by Michael Joseph
  by Duncan Campbell and   1986
  Steve Connor

POLICE & CONSTABULARY   Published by R Hazell & Co 1992
  ALMANAC

THE INTELLIGENCE GAME   Published by Bodley Head 1989
  by James Rushbridger

PRIVATE POLICE by Hilary Draper	Published by Penguin 1978
INDEPENDENT MAGAZINE	Published 1992
20/20 VISION Channel 4 Television	March 1985
FIRST TUESDAY Yorkshire Television	1988
SCOTTISH EYE Television	1990
SHROPSHIRE STAR	26th March 1984 – 12th September 1984
HANSARD	19th December 1984
DAILY STAR	12th–13th–14th–27th June 1988

SHROPSHIRE LEISURE
  SERVICES RECORDS &
  RESEARCH DEPARTMENT
	20th February 1992 (letter)

DAILY TELEGRAPH	7th August 1973 30th March 1974
THE SUN	4th August 1973
SUNDAY TIMES	22nd July 1973
SUNDAY TIMES	5th June 1983
LONDON EVENING NEWS	10th April 1979
DAILY TELEGRAPH	23rd January 1973
EVENING NEWS	13th July 1971
GUARDIAN	5th February 1972
DAILY TELEGRAPH	21st November 1974
SUNDAY TIMES	24th October 1980
DAILY MIRROR	19th February 1980
SUNDAY TIMES	10th November 1968
TIMES	14th March 1970
DAILY TELEGRAPH	17th June 1971
DAILY TELEGRAPH	21st November 1974
TODAY	20th February 1987

REFERENCES

TIMES	17th February 1987
THE OBSERVER	22nd February 1987
TODAY	5th January 1986
DAILY MAIL	17th February 1987
DAILY EXPRESS	17th February 1987
TIMES	25th May 1985
DAILY EXPRESS	August 1985
TIMES	6th January 1986
AFFIDAVIT OF CATRIONA GUTHRIE (TRINA)	10th June 1992
AFFIDAVIT OF PAT DAVIS	19th February 1986
STATEMENT OF HAZEL RENNIE	28th July 1988
STATEMENT OF JANE POWELL	13th August 1988
STATEMENT OF HASSAN ASSALI	28th July 1988
STATEMENT OF DR MICHAEL RYAN	7th April 1989
COPY OF JUDGE'S SUMMING-UP IN THE TRIAL OF HASSAN ASSALI	24th May1985
COPY STATEMENT OF ALAN WILLIAM FERADAY, SENIOR SCIENTIFIC OFFICER IN THE TRIAL OF HASSAN ASSALI	23rd July 1984
SANITY MAGAZINE	August 1986
SANITY MAGAZINE	March 1988
COPY TAPE RECORDINGS OF CUSTOMS & EXCISE INTER-VIEW OF HASSAN ASSALI	1984
COMPANY FILES OF RADIO-FORT SENTEK LTD	1983 – 1984 – 1985 – 1986
COMPANY FILES OF EURO-TEC PRIVATE INVESTIGATORS	1968 until present time

COMPANY FILES OF   1979–1984
  ECOROPA LTD

LETTERS WRITTEN BY   1979–1984
  HILDA MURRELL

STATEMENT AND PRESS   1984 until present time
  RELEASES FROM COMMANDER
  (RETIRED) ROB GREEN

Appendix

Ecoropa Information Sheet 11

FALKLANDS WAR
The Disturbing Truth

It is with deep regret and in the face of considerable pressure that we publish this leaflet. As the facts over the Falklands war have gradually become known, we have been forced to conclude that it was ordered by Mrs Thatcher for base political reasons; that it was completely unnecessary since alternatives existed; that it involved nuclear weapons; that news of it was manipulated; that it has left us dangerously over-committed financially and militarily and that it has not deterred Argentinian intentions toward the Falklands.

The war cost 255 British lives, with a further 770 seriously wounded (and over 800 Argentinians were killed). These casualties will have been incurred to the best of ends if, as a result of the truth being published, Parliament never again permits our political leaders to commit such an unforgivable folly. The Falklands war has been the subject of a sustained propaganda campaign in which Mrs Thatcher has sought to present herself as having saved Britain from humiliation inflicted by a fascist dictator. The reality is tragically different.

299

Through a series of questions and answers we attempt to put the record straight. This is not an apology for the Argentinians: the behaviour of the military junta was inexcusable from start to finish. Those who have acted irresponsibly stand accused. It is for the reader and the British public to decide who is guilty and what must now be done. The evidence is clear and simple.

Q.1. What led to the Argentine invasion?
A. The belief, instilled into successive generations of Argentine school children, that the 'Malvinas' were an integral part of their country, which had been snatched by British piracy in 1833. In 1910, so uncertain was the British Foreign Office about Britain's claim that it asked the Foreign Office lawyers to make a report. The view was expressed that our claim was doubtful – so doubtful that successive British governments never dared to go to the International Court at The Hague. From the mid-1960s until April 1982, successive British governments conducted negotiations – presumably in good faith – but lacking any determination to succeed. By planning to invade, Galtieri not only thought he could bring negotiations to a head, but could do so when he desperately needed to divert pubic attention from trade union upheaval, inflation, the growing clamour over the 'Disappeared Ones' and the mothers in the Plaza de Mayo.

Q.2. Did we receive warning that an invasion was intended?
A. Yes. MI6 performed superbly – though their task was not difficult in the environment of 100,000 Anglo-Argentinians and 17,000 British passport holders. Argentina's decision to invade was made on January 12, 1982, and the British agents were told, in the expectation that they would pass the information to London. This they did – and the SAS were informed that they were going to the Falklands in February, 1982. According to the Franks Committee, on March 3, 1982, Ambassador Williams in Buenos Aires sent an urgent telegram giving warning of precisely the military action suggested by the Joint Intelligence Committee in Whitehall (Franks, paragraph 95). Admittedly, the senior Foreign Office official did comment: 'He's only an emotional Welshman – not too much notice should be taken of him!' But Mrs Thatcher, in her own handwriting (Franks, paragraphs 147–152) did scribble on it: 'We must have contingency plans'. How can a person who wrote that, if she has any respect for the truth, tell the Commons (October 26, 1982) that the Falklands crisis came 'out of the blue' on Wednesday, March 31?

Q.3.   What attempts were made to bring about a diplomatic solution prior to the invasion?
A.   Seriously, none. The Argentinians were allowed to interpret British actions (such as the withdrawal of HMS *Endurance)* and American messages (through General Walters, Jean Kirkpatrick, Jose Sorsano and others) as a nod and a wink to get the problem solved by a *fait accompli.*

In international affairs it is generally acceptable to compromise by shifting form a hard position to a soft position. It is wholly unacceptable and totally irresponsible to give the impression of taking a soft position, and then instead, adopting an ultra hard one.

Q.4.   Could the war have been avoided?
A.   Almost certainly. It is 'the quarrel of two bald men fighting over a comb'. Prior to the Argentinian invasion, the British Foreign Secretary should have gone to Buenos Aires and sought an acceptable lease-back agreement, which would have avoided the conflict. If this proved unacceptable, Britain should have sought assurance that (a) those Falklanders who wished to leave be given compensation, (b) those who want to stay be given the same rights as the Welsh-speaking Patagonian communities, and (c) the work of the British Antartic Survey and the Scott Polar Research Institute would be guaranteed.

These assurances would almost certainly have been given. Yet even if this process of negotiation was thought unacceptable to Britain, the matter should have been placed in the hands of the United Nations, in which case the Argentine invasion would then have met with world-wide opposition – including that of Latin America. We have it on good authority that the Peruvian peace plan was acceptable to the junta – until the sinking of the *Belgrano.*

Q.5.   Who took the decision to engage in war?
A.   Margaret Thatcher.
'When you've spent half your political life dealing with humdrum issues like the environment . . . it's exciting to have a real crisis on your hands.' (Margaret Thatcher on May 14, 1982, during the Falklands campaign).

Q.6.   Was Parliament consulted in advance?
A.   In advance, no. The imprimature of Parliament was required for the despatch of the task force and in a truncated three-hour debate on Saturday, April 3, in which the most vigorous dissenters were not called by the Speaker, and in which Labour and SDP leaders revealed their ignorance of Latin America, the majority of an emotional House of Commons sent the task force on its way – few

MPs imagining that it would get beyond the Western Approaches. The shadow Foreign Secretary, Denis Healey, was in the United States, and it is still far from clear what discussion took place between Government ministers and the Shadow Defence Secretary.
'She has become a complete dictator, ordering war without consulting Parliament, and she is dragging the masses, shouting and cheering behind her' (A Message from the Falklands, Penguin, £1.95).

Q.7.   What military/diplomatic advice was given?
A.   Air Chief Marshal, Sir Michael Beetham, Chief of the Air Staff, expressed grave reservations, particularly about the shortage of air cover in the face of land-based Argentinian aircraft. The Army also had reservations largely for the same reasons. But the navy, particularly in the person of Sir Henry Leach (since the Chief of the Defence Staff, Admiral Lewin, was in New Zealand) were exceedingly anxious to send a task force – because they wanted to prove a justification for their surface ships, then under dire threat through Treasury defence cuts.

The considered and long-held Foreign Office view was that 'Fortress Falklands', as they have termed it over 15 years, was unsustainable in the event of a serious Argentine attack.

Q.8.   What use did we make of the UN?
A.   The skill of Sir Anthony Parsons and the contacts and goodwill he had fostered during his time in New York, were cleverly used to give a cloak of respectability to the sending of the task force, by getting what amounted to the neutralisation of the Security Council. The Government made cynical and selective use of UN Resolution 502: Mrs Thatcher's initial and sanctimonious endorsement of it was followed by her deliberately ignoring it since it called for the withdrawal of *all* forces. Privately, Secretary General Perez de Quellar was to observe that the Falklands were a problem which, with a little goodwill, could be solved in ten minutes.

Q.9.   Why was the General Belgrano sunk?
A.   There is strong reason to believe that on the morning of Sunday, May 2, 1982, the British Prime Minister, at Chequers, was faced with a compromise in the form of the Peruvian peace plan, endorsed by the UN, which most of the world, and the Labour opposition, expected her – and Argentina – to accept. Seemingly, she thought that were she to do so, and hold the task force back, she would be discredited in the eyes of the right-wing Tories, and that she would be unable to capitalise on the wave of euphoria that she had set in train. We therefore believe that, for the sake of her own

position, behind the back of her Foreign Secretary (who was in the US), without consulting our UN representatives to our American allies whose hemispheric relations were bound to be dangerously affected, in the clear knowledge that Argentina had ordered withdrawal of marine and land forces, Mrs Thatcher ordered a massacre *so as to make peace impossible.*

When the *Belgrano* (an antique ex-US cruiser, a survivor of Pearl Harbor, and due to become a floating museum in 1983) was torpedoed, she was 59 miles *outside* the total exclusion zone and steaming away from it. She was stated to present a major threat to the task force. In reality she was never such a threat and photographs reveal that she was not, as had been claimed, carrying Exocets. Her escorts, however, were – but to have sunk one of them would have caused far fewer casualties and thus might have still allowed a peaceful settlement.

Already that weekend three operations had been launched against Stanley airfield. The stated intention was to crater the runway. But, in reality, not just H.E. bombs, but cluster bombs and air-burst shells were used, entirely ineffective against the runway but causing many casualties – as intended.

Q.10. Is it true that nuclear weapons were taken to the South Atlantic?
A. Yes, both from Gibraltar and the RFA Fort Austin, on carriers, destroyers and frigates and from Portsmouth, – though after a major row some, not all, of the nuclear weapons were withdrawn before the fleet reached Ascension Island. Efforts to retrieve nuclear depth-bombs from the graves of Sheffield and Coventry have been only partially successful, and attempts to find nuclear-bombs from the two 'downed' Sea King helicopters have been unsuccessful.

Q.11. Who authorised this?
A. According to Keith Speed, sacked Navy Minister, he would have been extremely surprised and angry if the fleet had not taken nuclear weapons. On March 28, the crew of the RFA Fort Austin were told by the barmaids of the Gibraltar that they were going to the South Atlantic and not back to the UK as they anticipated after 5½ months in the sweltering Persian Gulf. Since the Prime Minister says that the Falklands crisis came 'out of the blue' three days later and since the fleet with nuclear weapons sailed two days earlier, how come that the barmaids of Gibraltar had better information on the destination of the fleet carrying nuclear weapons than she in Downing Street?

If Mrs Thatcher did not know that nuclear weapons were being moved to a theatre of war, vast ramifications follow for the control of nuclear weapons. If she did know – as we believe – no less vast consequences follow.

Q.12. Under what circumstances would these have been used?
A.   Conceivably, if Britain had lost *Invincible* or *Hermes* and was facing defeat. There were contingency plans for nuclear attacks on the Argentine mainland. Nuclear weapons would have been necessary since Britain lacked the capability for collective conventional attack. Britain, as a signatory of the Treaty of Tlatelolco, has clearly and unforgivably infringed the Treaty by taking nuclear weapons to the South Atlantic.

'*What is happening here is barbaric and totally unnecessary.*' (A message from the Falklands, Penguin, £1.95)

Q.13. Did the Argentinians have any such weapons?
A.   Some reports suggest that Argentina may have had and would have used them in response. They will certainly be available for use in the second Falklands war.

Q.14. Why did we have no adequate defence against Exocet?
A.   Because it is extremely difficult to counter air-launched missiles from aircraft that are out of range of ships' defences. In the second Falklands war, with the new Exocets bought from France since 1982, with the Gabriel missiles bought from Israel and fitted to the newly acquired A4 Skyhawks, the results could be still more devastating.

Q.15. Is it true that many of the Argentine weapons were supplied by Britain?
A.   Alas, yes, forty British companies were involved. Crucial Exocet guidance parts came from Bepi of Galashiels, £50 million worth of Argentine ammunition from a firm in Mrs Thatcher's home town of Grantham (which she sponsored as a candidate for the Queen's Award for Industry prize in 1982), and a mass of high technology has gone to the Argentine military from British Aerospace, Hawker Siddeley, Rolls-Royce and many other big names of British industry. For further details of Britain's part in promoting the arms trade, see Ecoropa leaflet no. 9.

'*The picture that Nott and his cronies are giving is not true. The Argentinian air force has the latest attack aircraft and missiles, which we just do not have.*' (A Message from the Falklands, Penguin, £1.95)

Q.16. Did our allies really support us?
A.   Leading newspapers in France, Germany and Italy were

amazed and contemptuous of the British reaction – a response that had deepened as the facts have become known. Governments that had reacted against the invasion became increasingly critical and their support was largely cosmetic. The French, for example, never recalled the technical team who taught the Argentinians how to marry an Exocet to the wing of an aircraft. The Germans carried on completing the Argentinian frigates (for which Rolls-Royce supplied the engines). The Canadians carried on supplying uranium fuel to start their nuclear reactors in the Argentine.

Q.17. Was it an easy victory?
A.   No. Although our forces did all – and more – that could possibly have been expected of them. If the German-made bombs that hit our ships had exploded, we would have lost nine more. If the torpedo which struck *Invincible* had exploded, the task force would have been in terrible difficulty. The 'Canberra' and other ships were sitting targets for crucial hours during the landings. The troops' guns immediately before the surrender of Stanley were down to 20 rounds a gun. The task force, which comprised over 70% of our sea fighting capability and which carried a significant part of our best assault troops, came exceedingly near to disaster. Of course risks are taken in war, but the task force had been irresponsibly committed to a task for which it lacked the air cover and, in the event, was saved not only by the gallantry and efficiency of the services, but by *luck*. Without this luck, Britain would have suffered a military catastrophe.

'. . . and above all, the tragedy, and horror of the British lives that have been lost which have been spent quite willingly by Mrs Thatcher and Mr Nott to make up for the political ineptitude and pig-headedness of the Government.' (A Message from the Falklands, Penguin, £1.95)

Q.18. Who actually suffered as a result of the war?
A.   Not the Prime Minister, whose war it was, and whose Government's popularity soared. Not the military junta who largely reside in retirement writing their memoirs. Not the politicians on the benches of the House of Commons who despatched the task force. The people who lost were the British and Argentinian parents, widows and children of those who will never return, and those who did return but are dreadfully maimed. And the 1,800 Falkland Islanders whose land is mined, who still have absolutely no long-term security and who continue to be treated by Whitehall as junior colonials.

When, in due course, negotiations cede sovereignty to the Argentine, the huge post-invasion investment made by Britain will fall straight into the Argentine pocket.

'The place I wanted to bring my children up has been spoilt, spoilt by this invasion. The life-style I came down here to find is gone. It's gone forever.' (An islander in *Eyewitness Falklands* by Robert Fox.)

Q.19. What is the cost of the war?
A.   To date £3,800,000,000 – about £160 per household in Britain. The cost of keeping the forces on full alert, in the face of low-intensity Argentine operations, is mind boggling. This money will have to be found by the British taxpayer.

Q.20. How vulnerable are the Falklands now?
A.   Against direct invasion probably not very vulnerable, if an £800,000,000 airport is built, and hugely expensive diversionary runways are constructed. Against bee-sting attack, taking out one or two ships, or against delayed-action mines, very vulnerable indeed. The Argentines have *carte blanche* for war of financial attrition.

Q.21. Have the Argentines any weapons left?
A.   Helped by international loans, to which Britain contributes, Argentina has more than replaced her armament, mostly from Britain's 'allies' including the US, and her services have learned many lessons. As the military establishment chillingly put it: 'We have a debt to cancel.'

Q.22. What did the Franks Committee conclude?
A.   They took nothing after April 2, 1982, into consideration. Their conclusions that no blame attached to the Government up to that time was inconsistent with facts in the body of the report.

Q.23. What about the Falkland Islanders and their future?
A.   Their fragile life-style has gone for ever. In the absence of negotiations about sovereignty, they live under the shadow of a second Malvinas/Falklands war. A peace treaty has not been signed. With up to 25 per cent of our naval capability tied down in their defence, it grows daily more obvious that this intolerable expense will only be sustained until Mrs Thatcher's personal future, for whatever reason, is no longer directly tied to this untenable situation.

'Their attitude to the British is a mixture of continued deep distrust, disappointment and a sullen acceptance of the military, the realities of the new occupying army amongst them. Six weeks have passed since liberation and the Falklands people – as distinct from the Falklands establishment – are profoundly disillusioned.' (Simon Winchester of the *Sunday Times*. The Falklands War.)

Q.24. What can I do about it?
A.   Publishing the truth is but the first step: it falls to the readers to act upon it. Here are some suggestions:
1.   Buy as many leaflets as you can afford and spread them around – see below for Hints on Easy Leafleting and Order Form.
2.   Write, in your own words, to your MP and say what you think about it. His or her address is – The House of Commons, London, SW1A 0AA. If you don't know his/her name, address it to 'The Member for . . . (name of town or borough). Send a copy to your local paper.

The Questions in this leaflet were posed by Ecoropa and were answered by Tam Dalyell, MP, formerly chairman of the Parliamentary Labour Party Foreign Affairs Group (1974–76) and opposition spokesman on Science until being sacked by Michael Foot in 1982 for his courageous and outspoken views on the Falklands war. He was called to give evidence before the Franks Enquiry into the Falklands in October 1982. He has written *One Man's Falklands* published by Woolf at £1.95. The information he gives has been corroborated by many others.

Originally published by Ecoropa, Crickhowell, Powys, NP8 1TA as a leaflet and printed on recycled paper by P.G. Printing, Caerphilly.

Index

(Numerals in bold face indicate a chapter/section devoted to the subject entry. Gary Murray is referred to as GM throughout. For list of individuals and organizations targeted for investigation, see pages 128–9.)